MCSE Training Guide: Networking Essentials

Networking Essentials Exam Objectives		Located Here...	
Exam Section	**Exam Objective**	**Chapter**	**Chapter Section**
Standards and Terminology	Define common networking terms for LANs and WANs	Chapter 1	Entire chapter
	Compare a file-and-print server with an application server	Chapter 1	"Server-Based Networking"
	Compare user-level security with access permission assigned to a shared directory on a server	Chapter 1	"Network Security"
	Compare a client/server network with a peer-to-peer network	Chapter 1	"Network Models: Comparing Server-Based to Peer-to-Peer Configurations"
	Compare the implications of using connection-oriented with connectionless communications	Chapter 2	"Connection-Oriented and Connectionless Modes"
	Distinguish whether SLIP or PPP is used as the communications protocol for various situations	Chapter 2	"Serial Line Protocol (SLIP) and Point-to-Point Protocol (PPP)"
	Define the communications devices that communicate at each level of the OSI model	Chapter 2	"Communication Devices and OSI"
	Describe the characteristics and purpose of the media used in IEEE 802.3 and IEEE 802.5 standards	Chapter 2	"IEEE 802.3 and IEEE 802.5 Media"
	Explain the purpose of NDIS and Novell ODI network standards	Chapter 2	"NDIS and ODI"
Planning	Select the appropriate media for various situations. Media choices include: twisted-pair cable, coaxial cable, fiber-optic cable, and wireless. Situational elements include cost, distance limitations, and number of nodes	Chapter 3	Entire chapter
	Select the appropriate topology for various Token Ring and Ethernet networks	Chapter 4	Entire chapter
	Select the appropriate network and transport protocol or protocols for various Token Ring and Ethernet networks. Protocol choices include: DLC, AppleTalk, IPX, TCP/IP, NFS, and SMB	Chapter 5	Entire chapter

Networking Essentials Exam Objectives		Located Here...	
Exam Section	**Exam Objective**	**Chapter**	**Chapter Section**
Planning	Select the appropriate connectivity devices for various Token Ring and Ethernet networks. Connectivity devices include: repeaters, bridges, routers, brouters, and gateways	Chapter 6	Entire chapter
	List the characteristics, requirements, and appropriate situations for WAN connection services. WAN connection services include: X.25, ISDN, Frame Relay, and ATM	Chapter 7	Entire chapter
Implementation	Choose an administrative plan to meet specified needs, including performance management, account management, and security	Chapter 8	Entire chapter
	Choose a disaster recovery plan for various situations	Chapter 9	Entire chapter
	Given the manufacturer's documentation for the network adapter, install, configure, and resolve hardware conflicts for multiple network adapters in a Token Ring or Ethernet network	Chapter 10	Entire chapter
	Implement a NetBIOS naming scheme for all computers on a given network	Chapter 11	Entire chapter
	Select the appropriate hardware and software tools to monitor trends in the network	Chapter 12	Entire chapter
Troubleshooting	Identify common errors associated with components required for communications	Chapter 13	"Troubleshooting Connectivity and Communication"
	Diagnose and resolve common connectivity problems with cards, cables, and related hardware	Chapter 13	"Troubleshooting Connectivity and Communication"
	Resolve broadcast storms	Chapter 13	"Broadcast Storms"
	Identify and resolve network performance problems	Chapter 13	"Troubleshooting Network Performance"

JOE CASAD
DAN NEWLAND, MCSE, MCT

MCSE
TRAINING GUIDE

NETWORKING
ESSENTIALS

New
Riders

MCSE Training Guide: Networking Essentials

By Joe Casad and Dan Newland, MCSE, MCT

Published by:
New Riders Publishing
201 West 103rd Street
Indianapolis, IN 46290 USA

Copyright © 1997 by New Riders Publishing

Printed in the United States of America   3 4 5 6 7 8 9 0

Library of Congress Cataloging-in-Publication Data

CIP data available upon request

ISBN: 1-56205-749-9

Warning and Disclaimer

This book is designed to provide information about Microsoft's Networking Essentials exam. Every effort has been made to make this book as complete and as accurate as possible, but no warranty or fitness is implied.

The information is provided on an "as is" basis. The authors and New Riders Publishing shall have neither liability nor responsibility to any person or entity with respect to any loss or damages arising from the information contained in this book or from the use of the discs or programs that may accompany it.

Associate Publisher	*David Dwyer*
Publishing Manager	*Emmett Dulaney*
Marketing Manager	*Mary Foote*
Managing Editor	*Carla Hall*
Director of Development	*Kezia Endsley*

Product Development Specialist
Sean Angus, Jack Belbot, Mary Foote

Acquisitions Editor
Nancy Maragioglio

Senior Editors
Sarah Kearns
Suzanne Snyder

Development Editor
Linda LaFlamme

Project Editor
Dayna Isley

Copy Editors
Krista Hansing, Daryl Kessler

Technical Editor
Robert Reinsch, Patrick Koepsell

Software Product Developer
Steve Flatt

Software Acquisitions and Development
Dustin Sullivan

Assistant Marketing Manager
Gretchen Schlesinger

Editorial Assistant
Karen Opal

Manufacturing Coordinator
Brook Farling

Cover Designer
Karen Ruggles

Cover Production
Nathan Clement

Book Designer
Glenn Larsen

Director of Production
Larry Klein

Production Team Supervisors
Laurie Casey, Joe Millay

Graphics Image Specialists
Kevin Cliburn, Wil Cruz, Oliver Jackson, Casey Price

Production Analysts
Dan Harris, Erich J. Richter

Production Team
Lori Cliburn, Malinda Kuhn, Laure Robinson, Maureen West

Indexer
Kevin Fulcher

About the Authors

Joe Casad is a freelance writer and editor who specializes in programming and networking topics. He was the managing editor of the short-lived but well-received *Network Administrator Magazine*, a journal of practical solutions for network professionals. Casad received a B.S. in engineering from the University of Kansas in 1980 and, before becoming a full-time writer and editor, spent ten years in the computer-intensive areas of the structural engineering profession. He now lives in Lawrence, Kansas, with wife Barb Dineen and a pair of pint-sized hackers named Xander and Mattie. Look for his recently published book, *MCSE Training Guide: Windows NT Server 4*, by New Riders Publishing.

Daniel Lee Newland is a Microsoft Certified Trainer as well as a Microsoft Certified Systems Engineer for both the 3.51 and 4.0 MCSE tracks. He is currently training and consulting on Microsoft networking and messaging products. Newland also holds a Novell CNA certification and is the owner of an Internet consulting and design company. He obtained a bachelors degree in history from Moorhead State University in Moorhead, MN, and is currently pursuing both a Master of Arts degree in history and additional networking-related certifications. He welcomes comments and can be reached at dnewland@corpcomm.net.

Dedications

From Dan Newland

To my parents, who instilled in me a desire to understand and allowed me the opportunity to learn.

Acknowledgments

Joe Casad's Acknowledgments

Thanks to Dayna Isley, Emmett Dulaney, Nancy Maragioglio, Linda LaFlamme, Bob Reinsch, and the staff of New Riders. A special thanks to Jack Belbot for his confidence and support.

Dan Newland's Acknowledgments

Thanks to the adminstration and staff of my ATEC, Corporate Technologies in Fargo, ND, for providing an enjoyable and edu-cating work environment in which to learn the information I have written about here. Also to my students for constantly driving me to find better answers, and to the people at New Riders for their assistance and encouragement. Specifically, I would like to thank Nancy Maragioglio for inviting me to work on this project and Dayna Isley for providing much needed support during the au-thoring process.

Contents at a Glance

Table of Contents

Part V: Appendixes

Introduction

MCSE Training Guide: Networking Essentials is designed for advanced end-users, service technicians, and network administrators who are considering certification as a Microsoft Certified System Engineer (MCSE). The Networking Essentials exam ("Exam 70-58: Networking Essentials") tests your ability to implement, administer, and troubleshoot systems, as well as your ability to provide technical support to users of the Microsoft suite of networking products.

Who Should Read This Book

This book is designed to help advanced users, service technicians, and network administrators who are working for MCSE certification prepare for the MCSE "Networking Essentials" exam (#70-58).

This book is your one-stop shop. Everything you need to know to pass the exam is in here, and the book has been certified by Microsoft as study material. You do not *need* to take a class in addition to buying this book to pass the exam. However, your personal study habits may benefit from taking a class in addition to the book, or buying this book in addition to a class.

This book also can help advanced users and administrators who are not studying for the MCSE exam but are looking for a single-volume reference on Networking Essentials.

How This Book Helps You

This book takes you on a self-guided tour of all the areas covered by the MCSE Networking Essentials exam and teaches you the specific skills you need to achieve your MCSE certification. You'll also find helpful hints, tips, real-world examples, exercises, and references to additional study materials. Specifically, this book is set up to help you in the following ways:

▶ **Organization.** This book is organized by major exam topics (4 in all) and exam objectives. Every objective you need to know for the "Networking Essentials" exam is covered in this book; we've included a margin icon, like the one in the margin here, to help you quickly locate these objectives. Pointers at different elements direct you to the appropriate place in the book if you find you need to review certain sections.

▶ **Decide how to spend your time wisely.** Pre-chapter quizzes at the beginning of each chapter test your knowledge of the objectives contained within that chapter. You can find the answers to each pre-chapter quiz at the end of the chapter. If you already know the answers to those questions, you can make a time management decision accordingly.

▶ **Extensive practice test options.** Plenty of questions at the end of each chapter test your comprehension of material covered within that chapter. An answer list follows the questions so you can check yourself. These practice test options will help you decide what you already understand and what requires extra review on your part. You'll also get a chance to practice for the certification exams using the test engine on the accompanying CD-ROM. The questions on the CD-ROM provide a more thorough and comprehensive look at what the certification exams really are like.

For a complete description of New Riders's newly developed test engine, please see Appendix D, "All About TestPrep."

For a complete description of what you can find on the CD-ROM, see Appendix C, "What's on the CD-ROM."

On the CD-ROM accompanying this book, you'll find TestPrep and Flash.

This book also can help you by serving as a desktop reference for information on the basics of networking technology.

Understanding What the "Networking Essentials" Exam (#70-58) Covers

The "Networking Essentials" exam (#70-58) covers four main topic areas, arranged in accordance with test objectives.

Standards and Terminology

- ▶ Define common networking terms for LANs and WANs

- ▶ Compare a file-and-print server with an application server

- ▶ Compare a client/server network with a peer-to-peer network

- ▶ Compare the implications of using connection-oriented communications with connectionless communications

- ▶ Distinguish whether SLIP or PPP is used as the communications protocol for various situations

- ▶ Define the communication devices that communicate at each level of the OSI model

- ▶ Describe the characteristics and purpose of the media used in IEEE 802.3 and IEEE 802.5 standards

- ▶ Explain the purpose of NDIS and Novell ODI network standards

Planning

▶ Select the appropriate media for various situations. Media choices include:

 ▶ Twisted-pair cable

 ▶ Coaxial cable

 ▶ Fiber-optic cable

 ▶ Wireless

▶ Situational elements include:

 ▶ Cost

 ▶ Distance limitations

 ▶ Number of nodes

▶ Select the appropriate topology for various Token Ring and Ethernet networks

▶ Select the appropriate network and transport protocol or protocols for various Token Ring and Ethernet networks. Protocol choices are:

 ▶ DLC

 ▶ AppleTalk

 ▶ IPX

 ▶ TCP/IP

 ▶ NFS

 ▶ SMB

▶ Select the appropriate connectivity devices for various Token Ring and Ethernet networks. Connectivity devices include:

 ▶ Repeaters

 ▶ Bridges

- ▶ Routers

- ▶ Brouters

- ▶ Gateways

▶ List the characteristics, requirements, and appropriate situations for WAN connection services. WAN connection services include:

- ▶ X.25

- ▶ ISDN

- ▶ Frame Relay

- ▶ ATM

Implementation

▶ Choose an administrative plan to meet specified needs, including performance management, account management, and security

▶ Choose a disaster recovery plan for various situations

▶ Given the manufacturer's documentation for the network adapter, install, configure, and resolve hardware conflicts for multiple network adapters in a Token Ring or Ethernet network

▶ Implement a NetBIOS naming scheme for all computers on a given network

▶ Select the appropriate hardware and software tools to monitor trends in the network

Troubleshooting

▶ Identify common errors associated with components required for communications

▶ Diagnose and resolve common connectivity problems with cards, cables, and related hardware

▶ Resolve broadcast storms

▶ Identify and resolve network performance problems

Hardware and Software Needed

As a self-paced study guide, much of the book expects you to use Microsoft products and follow along through the exercises while you learn.

Tips for the Exam

Remember the following tips as you prepare for the MCSE certification exams:

▶ **Read all the material.** Microsoft has been known to include material not specified in the objectives. This book includes additional information not required by the objectives in an effort to give you the best possible preparation for the examination and for the real-world network experiences to come.

▶ **Complete the exercises in each chapter.** The exercises will help you gain experience using the Microsoft product. All Microsoft exams are experience-based and require you to have used the Microsoft product in a real networking environment. Exercises for each objective are placed at the end of each chapter.

▶ **Take each pre-chapter quiz to evaluate how well you know the topic of the chapter.** Each chapter opens with questions related to the exam objectives covered in the chapter. You can find the answers to the quiz at the end of the chapter.

▶ **Complete all the questions in the "Review Questions" sections.** Complete the questions at the end of each chapter—they will help you remember key points. The questions are fairly simple, but be warned, some questions may have more than one answer.

Although this book is designed to prepare you to take and pass the "Networking Essentials" certification exam, there are no guarantees. Read this book, work through the exercises, and take the practice assessment exams.

When taking the real certification exam, make sure you answer all the questions before your time limit expires. Do not spend too much time on any one question. If you are unsure about an answer, answer the question as best you can and mark it for later review when you have finished all the questions. It has been said, whether correctly or not, that any questions left unanswered will automatically cause you to fail.

Remember, the objective is not to pass the exam, it is to understand the material. After you understand the material, passing is simple. Knowledge is a pyramid; to build upward, you need a solid foundation. The Microsoft Certified System Engineer program is designed to ensure that you have that solid foundation.

Good luck!

New Riders Publishing

The staff of New Riders Publishing is committed to bringing you the very best in computer reference material. Each New Riders book is the result of months of work by authors and staff who research and refine the information contained within its covers.

As part of this commitment to you, the NRP reader, New Riders invites your input. Please let us know if you enjoy this book, if you have trouble with the information and examples presented, or if you have a suggestion for the next edition.

Please note, though: New Riders staff cannot serve as a technical resource during your preparation for the MCSE certification exams or for questions about software- or hardware-related problems.

If you have a question or comment about any New Riders book, you can contact New Riders Publishing in several ways. We will respond to as many readers as we can. Your name, address, or phone number will never become a part of a mailing list or be used for any purpose other than to help us continue to bring you the best books possible. You can write us at the following address:

New Riders Publishing

Attn: Publisher

201 West 103rd Street

Indianapolis, IN 46290

If you prefer, you can fax New Riders at (317) 817-7448.

You can also send e-mail to New Riders at the following Internet address:

mfoote@newriders.mcp.com

New Riders Publishing is an imprint of Macmillan Computer Publishing. To obtain a catalog or information, or to purchase any Macmillan Computer Publishing book, call (800) 428-5331.

Thank you for selecting *MCSE Training Guide: Networking Essentials*!

Part 1

Standards and
Terminology

Chapter 1

Networking Terms and Concepts

As one of the required exams in the Microsoft MCSE program, the test for Networking Essentials is intended to challenge your knowledge of computer networking components, theory, and implementation. This chapter covers mostly theory and acquaints you with some of the basic terms and concepts used in networking. Study this chapter carefully—you will use these terms and concepts often throughout the rest of this book. Realize also that the topics covered in this chapter are generally applicable to all networking models. In addition, although most of the examples are given in terms of Microsoft solutions, all other successful networking models must accomplish the same tasks.

Chapter 1 targets the following objectives in the Standards and Terminology section of the Networking Essentials exam:

Test Objectives

- ▶ Define common networking terms for LANs and WANs

- ▶ Compare a file-and-print server with an application server

- ▶ Compare user-level security with access permission assigned to a shared directory on a server

- ▶ Compare a client/server network with a peer-to-peer network

Test Yourself

Stop! Before reading this chapter, test yourself to determine how much study time you will need to devote to this section.

1. Which two of the following are indicative of the server-based network model?

    A. The model is better for smaller networks (fewer than 10 users).

    B. The model has single point of failure.

    C. The model relies on centralized administration.

    D. The model makes it harder to implement RAID.

2. The size limit for a WAN is _____.

    A. 100 kilometers

    B. 1,000 kilometers

    C. 10,000 kilometers

    D. worldwide (no limit)

3. The _____ routes I/O requests from the local machine to the network.

    A. router

    B. redirector

    C. network driver

    D. none of the above

4. A _____ network typically demands more knowledgeable users.

    A. server-based

    B. peer-to-peer

    C. local area

    D. wide area

In the 1980s, the desktop computer emerged as a low-cost alternative to terminals connected to a high-priced mainframe. Each desktop computer was capable of integrating peripherals and software to accomplish certain tasks, but data transfer between systems all too often required the cumbersome intervention of a human with a floppy disk. As the computer industry grew, PC managers, marketers, users, and designers began to see the advantages of sharing data and hardware among a group of individual, but cooperating, PCs. The first PC network operating systems (such as Novell NetWare and Microsoft LAN Manager) were designed as add-ons to existing desktop operating systems. A new breed of PC operating systems, such as Microsoft Windows 95 and Windows NT, now include a fully-integrated system of network services. The integration of network services within personal desktop operating systems and the public emergence of the worldwide network—the Internet—has generated incredible momentum in the movement to "get connected." Networks have become the primary means of disseminating information in most modern offices.

Networking Concepts and Components

 A *network* is a group of interconnected systems sharing services and interacting by means of a shared communications link (see fig. 1.1). A network, therefore, requires two or more individual systems with something to share (data). The individual systems must be connected through a physical pathway (called the *transmission medium*). All systems on the physical pathway must follow a set of common communication rules for data to arrive at its intended destination and for the sending and receiving systems to understand each other. The rules that govern computer communication are called *protocols*.

Figure 1.1

At its simplest, a computer network is two or more computers sharing information across a common transmission medium.

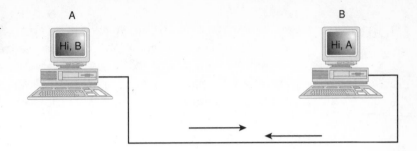

In summary, all networks must have the following:

▶ Something to share (data)

▶ A physical pathway (transmission medium)

▶ Rules of communication (protocols)

Merely having a transmission pathway does not produce communication. When two entities communicate, they do not merely exchange data; rather, they understand the data they receive from each other. The goal of computer networking, therefore, is not simply to exchange data, but to be able to understand and use data received from other entities on the network.

Because all computers are different, are used in different ways, and can be located at different distances from each other, enabling computers to communicate is often a daunting task that draws on a wide variety of technologies.

Remembering that the term *network* can be applied to human communication can be useful. When you are in a classroom, for example, the people in that class form a human information network (see fig. 1.2). In computer terms, the instructor is the server, and the students are network clients. When the instructor speaks, the language he uses is equivalent to a computer protocol. If the instructor speaks French, and the student understands only English, the lack of a common protocol makes productive communication difficult. Likewise, air is the transmission medium for human communication. Sound is really nothing more than wave vibrations transmitted across the air to our eardrums, which receive and interpret the signals. In a vacuum, we cannot communicate via speech because our transmission pathway is gone.

Figure 1.2

Human communication is a kind of network.

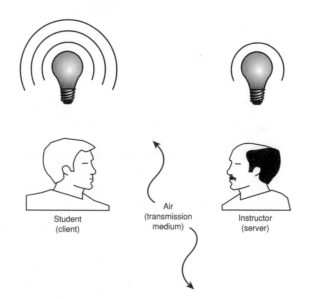

The goals of computer networking are to provide services and to reduce equipment costs. Networks enable computers to share their resources by offering services to other computers. Some of the primary reasons for networking PCs are as follows:

▶ Sharing files

▶ Sharing printers and other devices

▶ Enabling common administration and security

▶ Supporting network applications such as electronic mail and database services

You learn more about these important network functions later in this chapter.

Models of Network Computing

After you have the necessary prerequisites for network communication, a structure must be put in place that organizes the way communication and sharing occur. Three methods of organization, or *models*, are generally recognized. The three models for network computing are as follows:

▶ Centralized computing

▶ Distributed computing

▶ Collaborative or cooperative computing

These three models are the basis for the various types of computer networks you learn about in this book. The following sections discuss the three models for network computing.

Centralized Computing

The earliest computers were large, expensive, and difficult to manage. Originally, these large mainframe computers were not networked in the sense you are familiar with today. Jobs were entered into the system by reading commands from card decks. The computer would execute one job at a time and generate a printout when the job was complete. Terminals, which came later, enabled users to interact with the centralized computer, but terminals were merely input/output devices that had no independent processing power. All processing still took place on the mainframe, hence the name *centralized computing*. Networks, therefore, served little purpose other than to deliver commands to and results from the powerful centralized processing device. Large IBM and Digital (DEC) networks often still operate on this model, but Microsoft has largely ignored it.

In summary, the centralized computing model involves the following:

▶ All processing takes place in the central, mainframe computer.

▶ Terminals are connected to the central computer and function only as input/output devices.

▶ Networks may be employed to interconnect two or more mainframe computers. Terminals connect only to the mainframe, never to each other.

This early computing model worked well in large organizations, but was not flexible and did not scale down to meet the needs of smaller organizations. As such, new ways of sharing information were needed to allow computing power to be shared efficiently on smaller networks.

Distributed Computing

As personal computers were introduced to organizations, a new model of *distributed computing* emerged. Instead of concentrating computing to a central device, PCs made it possible to give each worker an independent, individual computer. Each of these PCs can process and store data locally, without assistance from another machine. This meant that groups who previously had found the cost of a mainframe environment prohibitive were able to gain the benefits of networking at a far reduced cost. Under the distributed computing model, networking has evolved to enable the many distributed computers to exchange data and share resources and services among themselves. Note that these machines need not be considered equals. A Windows NT file server, for instance, is considered to be a part of a distributed network. This server stores and retrieves files for other machines, but does not do the thinking for these machines as a mainframe would have done in the centralized computing model.

The term PC initially referred to a specific device, the IBM PC computer. Over time, though, *PC* has become a generic term referring to any IBM-compatible workstation computer.

In summary, distributed computing involves the following:

▶ Multiple computers are capable of operating independently.

▶ Tasks are completed locally on various computers.

▶ Networks enable the computers to exchange data and services but do not provide processing assistance.

Distributed computing was a major step forward in the way that businesses could leverage their hardware resources. However, it largely dealt with the sharing of data and printers. Processing was left to be done at each machine separately, without any specialization or assistance.

Collaborative Computing

Also called cooperative computing, *collaborative computing* enables computers in a distributed computing environment to share processing power in addition to data, resources, and services. In a collaborative computing environment, one computer might "borrow" processing power by running a program on other computers on the network. Or, processes might be designed so that they can run on two or more computers. Obviously, collaborative computing cannot take place without a network to enable the various computers to communicate.

Collaborative computing is exemplified in Microsoft networks by server-based products such as Exchange Server or SQL Server.

With both of these products, requests originate from intelligent client software (which uses the processor power of the workstation it is running on) but then are serviced from server software running on an NT Server. The server processes the request using its own resources and then passes the results back to the client. Processor and memory resources on both the client and the server are utilized in the completion of the task.

In summary, collaborative computing involves the following:

▶ Multiple computers cooperating to perform a task

▶ A network that enables the computers to exchange data and services

▶ Software designed to take advantage of the collaborative environment.

Now that we have looked at these three organizational models, you should realize that Microsoft networks are generally based on the distributed computing model and that many higher-end NT options incorporate collaborative computing elements as well. The next decision an administrator needs to make is what type of server the network will have.

Network Models: Comparing Server-Based and Peer-to-Peer Configurations

PC networks generally fall within one of these two network types:

▶ **Server-based.** A server-based network consists of a group of user-oriented PCs (called *clients*) that request and receive network services from specialized computers called *servers*. Servers are generally higher-performance systems, optimized to provide network services to other PCs. (Some common server types include file servers, mail servers, print servers, fax servers, and application servers.)

▶ **Peer-to-peer.** A peer-to-peer network is a group of user-oriented PCs that basically operate as equals. Each PC is called a *peer*. The peers share resources, such as files and printers, but no specialized servers exist. Each peer is responsible for its own security, and, in a sense, each peer is both a client (because it requests services from the other peers) and a server (because it offers services to the other peers). Small networks—usually under 10 machines—may work well in this configuration.

Many network environments are a combination of server-based and peer-to-peer networking models. For example, an organization may concurrently use Novell's server-based network operating system, NetWare, and Microsoft's peer-to-peer operating system, Windows for Workgroups. New desktop operating systems, such as Microsoft Windows 95, integrate easily into either network model.

Windows NT Server and Workstation

The two flavors of Windows NT—Windows NT Server and Windows NT Workstation—embody the different orientations of the server-based and peer-to-peer networking models (see fig. 1.3). Under the hood, the two operating systems are quite similar, yet they are outfitted and optimized for very different roles.

Windows NT Server—is optimized to act as a file, print, and application server and is designed to function as a server in server-based networks. NT Server can support unlimited concurrent incoming sessions (depending on the licensing agreement) and up to 256 inbound RAS connections. Windows NT Server can also act as a domain controller, maintaining a user account database for an entire domain. (See the section titled "Network Security" later in this chapter.)

Windows NT Workstation—is optimized for desktop performance. Windows NT Workstation can serve as a high-security, industrial strength desktop operating system and, therefore, is designed to function as a client in a server-based network or as a peer in a peer-to-peer network.

Figure 1.3

Windows NT Server is optimized for file, print, and application services. Windows NT Workstation is optimized for desktop performance, either as a network client or as a peer.

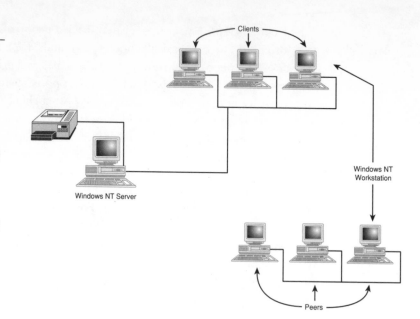

Server-Based Networking

In a *server-based* network environment, resources are located on a central server or group of servers. A *server* is a computer that is specifically designated to provide services for the other computers on the network. A *network client* is a computer that accesses the resources available on the server.

The server-based network model is more efficient for all but the smallest networks because hardware resources can be concentrated on relatively few highly-utilized network servers; client computers can be designed with minimal hardware configurations. A basic network client machine, for instance, might have a 486 processor and 8–16 megabytes of RAM. A typical server might have 32 megabytes of RAM (or more) and many gigabytes of file storage capacity.

Humans often specialize so that they become very good at one type of task. This approach has benefits for network servers as well. By dedicating a server to providing a specific set of services, it becomes possible to carefully tailor the computer to the requirements for that service, which results in optimal performance, simpler troubleshooting, and enhanced scalability. Both Exchange Server and SQL Server, for instance, are very resource-intensive services, and running these on a server that also provides file and print services often can result in decreased performance. Dedicating a single server to SQL Server, while expensive, greatly improves overall access to both the SQL databases and normal file and print requests.

A *file server* is a server that stores files on the network for users (see fig. 1.4). A user at a client machine can save a file to a hard drive located on the file server. If the user wants to access the file later, she can access the file from the client machine through a network connection to the file server. Maintaining a central location for file storage on the server makes it easier to provide a backup copy of important files and implement a fault-tolerance system, such as the RAID (Redundant Array of Inexpensive Disks) systems you learn about in Chapter 9, "Disaster Recovery."

A print server manages access to network printing resources, thus enabling several client machines to use the same printer (see fig. 1.5). Because files and printers are so basic and so important to most networks, file and print services are very basic components of most network operating systems, and a single machine commonly acts (or is able to act) as both a file server and a print server.

For licensing purposes, Microsoft uses the term *file-and-print server* to refer to a machine that provides either file or print service functions because the use of either a printer or hard drive space on the server is considered a client connection. Licensing compliance is an important and often confusing part of network administration, which is covered in Chapter 8, "Managing and Securing a Microsoft Network."

Figure 1.4

A file server stores files for users on other network machines.

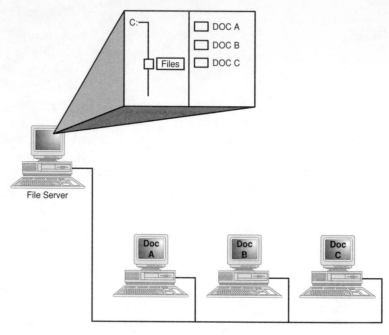

File Server

Figure 1.5

A print server manages access to a shared printer, making it accessible to users at other network machines.

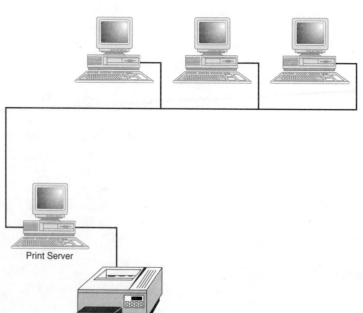

Print Server

An *application server* is a server that actually runs an application (or part of an application) for the client (see fig. 1.6). Whereas a file server simply holds data (in the form of a file) that then is retrieved and processed at the client, an application server performs all or part of the processing on the server end. An application server might search through a large database to provide a requested record for a client. Or, an application server might be part of a client/server application, in which both the client and the server perform some of the processing.

Figure 1.6

An application server runs all or part of an application on behalf of the client and then transmits the result to the client for further processing.

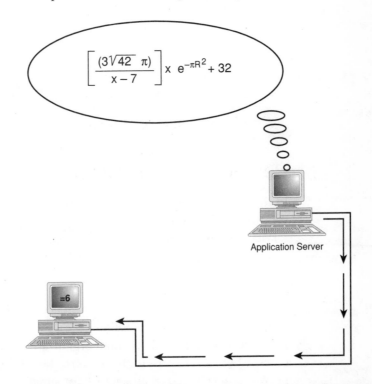

Application Server

The distinction between a file-and-print server and an application server is very important. Remember that a file-and-print server stores files, but it does not actually provide any processing. An application server provides processing and downloads the result to the client. A file-and-print server, therefore, generally requires a great deal of RAM, but is easy on the processor. An application server can be RAM intensive as well, but it definitely needs a more powerful processor.

Under the server-based model, a network administrator can easily control access to network resources. Through the network operating system, the network administrator can give or withhold permission for a user to access files, printers, and other resources located on the server.

The following network operating systems are designed to implement LANs based on server-based models:

▶ Novell NetWare

▶ Banyan VINES

▶ OpenVMS

▶ IBM OS/2 LAN Server

▶ Microsoft Windows NT Server

Peer-to-Peer Networking

In the *peer-to-peer* network environment, resources are distributed throughout the network on computer systems that may act as both service requesters and service providers. In a peer-to-peer network, the user of each PC is responsible for the administration and sharing of resources for his PC, which is known as distributed or workgroup administration.

A peer-to-peer network sometimes is called a *workgroup*. Peer-to-peer networks are ideal for small organizations (fewer than ten users) where security is not of concern. Peer-to-peer networks also provide a decentralized alternative for situations in which server administration would be too large or complex a task.

Because a peer-to-peer network does not attempt to centralize security, and because peer-to-peer networks are generally much smaller and simpler than server-based networks, the software required to operate a peer-to-peer network can be much simpler. Several desktop operating systems, including the Microsoft operating systems Windows for Workgroups, Windows 95, and Windows NT Workstation, come with built-in peer-to-peer networking functionality.

When deciding whether to build a peer-to-peer network around NT Workstation or a server-based network around NT Server, remember that a key difference between the two is that NT Workstation supports a *maximum* of ten concurrent, logged-on users. This means that no more than ten other computers can access resources on a Workstation at one time. NT Server, however, has no such limitation and is capable of supporting dozens, even hundreds, of connections at once by the addition of more access licenses.

Aside from Microsoft's NT Workstation, Windows 95, and Windows for Workgroups, numerous other operating systems, including the following, are designed to implement peer-to-peer networking models:

▶ Novell Personal NetWare

▶ AppleTalk (the networking system for Apple Macintosh computers)

▶ Artisoft LANtastic

Remember that many of these peer-to-peer products can be integrated with networks that are primarily managed in a server-based environment. Macintosh computers, for example, can access resources on an NT Server system that is configured to receive them.

Network Security

Because the purpose of a network is to make accessing resources easy, network administrators and designers are constantly concerned with how to protect network resources so that unauthorized users can't gain access to them. All commercial network operating systems provide some form of security system that limits access to shared files, printers and other resources, and the system itself. Chapter 8 describes how to secure resources in Microsoft networks. The following are the elements of network security:

▶ **Authentication.** A user must provide a username and password to gain access to the system. The logon process is like a front door to the system, and the user's credentials (a username and a password) are the key. If you have the key, you can go inside. Otherwise, you are "out" of the system.

▶ **Access permissions.** Specific resources (such as files, directories, or printers) have their own access lists. The operating system checks the access list to determine whether a user has permission to access the resource. Some kind of authentication method (see preceding bullet) must accompany the access permission system—the operating system has to know the identity of the user to determine whether the user has the required permissions.

▶ **Password-protected shares.** Specific resources (such as files, directories, or printers) are protected with passwords. To access the resource, the user must type the correct password. This method does not require an initial authentication procedure. The operating system does not have to verify the identity of the user—it just checks to see whether the user knows the password.

On Windows NT networks, a *domain* is a collection of computers with a common account database. The account database resides on special Windows NT Server systems called domain controllers. When a user logs on to the domain from a client machine (attempts to gain access to the domain), the user's credentials are forwarded via the network to the domain controller for authentication.

Windows NT enables you to directly set access permissions for files, directories, printers, and other resources (see the following sidebar). To simplify the task of assigning access permissions to users, Windows NT uses a concept called a *group*. A group is a predefined collection of access permissions and rights assigned to a collection of users. Permissions are initially assigned to the group, and any user who becomes a member of the group assumes those permissions. Rather than configuring an individual set of permissions for each user, add the user to a group that possesses the permissions you want the user to have.

Some of the Windows NT access permissions are as follows:

- ▶ **Read.** Grants permission to read and copy files.

- ▶ **Write.** Grants permission to create new files.

- ▶ **Execute.** Grants permission to execute files.

- ▶ **Delete.** Grants permission to delete files.

- ▶ **No Access.** Denies all access to the resource.

When using Windows NT, you can set user-level security for a file or directory only if the file directory is on a partition that uses the NTFS files system (New Technology File System or NT File System). The permissions then become part of the access control list for the file or directory. The older FAT (File Allocation Table) file system doesn't support access permissions for file or directory objects; however, Windows NT enables you to define access permissions for a directory share whether or not the share is on a FAT or an NTFS partition. (See Chapter 8.)

A *share* is an object that has been made available for network access. You learn more about shares and permissions in Chapter 8.

Share permissions in NT are known as ATS (Access through Share) permissions. ATS permissions are independent of any local NTFS file- or directory-level permissions (see fig. 1.7). Think of a share as an object that is distinct from the object you are sharing. The available access types for an ATS share are more limited than the access types available through directory permissions for an NTFS directory. (Your choices are No Access, Read, Change, and Full Control. NTFS directory permissions offer several other access types, such as List, Add, Add & Read, and Special Access.) If you have directly specified permissions for an NTFS file or directory and also specified ATS permissions for that file or directory through a directory share, the most restrictive permissions apply.

Figure 1.7

Access through ATS permissions applies to the share, while NTFS file or directory permissions apply to the actual file or directory.

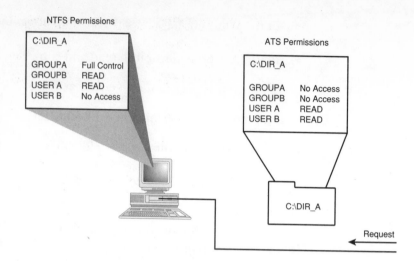

ATS permissions apply only to access via the network. Set ATS permissions through the Sharing tab of the directory Properties dialog box (see the following sidebar). Set file- or directory-level access permissions through the Security tab of the file/directory Properties dialog box.

Windows NT Permissions

You can set permissions for a Windows NT 4.0 object (such as a file, directory, printer, drive, or network share) by using the object's Security tab. You can find the Security tab in the Properties dialog box for the object (right-click on an icon for the object and choose Properties). Clicking on the Permissions button in the Security tab invokes a Permissions dialog box that enables you to specify the level of access you want to extend to specific groups and users.

The FAT file system doesn't support file-level access permissions, so if your partition is formatted for the FAT file system, you won't find a Security tab in the Properties dialog box. If you share the file or directory, however, you can still define permissions for the share. Select the Sharing tab and click on the Permissions button to invoke a Permissions dialog box similar to the one shown in figure 1.8.

Figure 1.8

The Access Through Share Permissions dialog box.

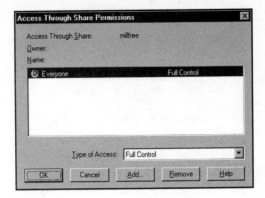

A Windows 95 machine can share its resources either through user-level permissions or through password-protected shares. If you choose to assign permissions using user-level security, you must tell Windows 95 where to obtain a list of users because Windows 95 does not support its own user account database. Requests to access the resource then are passed to a security provider (a Windows NT computer or a NetWare server) on the network.

Another major advantage of a server-based Windows NT domain over a Windows peer-to-peer workgroup is the capability to share user information. If you have nine machines in a peer-to-peer workgroup with NT Workstation, and you need to add a user to a group that has access to them all, for example, you need to go to each individual machine and create an account for the user. You then add this new user to the appropriate group on each machine. If you have eight workstations and an NT Server acting as a domain controller in a properly constructed domain, things are far easier. You create the user on the server, add the user to the proper Global group (also on the server), and add this Global group into Local groups on each machine. The user then has rights on all nine machines. You can find more on this in Chapter 8.

Local and Wide Area Networks

Networks come in all shapes and sizes. Network administrators often classify networks according to geographical size. Networks of similar size have many similar characteristics, as you learn in later chapters. The most common size classifications are the following:

- ▶ Local area networks (LANs)

- ▶ Wide area networks (WANs)

Each of these size classifications is described in the following sections.

Local Area Networks (LANs)

A *local area network (LAN)* is a group of computers and network communication devices interconnected within a geographically limited area, such as a building or campus. A LAN tends to use only one type of transmission medium—cabling.

LANs are characterized by the following:

- ▶ They transfer data at high speeds.

- ▶ They exist in a limited geographical area.

- ▶ Their technology is generally less expensive.

Wide Area Networks (WANs)

A *wide area network (WAN)* interconnects LANs. A WAN may be located entirely within a state or country, or it may be interconnected around the world.

WANs are characterized by the following:

- ▶ They exist in an unlimited geographical area.

- ▶ They are more susceptible to errors due to the distances data travels.

- ▶ They interconnect multiple LANs.

▶ They are more sophisticated and complex than LANs.

▶ Their technology is expensive.

WANs can be further classified into two categories: enterprise WANs and global WANs. An *enterprise WAN* is a WAN that connects the widely separated computer resources of a single organization. An organization with computer operations at several distant sites can employ an enterprise WAN to interconnect the sites. An enterprise WAN can use a combination of private and commercial network services but is dedicated to the needs of a particular organization. A *global WAN* interconnects networks of several corporations or organizations. An example of a global WAN is the Internet.

WANs are often a natural outgrowth of the need to connect geographically separate LANs into a single network. For instance, a company might have several branch offices in different cities. Every branch would have its own LAN so that branch employees could share files and other resources, and all the branches together would be part of a WAN, a greater network that enables the exchange of files, messages, and application services between cities.

Much of the complexity and expense of operating a WAN is caused by the great distances that the signal must travel to reach the interconnected segments. WAN links are often slower and typically depend on a public transmission medium leased from a communications service provider.

Network Operating Systems

The PCs in a network must have special system software that enables them to function in a networking environment. The early network operating systems were really add-on packages that supplied the networking software for existing operating systems, such as MS-DOS or OS/2. More recent operating systems, such as Windows 95 and Windows NT, come with the networking components built in.

Client and server machines require specific software components. A computer that is in a peer-to-peer network is functioning as both a client and a server and thus requires both client and server software. Operating systems, such as Windows NT, include dozens of services and utilities that facilitate networking. You learn about some of those components in other chapters, and some are beyond the scope of the Networking Essentials exam. (You'll get to know them when you study for the Windows NT Server or Windows NT Workstation exam.) This section introduces you to a pair of key network services —the redirector and the server— that are at the core of all networking functions.

A network client must have a software component called a *redirector*. In a typical stand-alone PC, I/O requests pass along the local bus to the local CPU. The redirector intercepts I/O requests within the client machine and checks whether the request is directed toward a service on another computer. If it is, the redirector directs the request toward the appropriate network entity. The redirector enables the client machine to perform the following tasks:

- ▶ Log on to a network

- ▶ Access shared resources

- ▶ Access and participate in distributed applications

In some operating environments, the redirector is called the *requester.* The Workstation service acts as a redirector on Windows NT systems.

A network server machine must have a component that accepts I/O requests from clients on the network and fulfills those requests by routing the requested data back across the network to the client machine. In Windows NT, the Server service performs the role of fulfilling client requests.

File Services

File services enable networked computers to share files. This capability was one of the primary reasons networking personal computers initially came about. File services include all network functions centering on the storage, retrieval, or movement of data files. A common feature of file services is access control and transaction logging. File services enable users to read, write, and manage files and data, but they also should restrict users to authorized file operations so that files aren't accidentally overwritten or deleted. In addition, file services should track unauthorized actions.

File services are an important part of server-based and peer-to-peer networks. Two types of servers exist: dedicated and non-dedicated. Dedicated servers do nothing but fulfill requests to network clients. These are commonly found in client-server environments. Non-dedicated servers do double duty by requesting and providing services, and they are the backbone of the peer-to-peer structure. (A Windows 95 machine used to access files on the network and to provide access to a shared printer is an example of a non-dedicated server.)

Dedicated file servers have the following benefits:

- ▶ Files are in a specific place where they can be reliably archived.

- ▶ Central file servers can be managed more efficiently, with user and security data located in a single database.

- ▶ Central file servers can contain expensive, high-performance hardware that expedites file services and makes the file servers more reliable.

- ▶ The cost of specialized file server technology is shared by a large number of users.

- ▶ Centralized networks are more scaleable.

The following drawbacks, however, should be considered with regard to centralized file services:

▶ When all data is stored on a single server, a single point of failure exists. If the server fails, all data becomes unavailable, making proper design, management, and backup of the server essential.

▶ Because all clients contend for file services from a single source, average file-access times might be slower with a centralized file server than when files are stored on individual, local hard drives.

Centralized file services generally are chosen for organizations that want to achieve the highest levels of protection for their data files.

> Take care when discussing the words "centralized" and "distributed." These terms describe the utilization method of processor resources, file resources, or administrative tasks. For instance, a single administrator can watch over a network with a single file server and many PC clients. This network utilizes centralized administration and provides for centralized file access, but because the clients do their own processing, the network itself fits under the distributed computing model.

In a peer-to-peer network environment, any computer can share its files and applications with any other computer. The sharing of services must be established for each individual computer, and each user must have the skills required to manage the networking services on her PC. Because services are provided by many different computers, users must become aware of which computers are providing which services. Clearly, the skills and responsibility required of users are greater than for centralized file services.

Some advantages of distributed file storage include the following:

▶ No single point of failure exists. When a computer fails, only the files stored on that computer become unavailable.

▶ Individuals typically experience faster access for files located on local hard drives than for files on centralized file servers.

> ▸ No specialized server hardware is required. File services can be provided with standard PCs.

Some negative issues related to distributed file storage include the following:

> ▸ It's more difficult to manage the file service and to protect the integrity of files. File backup is more difficult when files are distributed across many PCs.

> ▸ Individual PCs generally don't have high-reliability hardware, such as uninterruptible power supplies and disk mirroring.

> ▸ File services provided by peers typically are not as fast or as flexible as file services provided by a central file server that is specifically designed for the purpose.

> ▸ Instead of upgrading one central file server when higher performance is required, you must upgrade each computer.

Organizations tend to choose peer-to-peer networking for two primary reasons. One is a desire to network with their current stock of PCs without the expense of a centralized server. Another is that peer-to-peer is an informal networking approach that fits the working style of many organizations. Microsoft implements peer-to-peer networking components into Windows for Workgroups, Windows 95, and Windows NT Workstation. Any of these operating systems is capable of sharing and accessing network resources without the aid of a centralized server. These systems are not optimized for file and printer sharing, however, and this sort of network structure is only recommended for smaller networks with limited security concerns.

Some key file services include:

> ▸ File transfer

> ▸ File storage

> ▸ Data migration

- ▶ File archiving

- ▶ File-update synchronization

Each of these services is discussed in the following sections.

File Transfer

Without a network, the options for transferring data between computers are limited. You can, of course, exchange files on floppy disks. This process came to be called "sneaker-net" because it consisted of networking by physically running around and hand-delivering floppy disks from desk to desk. Otherwise, you can use communication software to dial another computer and transfer files via a modem or a direct serial connection. With a network, users have constant access to high-speed data transfer without leaving their desks or dialing anywhere. Moving a file is as easy as depositing it in a shared directory.

When users transfer confidential files, the need for network security rises. You might need to limit file transfers to authorized users who are using password-controlled security systems, to assign file attributes that restrict the operations that may be performed with a file, or to encrypt files so they may be read only by authorized users. Each of these options is possible with networking.

Another important file-management task of the NOS is to provide and regulate access to programs and data stored on the file server's hard drive, which is known as *file sharing*. File sharing is another main reason companies invest in a network. Companies save money by purchasing a single network version of an application rather than many single-user versions. Placing data files created by employees on a file server also serves several other purposes, such as security, document control, and backup.

One of the most difficult facts to convince your network users of is that their data is actually far more secure on the network file server than on their own workstation. The reasons for this are numerous, but they center on the fact that network servers are backed up more regularly and have more sophisticated authentication and permission structures than most workstations. Perhaps most important, servers generally are locked away and are not as vulnerable to physical damage or theft.

Centralized document control can be critical in a company where a document might need to be revised several times. In an architectural firm, for example, the design of a building might be created by using a drafting program, such as AutoCAD. The architects might produce several versions of the building plan as the client comes to a decision. If the plan is stored on the individual computers of each architect, the firm might not know which is the most recent version of the plan. The wrong version might have a more recent date (because of a backup, for example). If the plan is saved on a file server, however, each architect can work on the same file. The file sharing is regulated by the operating system.

A tape backup should always be installed on the network, forming the heart of a centralized backup strategy. All files located on the network can be backed up regularly. This strategy is much safer than relying on individual users to back up their workstations and can be more easily managed and controlled by the administrator.

File Storage

Most networks have some form of centralized file storage. For many years, companies have used the *online storage* approach to file storage. In the online storage scenario, data is stored on hard disks that are accessible on demand. The files that can be accessed on a server are limited to the amount of available hard drive space. Hard drives are fast, but even with drive prices decreasing in recent years, the cost to store a megabyte of data this way is still fairly high. Hard drives have another disadvantage; that is, generally, they cannot be removed for off-site storage or exchange or simply to build a library of files that are seldom required but must be fairly readily available.

Almost all companies have large amounts of infrequently used data. For example, there is usually no need to keep all the financial reports from the previous year online. However, those reports must be stored somewhere in case questions arise or an audit occurs.

Another common approach to file storage, therefore, is *offline storage*, which consists of removable media that is managed manually. After data is written to a tape or optical disk, the storage medium can be removed from the server and shelved. Users who require offline data might need to know which tape or optical disk to request. Some systems provide indexes or other aids that make requesting the proper offline storage element automatic. A system operator still has to retrieve the tape or disk and mount it on the server, however.

When the slow response of offline storage is unacceptable, a *near-line storage* approach may be selected. Near-line storage employs a machine, often called a *jukebox*, to manage large numbers of tapes or optical disks automatically. The proper tape or disk is retrieved and mounted by the jukebox without human intervention. With near-line storage, huge amounts of data can be made available with only slight delays, but at a much lower cost than would be required to store the data on hard drives.

Data Migration

Data migration is a technology that automatically moves less-used data from online storage to near-line or offline storage. The criteria for moving files can depend on when the files were last used, the owner of the files, file size, or a variety of other factors. An efficient data-migration facility makes locating migrated files easier for users. Figure 1.9 illustrates one approach to data migration.

Figure 1.9

Data migration.

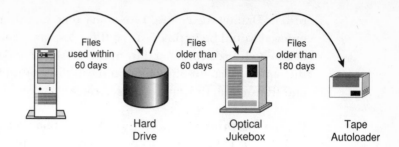

File Archiving

File archiving (also known as backup) is basically offline storage that is primarily geared to creating duplicate copies of online files. These backup copies serve as insurance against minor or major system failures by creating a redundant copy of important system and data files.

Generally, network administrators enable file archiving from a centralized location. A single site, for example, can back up all the servers on a network. Many current backup systems also offer the capability to back up various client workstations, making it feasible to archive all files on the network to a central facility, whether the files are located on network servers or clients. This archive then is stored in a safe location, and a duplicate often is made and placed off the premises in case of disaster.

File-Update Synchronization

In its simplest form, *file-update synchronization* is a means of ensuring that all users have the latest copy of a file. File-update synchronization services can manage files by monitoring the date and time stamps on files to determine which files were saved most recently. By tracking the users who access the file, along with the date and time stamps, the service can update all the copies of the file with the most recent version.

File-update synchronization, however, can be considerably more involved. In a modern computing environment, it is not always feasible for all users to access all files in real time. A salesman, for example, might carry a notebook computer on which to enter orders. Dialing the central LAN every time an order was to be entered would be impractical, so the salesman would enter orders offline (while disconnected from the network) and store them in the laptop. That evening, he would call the central LAN, log in, and transmit all the day's orders at once.

During this process, files on the LAN must be updated to reflect new data in the salesman's portable computer. In addition, the salesman's PC might need to be updated, for example, with order confirmations or new pricing information. The process of bringing the local and remote files into agreement is also known as file-update synchronization.

File-update synchronization becomes considerably more challenging when additional users are sharing data files simultaneously. Complex mechanisms must be in place to ensure that users do not accidentally overwrite each other's data. In some cases, the system simply flags files that have multiple, conflicting updates and require a human to reconcile the differences. In Windows 95 and NT 4.0, the My Briefcase program provides this service.

Network Printing

After file services, printing is the second biggest incentive for installing a LAN. The following are just some of the advantages of network print services:

▶ Many users can share the same printers—a capability that is especially useful with expensive devices, such as color printers and plotters.

▶ Printers can be located anywhere, not just next to a user's PC.

▶ Queue-based network printing is more efficient than direct printing because the workstation can begin working again as soon as a job is queued to the network.

▶ Modern printing services can enable users to send facsimile (fax) transmissions through the network to a fax server.

In this book, print services are defined as network applications that control and manage access to printers, network fax, and other similar devices.

Network Applications

Application services enable applications to leverage the computing power and specialized capabilities of other computers on a network.

For example, business applications often must perform complex statistical calculations beyond the scope of most desktop PCs. Statistical software with the required capabilities might need to run on a mainframe computer or on a minicomputer. The statistical package, however, can make its capabilities available to applications on users' PCs by providing an application service.

The client PC sends the request for a calculation to the statistics server. After the results become available, they are returned to the client. This way, only one computer in an organization requires the expensive software license and processing power required to produce the statistics, but all client PCs can benefit.

Application services enable organizations to install servers that are specialized for specific functions. Currently, the most common application servers are database servers, which are discussed in the next section. Other application services, however, are beginning to emerge, such as fax and e-mail messaging services.

Application servers are an effective strategy for making a network more scaleable. Additional application servers can be added as new types of application needs emerge. If more power is needed for the application, only the application server needs to be upgraded. A database server, for example, might grow from a PC to a multiprocessor RISC system running Unix or Windows NT without requiring many (or even any) changes to the client PCs.

If demand for a server-based application begins to affect a server's performance, it's easy to move the application to a different server or even to dedicate a server specifically to that application.

This isolates the application and enables it and applications remaining on the other server to run more efficiently This scalability is one of the advantages of a LAN architecture.

Some common forms of network applications are as follows:

- ▶ Database services

- ▶ Electronic mail

- ▶ Groupware

Each of these applications is discussed in the following sections.

Database Services

Database servers are the most common examples of application servers. Because database services enable applications to be designed in separate client and server components, such applications are frequently called client/server databases.

With a client/server database, the client and server applications are designed to take advantage of the specialized capabilities of client and database systems, as follows:

- ▶ The client application manages data input from the user, generation of screen displays, some of the reporting, and data-retrieval requests that are sent to the database server.

- ▶ The database server manages the database files; adds, deletes, and modifies records in the database; queries the database and generates the results required by the client; and transmits results back to the client. The database server can service requests for multiple clients more or less at the same time.

Database services relieve clients of most responsibilities for managing data. A modern database server is a sophisticated piece of software that can perform the following functions:

- ▶ Provide database security

- ▶ Optimize the performance of database operations

- ▶ Determine optimal locations for storing data without requiring clients to know where the data is located

- ▶ Service large numbers of clients by reducing the time any one client is accessing the database

- ▶ Distribute data across multiple database servers.

> Microsoft SQL Server and Exchange are two examples of applications that run at the server but are able to perform tasks requested by clients. Because of the way in which these applications are designed, both of these require a "back-end," or server, component and a "front-end," or client, component.

Distributed databases are becoming increasingly popular. They enable portions of databases to be stored on separate server computers, which may be in different geographic locations. This technique, known as *distributed data*, looks like a single logical database to users, but places the data users need in the most accessible location. East Coast sales data, for example, might be located on a database server in Boston, whereas West Coast sales data is on a server in San Diego. Special database mechanisms must be in place to keep the data in the copies of the database synchronized.

More simply, databases can be replicated. Complete copies of the database can be stored in various locations, which provides a redundancy factor because disaster is unlikely to strike all copies at once. Additionally, database replication improves application response time over low-bandwidth connections because users can access the database on the LAN rather than over a comparatively slow WAN link.

As shown in figure 1.10, the most popular strategies for replication databases are the following:

- ▶ **Master driven updates.** A single master server receives all updates and, in turn, updates all replicas.

▶ **Locally driven updates.** Any local server can receive an update and is responsible for distributing the change to other replicas.

Figure 1.10

Master driven and locally driven data-base replications.

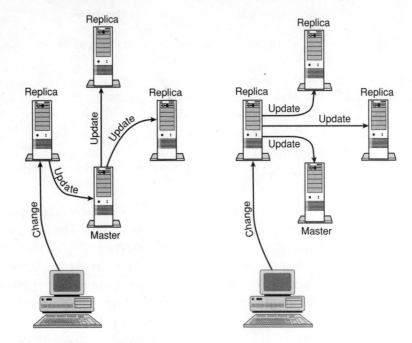

Electronic Mail

Electronic mail (e-mail) is technology for electronically transferring messages between networked computers. A LAN is an excellent platform for e-mail because it provides reliable, high-speed service at a low cost.

E-mail systems can service anything from a local workgroup, to a corporation, to the world. By installing e-mail routing devices, you can transfer mail smoothly and efficiently among several LANs. Moreover, e-mail also can be routed to and received from the Internet, which enables users in dozens of countries throughout the world to exchange electronic messages.

Early text-based e-mail has given way to elaborate systems that support embedded sound, graphics, and even video data.

The preferred e-mail system for Microsoft networks is Exchange, which is an advanced e-mail server included in Microsoft's Back-Office. Other major e-mail packages include Novell's Groupwise and Lotus Notes.

> BackOffice is a suite of Microsoft products that are designed to run only on NT Server. These products include Exchange, Systems Management Server, Internet Information Server, SQL Server, and SNA Server.

Groupware

Groupware is a recent technology that enables several network users to communicate and cooperate on solving a problem through real-time document management. Interactive conferencing, screen sharing, and bulletin boards are examples of groupware applications. Examples of applications with groupware features are Microsoft Exchange, Novell's Groupwise and Lotus Notes.

Summary

This chapter has introduced you to a number of terms that are commonly used in computer networking and has examined many of the basic networking structures you need to understand as an administrator. Use the following exercises to put this information to use and then use the quiz to see how well you remember.

Exercises

Exercise 1.1: Logging on as a Peer

Objective: Explore the distinction between logging on locally and logging on to a domain from Windows NT Workstation.

Estimated time: 15 minutes

1. Boot a domain-based Windows NT Workstation computer. Press Ctrl+Alt+Del to reach the Logon Information dialog box.

2. The box labeled Domain should display the name of the Windows NT domain to which the Windows NT Workstation belongs. This option logs you in by using the domain account database located on a domain controller. Click the down arrow to the right of the Domain box. At least one other option—the name of the workstation itself—should appear in the domain list. This option logs you in by using the workstation's local account database. The local account database is completely separate from the domain database, and it gives you access only to the local computer.

 note

> If the workstation were a member of a peer-to-peer workgroup instead of a domain, the local logon option would be the only option. In fact, if a Windows NT workstation is a member of a workgroup, the Domain box doesn't even appear in the Logon Information dialog box—you automatically log on to the local account database.

3. Select the computer name in the Domain box. Type in a username and password for the local account.

If you rarely or never use the local logon option, you may not even remember a username or password for a local account. If you can't remember a local username and password, log on to the domain from the workstation and find a local account by using the workstation's User Manager application (in the Administrative Tools group). Double-click on an account name to check the properties. Reset the password if necessary.

4. After you have successfully logged on to the local workstation account, you are operating as a peer in a peer-to-peer network would operate. Your credentials will carry you no farther than the local system. Try to access another network computer using Network Neighborhood. Windows NT will display a dialog box asking for a username and password. The computer you are accessing will validate your credentials separately.

Exercise 1.2:   Windows NT Access Permissions

Objective: Explore Windows NT access permissions.

Estimated time: 10 minutes

1. Log on to a Windows NT system as an Administrator.

2. Right-click the Start button and choose Explore to start Explorer. (This exercise assumes you are using a Windows NT 4.0 system. If you are using Windows NT 3.x, start File Manager. The remaining steps are similar.)

3. Right-click on a directory in Explorer. The Directory Properties dialog box appears. Click on the Sharing tab.

4. In the Directory Properties Sharing tab, click on the Share As button and then click the Permissions button.

5. The Access Through Share Permissions dialog box appears. Through this dialog box, you can define which users or groups can access the share. Click Add to add users and groups to the permissions list.

continues

Exercise 1.2:   Continued

---

      6. If the directory is on an NTFS partition, you also see a
Security tab in the Directory Properties dialog box. Click
on the Security tab. From the Security tab, click on the
Permissions button. The subsequent Directory Permissions
dialog box enables you to set permissions for the directory
itself (as opposed to the share).

> A hard drive partition must be formatted for a specific file sys-
> tem. Windows NT uses the FAT and NTFS file systems. NTFS
> is a disk file system designed to make use of Windows NT's
> finest features, including file-level access permissions.

Exercise 1.3:   Exploring the NT Workstation Service

Objective: Examine the effect of stopping Windows NT's redirector: the Workstation service.

Estimated time: 15 minutes

      1. Log on to a Windows NT Workstation system as an
Administrator.

      2. Browse a shared directory on another computer by using
Network Neighborhood or the Network Neighborhood icon
in Explorer. You should see a list of the files on the shared
directory.

      3. From the Start menu, click Settings and choose Control
Panel. Double-click the Services icon to start the Control
Panel Services application.

      4. From the Control Panel Services application, scroll down
to the Workstation service and click the Stop button. This
stops the Workstation service on your computer. Windows
NT asks if you want to stop some other dependent services
also. Click Yes.

5. Now try to access the shared directory by using Network Neighborhood. Without the redirector (the Workstation service) you will be unable to access the other computers on the network.

Review Questions

The following questions test your knowledge of the information in this chapter. For additional exam help, visit Microsoft's site at www.microsoft.com/train_cert/cert/Mcpsteps.htm.

1. You have a small office network of Windows NT and Windows 95 machines. One Windows NT machine will maintain a user account database for the network. Your network is a _____.

   A. workgroup

   B. domain

   C. coterie

   D. none of the above

2. _____ is a common fault-tolerance method.

   A. Remote access

   B. File service

   C. RAIN

   D. RAID

3. Your client computer isn't able to access services on other network PCs. It could be a problem with the _____ on your client computer.

   A. reflector

   B. redirector

   C. server service

   D. none of the above

4. You need to add a server to your domain that will compensate for the shortage of disk space on many of the older machines. You will be adding _____.

    A. a peer

    B. an application server

    C. a file-and-print server

    D. both A and C

5. You have a small office of Windows NT and Windows 95 computers. Each machine is responsible for its own security. Your network is a _____.

    A. workgroup

    B. domain

    C. WAN

    D. none of the above.

6. You need to add a server to your domain that will provide services designed to alleviate the problems caused by slow processor speeds on many of the older machines. You will be adding _____.

    A. a peer

    B. an application server

    C. a file-and-print server

    D. both A and C

7. You are designing a small network for a single office. The network will have nine users, each operating from one of nine networked PCs. The users are all accustomed to working with computers. The best solution is to use the _____ networking model.

    A. server-based

    B. peer-to-peer

    C. a combination of A and B

    D. any of the above

8. You are designing a small network for a single office. The network will have approximately 19 users who will roam freely among the 14 participating PCs. The best solution is to use the _____ networking model.

    A. server-based

    B. peer-to-peer

    C. a combination of A and B

    D. any of the above

9. Which type of network is most likely confined to a building or a campus?

    A. Local area

    B. Metropolitan area

    C. Wide area

    D. Departmental

10. Which of the following can concurrently provide and request services?

    A. Server

    B. Client

    C. Peer

    D. None of the above

11. The rules that govern computer communication are called _____.

    A. protocols

    B. media

    C. services

    D. network operating systems

12. Which file service is responsible for creating duplicate copies of files to protect against file damage?

    A. File transfer

    B. File-update synchronization

    C. File archiving

    D. Remote file access

13. Which two of the following are file services?

    A. Archiving

    B. Remote file access

    C. Update synchronization

    D. Data integrity

14. Which three statements are true regarding application services?

    A. Clients request services.

    B. Application services lack scalability.

    C. Application servers can be optimized to specialize in a service.

    D. Multiple services can be offered by the same server PC.

15. Which three statements are true regarding database services?

    A. A database server improves data security.

    B. All data must be located on the main database server.

    C. Database performance may be optimized.

    D. Database services enable multiple clients to share a database.

16. Which are the two most popular strategies for replication databases?

    A. Remote file access

    B. File-update synchronization

    C. Locally driven update

    D. Master server update

17. Which three are advantages of a centralized approach to providing file services?

    A. Centralized files may be readily archived.

    B. It provides the best possible performance.

    C. Management is efficient.

    D. The cost of high-performance, high-reliability servers can be spread across many users.

18. Which two are advantages of a distributed approach to providing file services?

    A. There is no central point of failure.

    B. It's less difficult to manage than a complex, centralized server.

    C. It's easily scaled to improve performance for all users.

    D. Specialized equipment is not required.

Pretest Answers

1. B, C (see section titled "Server-Based Networking")

2. D (see section titled "Wide Area Networks (WANs)")

3. B (see section tilted "Network Operating Systems")

4. B (see section titled "Peer-to-Peer Networking")

Review Answers

1. B

2. D

3. B

4. C

5. A

6. B

7. B

8. A

9. A

10. C

11. A

12. C

13. A, C

14. A, C, D

15. A, C, D

16. C, D

17. A, C, D

18. A, D

Chapter

Networking Standards

2

Before servers can provide services to clients, communications between the two entities must be enabled. Besides the cables that you see, numerous processes operate behind the scenes to keep things running smoothly. For these processes to interoperate smoothly in a diverse networking environment, the computing community has settled on several standards and specifications that define the interaction and interrelation of the various components of network architecture. This chapter explores some of those standards, including the Open Systems Interconnection (OSI) reference model, Serial Line Internet Protocol (SLIP), Point-to-Point Protocol (PPP), the IEEE 802 standards, Network Driver Interface Specification (NDIS), and Open Data-Link Interface (ODI).

Chapter 2 targets the following objectives in the Standards and Terminology section of the Networking Essentials exam:

Test Objectives

▶ Define the communication devices that communicate at each level of the OSI model

▶ Compare the implications of using connection-oriented communications with connectionless communications

▶ Distinguish whether SLIP or PPP is used as the communications protocol for various situations

▶ Describe the characteristics and purpose of the media used in IEEE 802.3 and IEEE 802.5

▶ Explain the purpose of the NDIS and Novell ODI network standards

Test Yourself

Stop! Before reading this chapter, test yourself to determine how much study time you will need to devote to this section.

1. Routers operate at the OSI _____ layer.

    A. Transport

    B. Network

    C. Data Link

    D. Physical

2. _____ communication provides flow control at internal nodes.

    A. Transport

    B. Internal

    C. Connection-oriented

    D. Internet

3. _____ supports serial line communication under the TCP/IP transport protocol.

    A. SLIP

    B. PPP

    C. Both A and B

    D. None of the above

4. 10BASE-T networks are defined in the _____ standard.

    A. IEEE 802.1

    B. IEEE 802.5

    C. Both A and B

    D. None of the above

Standards

The network industry uses two types of standards: *de facto standards* and *de jure standards*. To understand the concept of open systems architecture, you must be familiar with the concepts of de facto and de jure standards.

De facto standards arise through widespread commercial and educational use. These standards often are proprietary and usually remain unpublished and unavailable to outside vendors. Unpublished and unavailable standards are known as *closed system standards*. Published and accessible standards, on the other hand, are known as *open system standards*. Through the introduction of the OSI model, which is discussed later in this chapter, and the growing acceptance of the concept of interoperability, many closed proprietary systems (such as IBM's Systems Network Architecture) have started to migrate toward open system standards. Certainly, de facto standards are not always closed system standards—examples of proprietary open system standards include Novell's NetWare network operating system and Microsoft's Windows.

The second type of standards, de jure standards, are nonproprietary, which means that no single company creates them or owns the rights to them. De jure standards are developed with the intent of enhancing connectivity and interoperability by making specifications public so that independent manufacturers can build to such specifications. TCP/IP is an example of a nonproprietary de jure standard.

Several permanent committees comprised of industry representatives develop de jure standards. Although these committees are supported by manufacturer subscriptions and major company end users, they are intended to represent the interests of the entire community and thus remain independent of any one manufacturer's interests. Subscribing to de jure standards reduces the risk and cost of developing hardware and software for manufacturers. After a standard has been finalized, a component manufacturer subscribing to it can develop products with some confidence that the products will operate with components from other companies.

Standards Organizations and the ISO

The development and implementation of de jure standards is regulated by standards organizations. For example, the International Telecommunication Union (ITU) and the Institute of Electrical and Electronic Engineers (IEEE), among other organizations, are responsible for several prominent network standards that support the International Standards Organization's objective of network interoperability.

The International Standards Organization (ISO)—whose name is derived from the Greek prefix *iso*, meaning "same"—is located in Geneva, Switzerland. ISO develops and publishes standards and coordinates the activities of all national standardization bodies. In 1977, the ISO initiated efforts to design a communication standard based on the open systems architecture theory from which computer networks would be designed. This model came to be known as the Open Systems Interconnection (OSI) model.

Rules and the Communication Process

Networks rely on many rules to manage information interchange. Some of the procedures governed by network standards are as follows:

- ▶ Procedures used to initiate and end an interaction

- ▶ Signals used to represent data on the media

- ▶ Methods used to direct a message to the intended destination

- ▶ Procedures used to control the rate of data flow

- ▶ Methods used to enable different computer types to communicate

- ▶ Ways to ensure that messages are received correctly

Enabling computers to communicate is an extremely complex process—one that is often too complex to solve all at once using just one set of rules. As a result, the industry has chosen to solve different parts of the problem with compatible standards so that the solutions can be put together like pieces of a puzzle—a puzzle that comes together differently each time to build a complete communication approach for any given situation.

The OSI Reference Model

Having a model in mind will help you understand how the pieces of the networking puzzle fit together. The most commonly used model is the Open Systems Interconnection (OSI) reference model. The OSI model, first released in 1984 by the International Standards Organization (ISO), provides a useful structure for defining and describing the various processes underlying open systems networking.

The OSI model is a blueprint for vendors to follow when developing protocol implementations. The OSI model organizes communication protocols into seven layers. Each layer addresses a narrow portion of the communication process. Figure 2.1 illustrates the layers of the OSI model.

Figure 2.1

The OSI model is composed of seven layers.

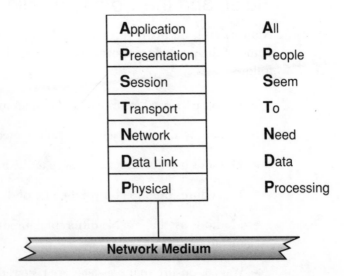

Application	**A**ll
Presentation	**P**eople
Session	**S**eem
Transport	**T**o
Network	**N**eed
Data Link	**D**ata
Physical	**P**rocessing

Network Medium

Although you will examine each layer in detail later in this chapter, a quick overview is in order. Layer 1, the Physical layer, consists of protocols that control communication on the network media. Layer 7, the Application layer, interfaces the network services with the applications in use on the computer. The five layers

in between—Data Link, Network, Transport, Session, and
Presentation—perform intermediate communication tasks.

> You should learn the names and the order of the seven OSI
> layers for the Networking Essentials exam. The following two
> phrases help you remember the first letters of the layers:
>
> **A**ll **P**eople **S**eem **T**o **N**eed **D**ata **P**rocessing (top down)
>
> **P**lease **D**o **N**ot **T**hrow **S**ausage **P**izza **A**way (bottom up)
>
> Choose one, depending on whether you are most comfortable
> working from the top of the model down or from the bottom up.

Protocol Stacks

Figure 2.1 illustrates the origin of the term *protocol stack*. The OSI
model (and other non-OSI protocol standards) break the complex process of network communication into *layers*. Each layer
represents a category of related tasks. A protocol stack is an implementation of this layered protocol architecture. The protocols
and services associated with the protocol stack interact to prepare,
transmit, and receive network data.

Two computers must run compatible protocol stacks before they
can communicate because each layer in one computer's protocol
stack must interact with a corresponding layer in the other computer's protocol stack. Figure 2.2, for example, shows the path of
a message that starts in the Transport layer. The message travels
down the protocol stack, through the network medium, and up
the protocol stack of the receiving computer. If the Transport
layer in the receiving computer understands the protocols used in
the Transport layer that originated the message, the message can
be delivered.

As long as their protocol stacks are compatible, computers of different types can communicate. TCP/IP, for example, is available
for almost all current computers and operating systems. If a
Macintosh and a Unix workstation both run TCP/IP, the Mac can
access files on the Unix workstation.

Figure 2.2

*Peer communica-
tion takes place
between protocol
stacks.*

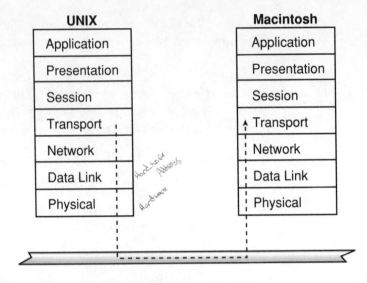

How Peer Layers Communicate

To communicate with its peer layer in another computer, each
protocol layer adds its own information to the message being sent.
This information takes the form of a *header* added to the beginning of the message (see fig. 2.3).

Figure 2.3

*Each protocol
layer, except the
Physical layer,
adds a header to
the frame.*

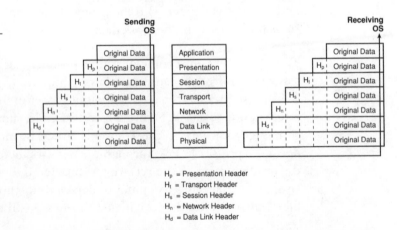

Headers are added as the message is prepared for transmission,
and headers are removed (stripped) by the receiving computer
after the information in the header has been utilized.

The Physical layer does not append a header because this layer deals with sending and receiving information on the individual bit level. The bits are assembled into longer message units in the Data Link layer.

OSI Physical Layer Concepts

Although the OSI Physical layer does not define the media used, this layer is concerned with all aspects of transmitting and receiving data on the network media. Specifically, the Physical layer is concerned with transmitting and receiving bits. This layer defines several key characteristics of the physical network, including the following:

▶ Physical structure of the network (physical topology)

▶ Mechanical and electrical specifications for using the medium (not the medium itself)

▶ Bit transmission encoding and timing

Although the Physical layer does not define the physical medium, it defines clear requirements that the medium must meet. These specifications differ depending on the physical medium. Ethernet for UTP, for example, has different Physical layer specifications from coaxial Ethernet (see Chapter 3, "Transmission Media").

You learn more about network transmission media in Chapter 3. In Chapter 4, "Network Topologies and Architectures," you learn about physical topologies.

OSI Data Link Layer Concepts

As you learned in the preceding section, the OSI Physical layer is concerned with moving messages at the machine level. Network communication, however, is considerably more involved than moving bits from one device to another. In fact, dozens of steps must be performed to transport a message from one device to another.

Real messages consist not of single bits but of meaningful groups of bits. The Data Link layer receives messages, called *frames*, from upper layers. A primary function of the Data Link layer is to disassemble these frames into bits for transmission and then to reconstruct the frames from the bits received.

The Data Link layer has other functions as well, such as addressing, error control, and flow control for a single link between network devices. (The adjacent Network layer, described later in this chapter, handles the more complex tasks associated with addressing and delivering packets through routers and across an internetwork.)

The IEEE 802 standard divides the Data Link layer into two sublayers:

- ▶ **Media Access Control (MAC).** The MAC sublayer controls the means by which multiple devices share the same media channel. This includes contention methods (see Chapter 4) and other media access details. The MAC layer also provides addressing information for communication between network devices.

- ▶ **Logical Link Control (LLC).** The LLC sublayer establishes and maintains links between communicating devices.

Hardware Access at the Data Link Layer

As the preceding section mentions, the Data Link layer's MAC sublayer provides an interface to the network adapter card. The details necessary to facilitate access to the network through the adapter card are thus assigned to the Data Link layer. Some of these details include the access control method (for example, contention or token passing—see Chapter 4) and the network topology.

The Data Link layer also controls the transmission method (for example, synchronous or asynchronous) used to access the transmission medium. See Chapter 6, "Connectivity Devices," for more on synchronous and asynchronous communications.

Addressing at the Data Link Layer

The Data Link layer maintains device addresses that enable messages to be sent to a particular device. The addresses are called *physical device addresses*. Physical device addresses are unique addresses associated with the networking hardware in the computer. In most cases (for example, Ethernet and Token Ring), the physical device address is burned into the network interface card at the time the card is manufactured.

The standards that apply to a particular network determine the format of the address. Because the address format is associated with the media access control method used, physical device addresses are frequently referred to as *MAC addresses*.

The device address is not actually used to route a message to a specific device. Frames on LANs are typically transmitted so that they are available to all devices on the network. Each device reads each frame far enough to determine the device address to which the frame is addressed. If the frame's destination address matches the device's own physical address, the rest of the frame is received. If the addresses do not match, the remainder of the frame is ignored.

As you learn in this chapter, *bridges* can be used to divide large networks into several smaller ones. Bridges use physical device addresses to determine which frames to leave on the current network segment and which to forward to devices on other network segments. (Chapter 6 covers bridges in more detail.)

Because they use physical device addresses to manage frame routing, bridges function at the level of the Data Link layer and are Data Link layer connectivity devices.

Error and Flow Control at the Data Link Layer

Several of the protocol layers in the OSI model play a role in the overall system of flow control and error control for the network. Flow control and error control are defined as follows:

▶ **Flow control.** Flow control determines the amount of data that can be transmitted in a given time period. Flow control prevents the transmitting device from overwhelming the receiver.

▶ **Error control.** Error control detects errors in received frames and requests retransmission of frames.

The Data Link layer's LLC sublayer provides error control and flow control for single links between communicating devices. The Network layer (described in the following section) expands the system of error control and flow control to encompass complex connections that include routers, gateways, and internetworks.

OSI Network Layer Concepts

As you learned in the preceding section, the Data Link layer deals with communication between devices on the same network. Physical device addresses are used to identify data frames, and each device is responsible for monitoring the network and receiving frames addressed to that device.

The Network layer handles communication with devices on logically separate networks that are connected to form *internetworks*. Because internetworks can be large and can be constructed of different types of networks, the Network layer utilizes routing algorithms that guide packets from their source to their destination networks. For more about routing and routing algorithms, see Chapter 6.

Within the Network layer, each network in the internetwork is assigned a *network address* that is used to route packets. The Network layer manages the process of addressing and delivering packets on complex networks.

Network Layer Addressing

You have already encountered the Data Link layer's physical device addresses, which uniquely identify each device on a network. On larger networks, it is impractical to deliver network data soley by means of physical addresses. (Imagine if your network adapter had to check every packet sent from anywhere on the Internet to look for a matching physical address.) Larger networks require a means of routing and filtering packets in order to reduce network traffic and minimize transmission time. The Network layer uses *logical network addresses* to route packets to specific networks on an internetwork.

Logical network addresses are assigned during configuration of the networks. A network installer must make sure that each network address is unique on a given internetwork.

The Network layer also supports *service addresses*. A service address specifies a channel to a specific process on the destination PC. The operating systems on most computers can run several processes at once. When a packet arrives, you must determine which process on the computer should receive the data in the packet. You do so by assigning service addresses, which identify upper-layer processes and protocols. These service addresses are included with the physical and logical network addresses in the data frame. (Some protocols refer to service addresses as *sockets* or *ports*.)

Some service addresses, called *well-known addresses*, are universally defined for a given type of network. Other service addresses are defined by the vendors of network products.

Delivering Packets

Many internetworks often include redundant data paths that you can use to route messages. Typically, a packet will pass from the local LAN segment of the source PC through a series of routers to the local LAN segment of the destination PC. (You learn more about routers in Chapter 6.) The OSI Network layer oversees the process of determining paths and delivering packets across the internetwork. Chapter 6 describes some of the routing algorithms used to determine a path. The following sections introduce some of the basic switching techniques, as follows:

- ▶ Circuit switching

- ▶ Message switching

- ▶ Packet switching

Circuit Switching

Circuit switching establishes a path that remains fixed for the duration of a connection (see fig. 2.4). Much as telephone switching equipment establishes a route between two telephones, circuit-switching networks establish a path through the internetwork when the devices initiate a conversation.

Figure 2.4

Circuit switching establishes a path between two devices much like a telephone connection.

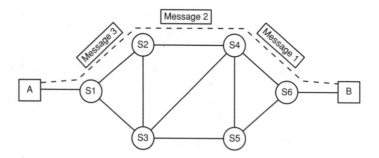

Circuit switching provides devices with a dedicated path and a well-defined bandwidth, but circuit switching is not free of disadvantages. First, establishing a connection between devices can be time-consuming. Second, because other traffic cannot share the dedicated media path, bandwidth might be inefficiently utilized. Finally, circuit-switching networks must have a surplus of bandwidth, so these types of switches tend to be expensive to construct.

Message Switching

Message switching treats each message as an independent entity. Each message carries address information that describes the message's destination, and this information is used at each switch to transfer the message to the next switch in the route. Message switches are programmed with information concerning other switches in the network that can be used to forward messages to their destinations. Message switches also may be programmed with information about the most efficient routes. Depending on network conditions, different messages may be sent through the network by different routes, as shown in figure 2.5.

Message switching transfers the complete message from one switch to the next, where the message is stored before being forwarded again. Because each message is stored before being sent on to the next switch, this type of network frequently is called a *store-and-forward network*. The message switches often are general-purpose computers and must be equipped with sufficient storage (usually hard drives) to enable them to store messages until forwarding is possible.

Figure 2.5

Message switching forwards the complete message one switch at a time.

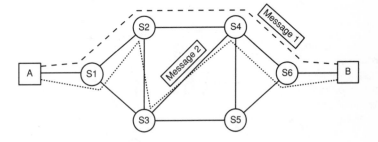

Message switching commonly is used in e-mail because some delay is permissible when delivering mail, unlike the requirements when two computers exchange data in real time. Message switching uses relatively low-cost devices to forward messages and can function well with relatively slow communication channels. Other applications for message switching include group applications such as workflow, calendaring, and groupware.

Message switching offers the following advantages:

▶ Data channels are shared among communicating devices, improving the efficiency of using available bandwidth.

▶ Message switches can store messages until a channel becomes available, reducing sensitivity to network congestion.

▶ Message priorities can be used to manage network traffic.

▶ Broadcast addressing uses network bandwidth more efficiently by delivering messages to multiple destinations.

The chief disadvantage of message switching is that message switching is not suited for real-time applications, including data communication, video, and audio.

Packet Switching

In packet switching, messages are divided into smaller pieces called *packets*. Each packet includes source and destination address information so that individual packets can be routed through the internetwork independently. As you can see in figure 2.6, the packets that make up a message can take very different routes through the internetwork.

Figure 2.6

Packet switching breaks up the message into smaller pieces that are routed independently.

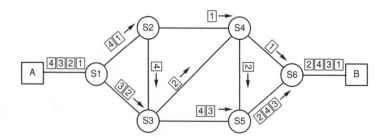

So far, packet switching looks considerably like message switching, but the distinguishing characteristic is that packets are restricted to a size that enables the switching devices to manage the packet data entirely in memory. This eliminates the need to store the data temporarily on disk. Packet switching, therefore, routes packets through the network much more rapidly and efficiently than is possible with message switching.

Several methods of packet switching exist. Two common methods of packet switching are as follows:

▶ Datagram

▶ Virtual circuit

These two methods are discussed in the following sections.

Datagram Packet Switching

Datagram services treat each packet as an independent message. Each packet is routed through the internetwork independently, and each switch node determines which network segment should be used for the next step in the packet's route. This capability enables switches to bypass busy segments and take other steps to speed packets through the internetwork (refer to fig. 2.6).

Datagrams are frequently used on LANs. Network layer protocols are responsible for delivering the frame to the appropriate network. Then, because each datagram includes destination address information, devices on the local network can recognize and receive appropriate datagrams.

> Packet switching meets the need to transmit large messages with the fairly small frame size that can be accommodated by the Physical layer. The Network layer is responsible for fragmenting messages from upper layers into smaller datagrams that are appropriate for the Physical layer. The Network layer also is responsible for reconstructing messages from datagrams as they are received.

Virtual Circuit Packet Switching

Virtual circuits operate by establishing a formal connection between two devices in communication. When devices begin a session, they negotiate communication parameters, such as maximum message size, communication windows, and network paths. This negotiation establishes a *virtual circuit*, which is a well-defined path through the internetwork by which the devices communicate. This virtual circuit generally remains in effect until the devices stop communicating.

Virtual circuits are distinguished by the establishment of a logical connection. *Virtual* means that the network behaves as though a dedicated physical circuit has been established between the communicating devices. Even though no such physical circuit actually exists, the network presents the appearance of a physical connection to the devices at the ends of the circuit.

Virtual circuits frequently are employed in conjunction with connection-oriented services, which are discussed later in this chapter.

Advantages of Packet Switching

Packet switching optimizes the use of bandwidth by enabling many devices to route packets through the same network channels. At any given time, a switch can route packets to several different destination devices, adjusting the routes as required to achieve the best efficiency.

Because entire messages are not stored at the switches prior to forwarding, transmission delays are significantly shorter than delays encountered with message switching.

Although the switching devices do not need to be equipped with large amounts of hard drive capacity, they might need a significant amount of real-time memory. In addition, the switching devices must have sufficient processing power to run the more complex routing protocols required for packet switching. A system must be in place by which devices can recognize when packets have been lost so that retransmission can be requested.

Connection-oriented and Connectionless Modes

The OSI Network layer determines the route a packet will take as it passes through a series of routers from the source PC to the destination PC. The complexity and versatility of Network layer addressing gives rise to two different communication modes for passing messages across the network, both of which are recognized under OSI:

▶ **Connection-oriented mode.** Error correction and flow control are provided at internal nodes along the message path.

▶ **Connectionless mode.** Internal nodes along the message path do not participate in error correction and flow control.

To understand the distinction between connection-oriented and connectionless communications, you must consider an important distinction between the OSI model's Data Link and Network layers. In theory, the Data Link layer facilitates the transmission of data across a single link between two nodes. The Network layer describes the process of routing a packet through a series of nodes to a destination elsewhere on the network. An example of this latter scenario is a message passing from a PC on one LAN segment through a series of routers to a PC on a distant part of the network. The internal nodes forwarding the packet also forward other packets between other end nodes.

In connection-oriented mode, the chain of links between the source and destination nodes forms a kind of logical pathway—a connection. The nodes forwarding the data packet can track which packet is part of which connection. This enables the internal nodes to provide flow control as the data moves along the path. For example, if an internal node determines that a link is malfunctioning, the node can send a notification message backwards through the path to the source computer. Furthermore, because the internal node distinguishes among individual, concurrent connections in which it participates, this node can transmit (or forward) a "stop sending" message for one of its connections without stopping all communications through the node. Another feature of connection-oriented communication is that internal nodes provide error correction at each link in the chain. Therefore, if a node detects an error, it asks the preceding node to retransmit.

Connectionless mode does not provide these elaborate internal control mechanisms; instead, connectionless mode relegates all error-correcting and retransmitting processes to the source and destination nodes. The end nodes acknowledge the receipt of packets and retransmit if necessary, but internal nodes do not participate in flow control and error correction (other than simply forwarding messages between the end nodes).

The advantage of connectionless mode is that connectionless communications can be processed more quickly and more simply because the internal nodes only forward data and thus don't have to track connections or provide retransmission or flow control.

Connectionless mode does have its share of disadvantages, however, including the following:

▶ Messages sometimes get lost due to an overflowing buffer or a failed link along the pathway.

▶ If a message gets lost, the sender doesn't receive notification.

▶ Retransmission for error correction takes longer because a faulty transmission can't be corrected across an internal link.

It is important to remember that OSI is not a protocol suite itself—OSI is a standard for designing protocol suites. As such, individual implementations of connectionless protocols can attenuate some of the preceding disadvantages. It is also important to remember that connection-oriented mode, although it places much more emphasis on monitoring errors and controlling traffic, doesn't always work either. Ultimately, the choice of connection-oriented or connectionless communications mode depends on interoperability with other systems, the premium for speed, and the cost of components.

Gateway Services

Routers can handle interconnection of networks whose protocols function in similar ways. When the rules differ sufficiently on the two networks, however, a more powerful device is required.

A *gateway* is a device that can reconcile the different rules used on two different networks. Gateways commonly are required to connect LANs to mainframe networks, which have completely different protocol architectures. Mainframe networks, such as IBM's SNA, for example, do not use the same device address schemes that LANs employ (these networks differ in many other ways as well). In these situations, you must fool the mainframe network into thinking that mainframe devices are on the LAN. This involves making the mainframe look like a LAN to devices on the LAN. Exercise 2.1, at the end of this chapter, explores Windows NT's Gateway Services for NetWare, which provides a gateway from a Microsoft network to NetWare resources.

Gateways can be implemented at the Network layer or at higher layers in the OSI model, depending on where the protocol translation is required.

OSI Transport Layer Concepts

The Transport layer, the next layer of the OSI model, can implement procedures to ensure the reliable delivery of messages to their destination devices. The term "reliable" does not mean that errors cannot occur; instead, it means that if errors occur, they are detected. If errors such as lost data are detected, the Transport layer either requests retransmission or notifies upper-layer protocols so that they can take corrective action.

The Transport layer enables upper-layer protocols to interface with the network but hides the complexities of network operation from them. Among its functions, the Transport layer breaks large messages into segments suitable for network delivery.

Transport Layer Connection Services

Some services can be performed at more than one layer of the OSI model. In addition to the Data Link and Network layers, the Transport layer can take on some responsibility for connection services. The Transport layer interacts with the Network layer's connection-oriented and connectionless services and provides some of the essential quality control features. Some of the Transport layers activities include the following:

▶ **Segment sequencing.** Segment sequencing is one connection-oriented service provided by the Transport layer. When large messages are divided into segments for transport, the Transport layer must resequence the segments when they are received before reassembling the original message.

▶ **Error control.** When segments are lost during transmission or when segments have duplicate segment IDs, the Transport layer must initiate error recovery. The Transport layer also detects corrupted segments by managing end-to-end error control using techniques such as checksums.

▶ **End-to-end flow control.** The Transport layer uses acknowledgments to manage end-to-end flow control between two connected devices. Besides negative acknowledgments, some Transport-layer protocols can request the retransmission of the most recent segments.

OSI Session Layer Concepts

The next OSI layer, the Session layer, manages dialogs between two computers by establishing, managing, and terminating communications. As illustrated in figure 2.7, dialogs can take three forms:

▶ **Simplex dialogs.** These dialogs are responsible for only one-way data transfers. An example is a fire alarm, which sends an alarm message to the fire station but cannot (and does not need to) receive messages from the fire station.

▶ **Half-duplex dialogs.** These dialogs handle two-way data transfers in which the data flows in only one direction at a time. When one device completes a transmission, this device must "turn over" the medium to the other device so that this second device has a turn to transmit.

CB radio operators, for example, converse on the same communication channel. When one operator is finished transmitting, he must release his transmit key so that the other operator can send a response.

▶ **Full-duplex dialogs.** This third type of dialog permits two-way simultaneous data transfers by providing each device with a separate communication channel. Voice telephones are full-duplex devices, and either party to a conversation can talk at any time. Most computer modems can operate in full-duplex mode.

Figure 2.7

Simplex and duplex communication modes.

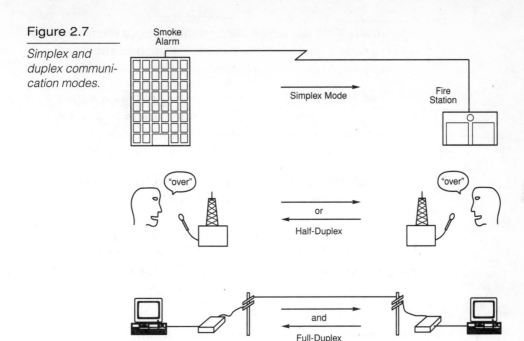

Costs rise for half- and full-duplex operation because the more complex dialog technologies are naturally more expensive. Designers of communications systems, therefore, generally use the simplest dialog mode that satisfies the communication requirements.

Half-duplex communication can result in wasted bandwidth during the intervals when communication is turned around. On the other hand, using full-duplex communication generally requires a greater bandwidth than half-duplex communication.

The Session layer also marks the data stream with checkpoints and monitors the receipt of those checkpoints. In the event of a failure, the sending PC can retransmit starting with the data sent after the last checkpoint, rather than resending the whole message.

Session Layer Session Administration

A *session* is a formal dialog between a service requester and a service provider. Sessions have at least three phases:

▶ **Connection establishment.** In this phase, a service requester requests initiation of a service. During the setup process, communication is established and rules are agreed upon.

▶ **Data transfer.** Because of the rules agreed upon during setup, each party to the dialog knows what to expect. Communication is therefore efficient, and errors are easy to detect.

▶ **Connection release.** When the session is completed, the dialog is terminated in an orderly fashion.

The connection establishment phase establishes the parameters for the communication session. Actually, the connection establishment phase is comprised of several tasks, including the following:

▶ Specification of required services

▶ User login authentication and other security procedures

▶ Negotiation of protocols and protocol parameters

▶ Notification of connection IDs

▶ Establishment of dialog control, as well as acknowledgment of numbering and retransmission procedures

After the connection is established, the devices involved can initiate a dialog (data transfer phase). Besides exchanging data, these devices exchange acknowledgments and other control data that manage the dialog.

The Session layer also can incorporate protocols to resume dialogs that have been interrupted. After a formal dialog has been established, devices recognize a lost connection whenever the connection has not been formally released. Therefore, a device realizes that a connection has been lost when the device fails to receive an expected acknowledgment or data transmission.

Within a certain time period, two devices can reenter the session that was interrupted but not released. The connection release phase is an orderly process that shuts down communication and releases resources on the service provider.

OSI Presentation Layer Concepts

The Presentation layer deals with the syntax, or grammatical rules, needed for communication between two computers. The Presentation layer converts system-specific data from the Application layer into a common, machine-independent format that will support a more standardized design for lower protocol layers.

The Presentation layer also attends to other details of data formatting, such as data encryption and data compression.

> The name "Presentation layer" has caused considerable confusion in the industry because some people mistakenly believe that this layer presents data to the user. However, the name has nothing to do with displaying data. Instead, this function is performed by applications running above the Application layer.
>
> The Presentation layer is so named because it presents a uniform data format to the Application layer. As a matter of fact, this layer is not commonly implemented because applications typically perform most Presentation layer functions.

On the receiving end, the Presentation layer converts the machine-independent data from the network into the format required for the local system. This conversion could include the following:

▶ **Bit-order translation.** When binary numbers are transmitted through a network, they are sent one bit at a time. The transmitting computer can start at either end of the number. Some computers start at the *most-significant digit (MSD);* others start at the *least-significant digit (LSD).*

▶ **Byte-order translation.** Complex values generally must be represented with more than one byte, but different computers use different conventions to determine which byte should be transmitted first. Intel microprocessors, for example, start with the least-significant byte and are called *little* *endian.* Motorola microprocessors, on the other hand, start with the most-significant byte and are called *big endian.* Byte-order translation might be needed to reconcile these differences when transferring data between a PC and a Macintosh.

▶ **Character code translation.** Different computers use different binary schemes for representing character sets. For instance: *ASCII,* the American Standard Code for Information Interchange, is used to represent English characters on all microcomputers and most minicomputers (see fig. 2.8); *EBCDIC,* the Extended Binary Coded Decimal Interchange Code, is used to represent English characters on IBM mainframes (see fig. 2.9); and *Shift-JIS* is used to represent Japanese characters.

▶ **File Syntax Translation.** File formats differ between computers. For instance, Macintosh files actually consist of two related files called a data fork and a resource fork. PC files, on the other hand, consist of a single file.

Many vendors are beginning to incorporate *Unicode* in their products. Unicode, a 16-bit code that can represent 65,536 characters in English and other languages, is organized into code pages devoted to the characters required for a given language. Unicode improves the portability of products between different language environments.

The redirector service (see Chapter 1, "Networking Terms and Concepts") operates at the OSI Presentation layer.

Figure 2.8

The ASCII character code represents English characters on microcomputers and most minicomputers.

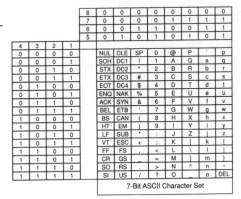
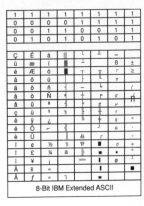

Figure 2.9

The EBCDIC character code represents English characters on IBM mainframes.

OSI Application Layer Concepts

The Application layer of the OSI reference model is concerned with providing services on the network, including file services, print services, e-mail services, and database services, among others.

A common misunderstanding is that the Application layer is responsible for running user applications such as word processors. This is not the case. The Application layer, however, does provide an interface whereby applications can communicate with the network.

The Application layer also advertises the available services to the network.

Communications Devices and OSI

 Each of the three lowest levels of the OSI model supports an important network hardware device. The function of these devices (and the differences between them) sheds some light on the functions of their corresponding OSI layers. This section describes how the following devices fit within the OSI model:

▶ **Repeaters.** Operate at the OSI Physical layer

▶ **Bridges.** Operate at the OSI Data Link layer

▶ **Routers (and brouters).** Operate at the OSI Network layer

These devices are discussed in greater detail in Chapter 6. The *network adapter* (an all-important connectivity component that operates at the OSI Data Link layer) is discussed in Chapter 10, "Network Adapter Cards."

Repeaters

A *repeater* is a network device that repeats a signal from one port onto the other ports to which it is connected (see fig. 2.10). Repeaters operate at the OSI Physical layer. A repeater does not filter or interpret anything; instead, it merely repeats (regenerates) a signal, passing all network traffic in all directions.

Figure 2.10

A repeater regenerates a weak signal.

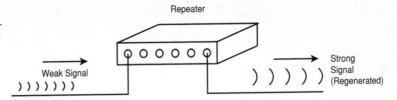

A repeater can operate at the OSI Physical layer because a repeater doesn't require any addressing information from the data frame. Therefore, the repeater doesn't have to pass the frame to upper layers where addresses and other parameters are interpreted. A repeater merely passes along bits of data, even if a data frame is corrupt. In fact, a repeater even will forward a broadcast storm caused by a malfunctioning adapter (see Chapter 13, "Troubleshooting," for details).

The primary purpose of a repeater is to enable the network to expand beyond the distance limitations of the transmission medium (see Chapter 3 for more details).

The advantages of repeaters are that they are inexpensive and simple. In addition, though they cannot connect networks with dissimilar data frames (such as a Token Ring network to an Ethernet network), some repeaters can connect segments with similar frame types but dissimilar cabling.

Bridges

A *bridge* is a connectivity device that operates at the OSI Data Link layer. The messaging parameters available at the Data Link layer enable a bridge to pass a frame in the direction of its destination without simultaneously forwarding it to segments for which it was not intended. In other words, a bridge can filter network traffic. This filtering process reduces overall traffic because the bridge segments the network, passing frames only when they can't be delivered on the local segment and passing frames only to the segment for which they are intended.

Figure 2.11 depicts a simple bridge implementation. In this process, a bridge filters traffic by tracking and checking the Data Link layer's MAC sublayer addresses of incoming frames. The bridge monitors the source addresses of incoming frames and builds a routing table that shows which nodes are on each of the segments. When a data frame arrives, the bridge checks the frame's destination address and forwards the frame to the segment that contains the destination node. If the destination node exists on the same segment as the source node, the bridge stops the frame so it doesn't pass unnecessarily to the rest of the network. If the bridge can't find the destination address in its routing table, it forwards the frame to all segments except the source segment.

Figure 2.11

A simple bridge configuration.

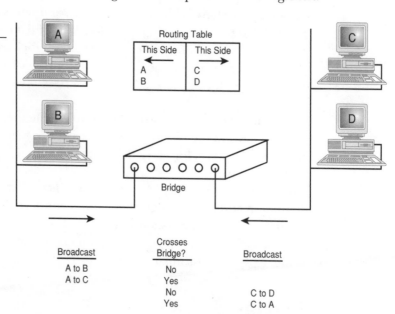

A bridge can perform the same functions a repeater performs, including expanding cabling distance and linking dissimilar cable types. In addition, a bridge can improve performance and reduce network traffic by splitting the network and confining traffic to smaller segments.

Routers

A *router* is a connectivity device that operates at the OSI Network layer. The information available at the Network layer gives a router far more sophisticated packet-delivery capabilities than a bridge provides. As with a bridge, a router constructs a routing table, but the Network layer addressing information (discussed earlier in this chapter) enables routers to pass packets through a chain of other routers, or even choose the best route for a packet if several routes exist. (See Chapter 6 for more information on routers and how they operate.)

A hybrid device called a *brouter* combines some characteristics of a router and a bridge. A brouter routes routable protocols using information available at the Network layer and acts as a bridge for nonroutable protocols. (A routable protocol is a protocol that can pass through a router. TCP/IP and IPX/SPX are examples of routable protocols—see Chapter 5, "Transport Protocols," for more information.)

Serial Line Internet Protocol (SLIP) and Point-to-Point Protocol (PPP)

Two other standards vital to network communication are *Serial Line Internet Protocol (SLIP)* and *Point-to-Point Protocol (PPP)*. SLIP and PPP were designed to support dial-up access to networks based on the Internet protocols. SLIP is a simple protocol that functions at the Physical layer, whereas PPP is a considerably enhanced protocol that provides Physical layer and Data Link layer functionality. The relationship of both to the OSI model is shown in figure 2.12.

Figure 2.12

The relationship of SLIP and PPP to the OSI reference model.

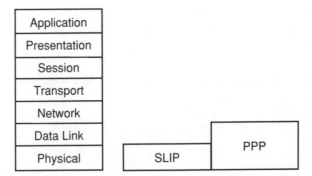

Developed to provide dial-up TCP/IP connections, SLIP is an extremely rudimentary protocol that suffers from a lack of rigid standardization, which sometimes hinders different implementations from interoperating.

Windows NT supports both SLIP and PPP from the client end using the Dial-Up Networking application. On the server end, Windows NT RAS (Remote Access Service) supports PPP but doesn't support SLIP. In other words, Windows NT can act as a PPP server but not as a SLIP server.

SLIP is most commonly used on older systems or for dial-up connections to the Internet via SLIP-server Internet hosts.

PPP was defined by the Internet Engineering Task Force (IETF) to improve on SLIP by providing the following features:

▶ Security using password logon

▶ Simultaneous support for multiple protocols on the same link

▶ Dynamic IP addressing

▶ Error control

Different PPP implementations might offer different levels of service and negotiate service levels when connections are made. Because of its versatility, interoperability, and additional features, PPP is presently surpassing SLIP as the most popular serial-line protocol.

Certain dial-up configurations cannot use SLIP for the following reasons:

▶ **SLIP supports the TCP/IP transport protocol only.** PPP, however, supports TCP/IP, as well as a number of other protocols, such as NetBEUI, IPX, AppleTalk, and DECnet. In addition, PPP can support multiple protocols over the same link.

▶ **SLIP requires static IP addresses.** Because SLIP requires static IP addresses, SLIP servers do not support Dynamic Host Configuration Protocol (DHCP), which assigns IP addresses dynamically. (DHCP enables clients to share IP addresses so that a relatively small number of IP addresses can serve a larger user base.) If the dial-up server uses DHCP to assign an IP address to the client, the dial-up connection won't use SLIP.

▶ **SLIP does not support dynamic addressing through DHCP.** Because of this, SLIP connections cannot dynamically assign a WINS or DNS server. (See exercise 2.2 at the end of this chapter.)

note

Windows NT RAS (using PPP) offers a number of other interesting features, including the following:

▶ **PPP Multilink Protocol.** Multilink enables a single connection to use several physical pathways (such as modems, ISDN lines, and X.25 cards). Utilizing multiple pathways for a single connection increases bandwidth and, therefore, performance.

▶ **NetBIOS Gateway.** A RAS server can connect a client running the NetBEUI protocol with a TCP/IP or IPX network by serving as a NetBIOS gateway.

▶ **IPX or IP Router.** A RAS server can act as a router for IPX/SPX and TCP/IP networks. (See Chapter 6 for more information on routers.)

The IEEE 802 Family

The Institute of Electrical and Electronic Engineers (IEEE) is the largest professional organization in the world and is extremely influential with regard to setting standards. The 802 committee of the IEEE, for example, has developed a series of standards for LANs and WANs. The IEEE standards govern lower-layer protocols and interactions with transmission media. These standards have been recognized and reissued by the ISO as the ISO 802 standards.

Twelve subcommittees oversee the 802 standards. (A thirteenth committee has been proposed for the development of the 100BASE-X standard.) Figure 2.13 illustrates the position each standard occupies in the OSI reference model.

Figure 2.13

The relationship between the IEEE 802 standards and the OSI reference model.

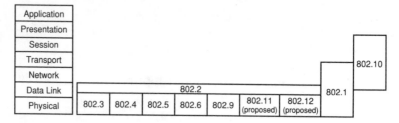

IEEE 802.2

The IEEE 802.2 standard defines an LLC sublayer that is used by other lower-layer protocols. Because these lower-layer protocols can use a single LLC protocol layer, Network layer protocols can be designed independently of both the network's Physical layer and MAC sublayer implementations.

The LLC appends to packets a header that identifies the upper-layer protocols associated with the frame. This header also declares the processes that are the source and destination of each packet.

IEEE 802.3

The IEEE 802.3 standard defines a network derived from the Ethernet network originally developed by Digital, Intel, and Xerox. This standard defines characteristics related to the MAC sublayer of the Data Link layer and the OSI Physical layer. With one minor distinction—frame type—IEEE 802.3 Ethernet functions identically to DIX Ethernet v.2. These two standards can even coexist on the same cabling system, although devices using one standard cannot communicate directly with devices using the other.

The MAC sublayer uses a type of contention access called *Carrier Sense Multiple Access with Collision Detection (CSMA/CD)*. This technique reduces the incidence of collision by having each device listen to the network to determine whether it's quiet ("carrier sensing"); a device attempts to transmit only when the network is quiescent. This reduces but does not eliminate collisions because signals take some time to propagate through the network. As devices transmit, they continue to listen so they can detect a collision should it occur. When a collision occurs, all devices cease transmitting and send a "jamming" signal that notifies all stations of the collision. Then, each device waits a random amount of time before attempting to transmit again. This combination of safeguards significantly reduces collisions on all but the busiest networks.

IEEE 802.4

The 802.4 standard describes a network with a bus physical topology that controls media access with a token mechanism. This standard was designed to meet the needs of industrial automation systems but has gained little popularity. Both baseband and broadband (using 75-ohm coaxial cable) configurations are available.

IEEE 802.5

The IEEE 802.5 standard was derived from IBM's Token Ring network, which employs a ring logical topology and token-based media-access control. Data rates of 1, 4, and 16 Mbps have been defined for this standard.

IEEE 802.6

The IEEE 802.6 standard describes a MAN standard called *Distributed Queue Dual Bus (DQDB)*. Much more than a data network technology, DQDB is suited to data, voice, and video transmissions. The network is based on fiber-optic cable in a dual-bus topology, and traffic on each bus is unidirectional. When operated in pairs, the two buses provide a fault-tolerant configuration. Bandwidth is allocated using time slots, and both synchronous and asynchronous modes are supported.

IEEE 802.9

The IEEE 802.9 standard supports a 10-Mbps asynchronous channel, along with 96 64-Kbps (6 Mbps total bandwidth) of channels that can be dedicated to specific data streams. The total bandwidth is 16 Mbps. This standard is called *Isochronous Ethernet (IsoEnet)* and is designed for settings with a mix of bursty and time-critical traffic.

IEEE 802.11

IEEE 802.11 is a standard for wireless LANs and is currently under development. A CSMA/CD method has been approved, but the final standard is pending.

IEEE 802.12

The IEEE 802.12 standard is based on a 100-Mbps proposal promoted by AT&T, IBM, and Hewlett-Packard. Called *100VG-AnyLAN*, the network is based on a star-wiring topology and a contention-based access method whereby devices signal the wiring hub when they need to transmit data. Devices can transmit only when granted permission by the hub. This standard is intended to provide a high-speed network that can operate in mixed Ethernet and Token Ring environments by supporting both frame types.

IEEE 802.3 and IEEE 802.5 Media

IEEE 802.2 (topology independent), IEEE 802.3 (based on Ethernet), and IEEE 802.5 (based on Token Ring) are the most commonly used IEEE 802 standards. Carefully read the following overview of the media each uses—Microsoft expects you to describe "the characteristics and purpose of the media used in IEEE 802.3 and IEEE 802.5" for the Networking Essentials exam. (Chapters 3 and 4 discuss Ethernet and Token Ring media in greater detail.)

The IEEE 802.3 Physical layer definition describes signaling methods (both baseband and broadband), data rates, media, and topologies. Several Physical layer variants also have been defined.

Each variant is named following a convention that states the signaling rate (1 or 10) in Mbps, baseband (BASE) or broadband (BROAD) mode, and a designation of the media characteristics.

The following list details the IEEE 802.3 variants:

- ▶ **1BASE5.** This 1-Mbps network utilizes UTP cable with a signal range up to 500 meters (250 meters per segment). A star physical topology is used.

- ▶ **10BASE5.** Typically called Thick Ethernet, or Thicknet, this variant uses a large diameter (10 mm) "thick" coaxial cable with a 50-ohm impedance. A data rate of 10 Mbps is supported with a signaling range of 500 meters per cable segment on a physical bus topology.

- ▶ **10BASE2.** Similar to Thicknet, this variant uses a thinner coaxial cable that can support cable runs of 185 meters. (In this case, the "2" only indicates an approximate cable range.) The transmission rate remains at 10 Mbps, and the physical topology is a bus. This variant typically is called Thin Ethernet, or Thinnet.

- ▶ **10BASE-F.** This variant uses fiber-optic cables to support 10-Mbps signaling with a range of 4 kilometers. Three subcategories include *10BASE-FL* (fiber link), *10BASE-FB* (fiber backbone), and *10BASE-FP* (fiber passive).

- ▶ **10BROAD36.** This broadband standard supports channel signal rates of 10 Mbps. A 75-ohm coaxial cable supports cable runs of 1,800 meters (up to 3,600 meters in a dual-cable configuration) using a physical bus topology.

- ▶ **10BASE-T.** This variant uses UTP cable in a star physical topology. The signaling rate remains at 10 Mbps, and devices can be up to 100 meters from a wiring hub.

- ▶ **100BASE-X.** This proposed standard is similar to 10BASE-T but supports 100 Mbps data rates.

Some disagreement exists in the industry regarding the proper use of the name "Ethernet." Xerox has placed the name "Ethernet" in the public domain, which means that no one can claim authority over it. Purists, however, often claim that "Ethernet" refers only to the original Digital-Intel-Xerox standard. More frequently, however, the term designates any network based on CSMA/CD access-control methods.

Usually, it is necessary to be specific about the standard that applies to a given network configuration. The original standard is called Ethernet version 2 (the older version 1 is still in occasional use) or Ethernet-II. The IEEE standard is distinguished by its committee title as 802.3.

This distinction is important because Ethernet version 2 and 802.3 Ethernet use incompatible frame types. Devices using one frame type cannot communicate with devices using the other frame type.

The IEEE 802.5 standard does not describe a cabling system. Most implementations are based on the IBM cabling system, which uses twisted-pair cable wired in a physical star. See Chapter 3 and Chapter 4 for more information on Token Ring cabling and topologies.

NDIS and ODI

The *Network Driver Interface Specification (NDIS)*, a standard developed by Microsoft and 3Com Corp., describes the interface between the network transport protocol and the Data Link layer network adapter driver. The following list details the goals of NDIS:

▶ To provide a vendor-neutral boundary between the protocol and the network adapter driver so that any NDIS-compliant protocol stack can operate with any NDIS-compliant adapter driver.

▶ To define a method for binding multiple protocols to a single driver so that the adapter can simultaneously support communications under multiple protocols. In addition, the method enables you to bind one protocol to more than one adapter.

The *Open Data-Link Interface (ODI)*, developed by Apple and Novell, serves the same function as NDIS. Originally, ODI was written for NetWare and Macintosh environments. Like NDIS, ODI provides rules that establish a vendor-neutral interface between the protocol stack and the adapter driver. This interface also enables one or more network drivers to support one or more protocol stacks.

Summary

This chapter discussed some of the important standards that define the networking environment. An understanding of these standards is essential for understanding the networking topics discussed in later chapters. This chapter covered the following:

▶ The OSI model

▶ SLIP and PPP

▶ The IEEE 802 Standards

▶ NDIS and ODI

Later chapters in this book look more closely at related topics, including transmission media, topologies, and connectivity devices.

Exercises

Exercise 2.1: Gateway Services for NetWare

Objective: Install and explore Windows NT Server's Gateway Services for NetWare, an example of a gateway service.

Estimated time: 15 minutes

Gateway Services for NetWare is a Windows NT service that enables a Windows NT Server system to act as a gateway to NetWare resources. A gateway (as described in this chapter) provides a conduit by which computers in one operating environment can access resources located in a dissimilar operating environment. A gateway works by stripping the incompatible protocol layers of an incoming packet and replacing them with the alternative headers needed for the packet to reach its destination. (See Chapter 6 for more information on gateways.) Gateway Services for NetWare provides a Microsoft Network with access to NetWare resources. To a Microsoft Network client that uses Server Message Block (such as Windows NT, Windows 95, and Windows for Workgroups), the NetWare resources will appear as Windows NT resources on the gateway machine.

1. Look in Windows NT's Server Control Panel for an icon labeled "GSNW" (Gateway Services for NetWare). If this icon is present, double-click on it and proceed to step 6. Otherwise, continue with step 2.

2. Double-click the Control Panel Network application and choose the Services tab.

3. In the Network application's Services tab, click on the Add button, which invokes the Select Network Services dialog box.

4. In the Select Network Services dialog box, double-click on Gateway (and Client) Services for NetWare. Windows NT will prompt you for the Windows NT Installation CD-ROM. Windows NT then will install Gateway Services for NetWare and the NWLink protocol (if it isn't already installed). If RAS is present on your system, Windows NT will ask if you want to add IPX/SPX to your RAS configuration. When the

installation is complete, shut down your system and log on again. As you log on, you might be asked to select a NetWare preferred server. Choose None and click OK.

5. Double-click on the GSNW icon in the Control Panel.

6. The Gateway Service for NetWare dialog box appears on your screen (see fig. 2.14). If you were configuring a real gateway, you would need to enter the NetWare server name in the Select Preferred Server box.

Figure 2.14

The Gateway Service for NetWare dialog box.

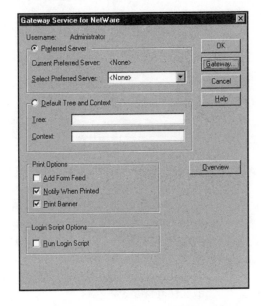

7. Click the Overview button for a directory of GSNW Help topics. You can browse through the topics if you have questions about configuring a NetWare gateway.

8. Click the Gateway button (refer to fig. 2.14) to configure a NetWare gateway. The Configure Gateway dialog box appears on your screen (see fig. 2.15). If you were configuring an actual gateway, you first would have to create a group called NTGATEWAY on the NetWare server, then set up a user account for the gateway on the Windows NT Server machine, and finally add the gateway user account to the NTGATEWAY group on the NetWare server. In the 9.In the

continues

Exercise 2.1: Continued

Configure Gateway dialog box, you then would check the Enable Gateway box, enter the gateway account and password, and click Add to invoke the New Share dialog box.

Figure 2.15

The Configure Gateway dialog box.

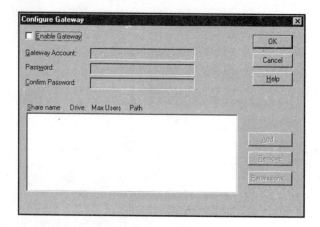

9. New Share dialog box, you can instruct the system to enable you to share NetWare resources on the Microsoft network. To do so, enter a share name and a network path and then enter a drive letter for a network drive mapping. In addition, you can specify a maximum number of users for the share. When you are finished, click Cancel (or click OK if you are actually connected to a NetWare network and you are setting up a real share).

10. If you configured an actual share in step 9, the share will appear in the share list of the Configure Gateway dialog box (refer to fig. 2.15). This new share will appear as a Windows NT share in the browse lists of Microsoft network clients.

GSNW also includes a client package, called Client Services for NetWare, which enables your computer to access NetWare resources as a NetWare client.

Exercise 2.2:   SLIP and PPP in Dial-Up Networking

Objective: Explore the Dial-Up Networking application and learn how to configure Dial-Up Networking for SLIP or PPP.

Estimated time: 10 minutes

1. From the Windows NT Start menu, choose Programs/ Administrative Tools and select Dial-Up Networking. The Dial-Up Networking application enables you to connect to another computer as a dial-up client using SLIP or PPP.

To get the full effect of this exercise, TCP/IP, NWLink, and Net-BEUI must be installed on your system and must be enabled for dial-out connections. Exercise 5.1 in Chapter 5 describes how to install protocols. To enable the protocols for dial-out connections, follow these steps:

   A. Start the Control Panel Network application and select the Services tab. If Remote Access Service isn't installed, click the Add button to install it.

   B. Double-click on Remote Access Service in the Services tab (or select Remote Access Service and click Properties).

   C. In the Remote Access Setup dialog box, click the Configure button and make sure either the Dial Out Only or Dial Out And Receive Calls button is selected under Port Usage. Click OK.

   D. In the Remote Access Setup dialog box, click the Network button. Select dial out protocols NetBEUI, TCP/IP, and IPX. Click OK.

   E. Click Continue in the Remote Access Setup dialog box.

2. In the Dial-Up Networking main screen, click the New button to set up a new connection. The New Phonebook Entry dialog box appears (see fig. 2.16). The tabs of the New Phonebook Entry dialog box enable you to enter a phone

continues

Exercise 2.2: Continued

---

number, modem information, security information, and a login script. In addition, you can enter information about the dial-up server to which you are connecting. Click the Server tab when finished.

Figure 2.16

The Dial-Up Net-working New Phonebook Entry dialog box enables you to enter information about the new connection.

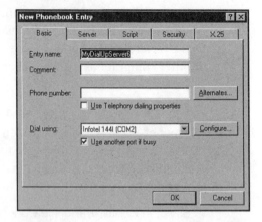

3. In the Dial-Up Networking Server tab (see fig. 2.17), click the arrow to the right of the box labeled Dial-up server type. Note that the default option is PPP: Windows NT, Windows 95 Plus, Internet. PPP enables you to connect to a Windows NT RAS server, a Windows 95 machine with the Windows 95 Plus Dial-up Server feature, or a server with an Internet-style TCP/IP configuration.

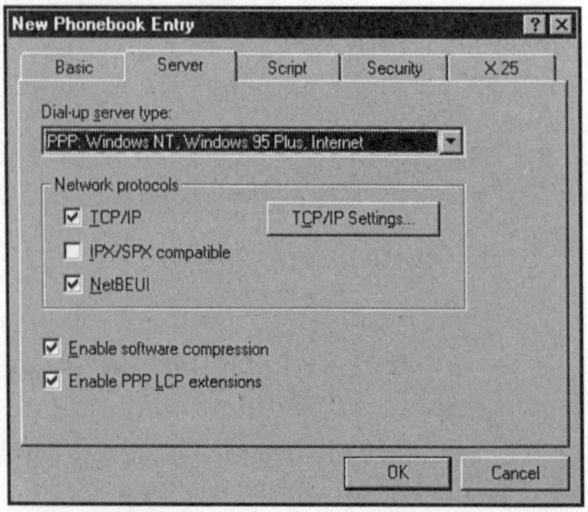

Figure 2.17

The Dial-Up Networking New Phonebook Entry Server tab.

4. In the Dial-up server type box, select the SLIP: Internet option. (TCP/IP must be installed on your machine.) Examine the rest of the Server tab options. The other protocols (IPX/SPX and NetBEUI) should be grayed out, as should software compression. Your only protocol option is TCP/IP. Check the TCP/IP check box and click the TCP/IP Settings button. Note the boxes for a static IP address and static DNS and WINS server addresses. Click Cancel.

5. In the New Phonebook Entry Server tab, click the down arrow to the right of the Dial-up server type box and choose PPP: Windows NT, Windows 95 Plus, Internet. Note that the IPX/SPX Compatible and NetBEUI protocol options are now available (if they are installed on your system and enabled for dial-out connections—see preceding note), as are software compression and PPP LCP extensions. Select the TCP/IP protocol and click the TCP/IP Settings button. Note that under a PPP connection, the TCP/IP Settings dialog box contains radio-button options for a server-assigned IP address and server-assigned name server addresses.

6. Click Cancel to exit TCP/IP Settings, Cancel to exit New Phonebook Entry, and Close to exit Dial-Up Networking.

Review Questions

The following questions test your knowledge of the information in this chapter. For additional exam help, visit Microsoft's site at www.microsoft.com/train_cert/cert/Mcpsteps.htm.

1. The OSI model organizes communication protocols into how many layers?

    A. 3

    B. 7

    C. 17

    D. 56

2. The layers of the OSI model (in order) are included in which of the following choices?

    A. Physical, Data Link, Network, Transport, System, Presentation, Application

    B. Physical, Data Link, Network, Transport, Session, Presentation, Application

    C. Physical, Data Link, Network, Transform, Session, Presentation, Application

    D. Presentation, Data Link, Network, Transport, Session, Physical, Application

3. In the OSI model, what is the relationship of a layer (N) to the layer above it (layer N+1)?

    A. Layer N provides services for layer N+1.

    B. Layer N+1 adds a header to information received from layer N.

    C. Layer N utilizes services provided by layer N+1.

    D. Layer N has no effect on layer N+1.

4. Two different computer types can communicate if
   _____.

   A. they conform to the OSI model

   B. they are both using TCP/IP

   C. they are using compatible protocol stacks

   D. they are a Macintosh and a Unix workstation

5. Which three of the following statements regarding protocol stacks are true?

   A. A given protocol stack can run on only one computer type.

   B. Layers add headers to packets received from higher layers in the protocol stack.

   C. A protocol stack is a hierarchical set of protocols.

   D. Each layer provides services for the next-highest layer.

6. Which protocol layer enables multiple devices to share the transmission medium?

   A. Physical

   B. MAC

   C. LLC

   D. Network

7. Which switching method employs virtual circuits?

   A. Message

   B. Circuit

   C. Packet

   D. All the above

8. Which OSI layer is concerned with data encryption?

   A. Network

   B. Transport

   C. Session

   D. Presentation

9. Which switching method makes the most efficient use of network bandwidth?

   A. Message

   B. Circuit

   C. Packet

   D. All methods are about equal

10. What is another name for a message-switching network?

   A. Connectionless

   B. Datagram

   C. Store-and-forward

   D. Virtual circuit

11. Which two statements about virtual circuits are true?

   A. They usually are associated with connection-oriented services.

   B. A virtual circuit represents a specific path through the network.

   C. A virtual circuit appears to the connected devices as a dedicated network path.

   D. Virtual circuits dedicate a communication channel to a single conversation.

12. Which three of the following terms are related?

    A. Port

    B. Connection ID

    C. Socket

    D. Service address

13. Which switching method fragments messages into small units that are routed through independent paths?

    A. Message

    B. Packet

    C. Circuit

    D. Virtual

14. Which two of the following methods of dialog control provide two-way communication?

    A. Simple duplex

    B. Simplex

    C. Half-duplex

    D. Full-duplex

15. Dialog control is a function of which layer of the OSI reference model?

    A. Network

    B. Transport

    C. Session

    D. Presentation

16. Which three of the following are functions of session administration?

    A. Connection establishment

    B. Checksum error detection

    C. Data transfer

    D. Connection release

17. Which two of the following are functions of connection establishment?

    A. Resumption of interrupted communication

    B. Verification of logon name and password

    C. Determination of required services

    D. Acknowledgment of data receipt

18. Which two of the following are possible functions of the Presentation layer?

    A. Data encryption

    B. Presentation of data on display devices

    C. Data translation

    D. Display format conversion

19. Which three of the following are possible functions of the Application layer?

    A. Network printing service

    B. End-user applications

    C. Client access to network services

    D. Service advertisement

20. PPP operates at which two of the following OSI layers?

    A. Physical

    B. Data Link

C. Network

D. Transport

21. SLIP supports which of the following transport protocols?

A. IPX/SPX

B. NetBEUI

C. TCP/IP

D. All the above

22. IEEE 802.3 is associated with which of the following network architectures?

A. Token Ring

B. Ethernet

C. Internet

D. None of the above

23. IEEE 802.5 is associated with which of the following network architectures?

A. Token Ring

B. Ethernet

C. Internet

D. None of the above

24. NDIS describes the interface between _____ and _____.

A. user

B. network transport protocol

C. Physical layer

D. network adapter driver

Pretest Answers

1. B (see the section titled "Routers")

2. C (see the section titled "Connection-oriented and Connection-less Modes")

3. C (see the section titled "Serial Line Internet Protocol (SLIP) and Point-to-Point Protocol (PPP)")

4. D (see the section titled "The IEEE 802 Family")

Review Answers

1. B

2. B

3. A

4. C

5. B, C, D

6. B

7. C

8. D

9. C

10. C

11. A, C

12. A, C, D

13. B

14. C, D

15. C

16. A, C, D

17. B, C

18. A, C

19. A, C, D

20. A, B

21. C

22. B

23. A

24. B, D

Part 2

Planning

Chapter

Transmission Media

3

On any network, the various entities must communicate through some form of media. Just as humans can communicate through telephone wires or sound waves in the air, computers can communicate through cables, light, and radio waves. Transmission media enable computers to send and receive messages but do not guarantee that the messages will be understood.

This chapter discusses some of the most common network transmission media, such as coaxial cable, shielded twisted-pair cable, and unshielded twisted-pair cable. You also learn about network fiber-optic cable and wireless communications. To lay the groundwork for these issues, the chapter begins with an introduction to radio frequency transmissions and a look at some important characteristics of transmission media.

This chapter targets one multipart objective in the Planning section of the Networking Essentials exam:

Test Objectives

▶ Select the appropriate media for various situations. Media choices include the following:

  ▶ Twisted-pair cable

  ▶ Coaxial cable

  ▶ Fiber-optic cable

  ▶ Wireless communications

▶ Situational elements include the following:

  ▶ Cost

  ▶ Distance limitations

  ▶ Number of nodes

Test Yourself

Stop! Before reading this chapter, test yourself to determine how much study time you will need to devote to this section.

1. The maximum range for Thicknet cable is approximately _____.

    A. 100 m

    B. 185 m

    C. 500 m

    D. 1000 m

2. The _____ is commonly used to connect coaxial Thinnet cable.

    A. N-connector

    B. DB-15

    C. RJ-45

    D. BNC

3. Which of the following cabling types is most expensive to install?

    A. Fiber-optic

    B. Unshielded twisted-pair

    C. Shielded twisted-pair

    D. Coaxial Thicknet

4. _____ is a technique for systematically switching frequencies in the middle of a spread-spectrum transmission.

    A. Frequency shifting

    B. Frequency switching

    C. Frequency hopping

    D. Frequency shopping

Transmission Media Types

The most common type of media is copper cable. The most common types of copper cabling are twisted-pair and coaxial. *Twisted-pair* cabling used in a LAN is similar to the cabling used to connect your telephone to the wall outlet. Network *coaxial* cabling, on the other hand, is similar to the cable used to connect your television set to the cable TV outlet.

Another type of LAN connection media quickly gaining popularity is fiber-optic cable. Consisting of a number of glass or high-grade plastic optical strands surrounded by a tough cloth-and-plastic wrap, *fiber-optic cables* resemble coaxial cables from the outside. Fiber-optic network cabling is similar to the fiber-optic strand used in the fiber-optic lamps found in novelty stores, in which colored lights feed into optical strands to create the appearance of dozens of pinpoints of light.

Wireless media, which is, in a sense, no media at all, is also gaining popularity. Wireless transmissions use radio waves or infrared light to transmit data. Many major network vendors now offer wireless network adapters.

Transmission Frequencies

Transmission media make possible the transmission of the electronic signals from one computer to another computer. These electronic signals express data values in the form of binary (on/off) impulses. The signals are transmitted through the network using a combination of electronic devices (such as network boards and hubs) and transmission media (such as cables and radio) until they reach the desired destination computer.

All signals transmitted between computers consist of some form of electromagnetic (EM) waveform, ranging from radio frequencies through microwave and infrared light. Different media are used to transmit the signals, depending on the frequency of the EM waveform. Figure 3.1 illustrates the range of electromagnetic waveforms (known as the electromagnetic spectrum) and their associated frequencies.

Figure 3.1

The electro-magnetic spectrum.

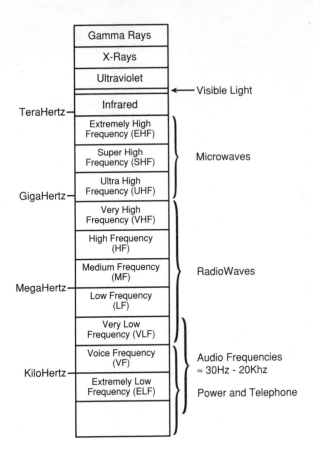

The electromagnetic spectrum consists of several categories of waveforms, including radio frequency waves, microwave transmissions, and infrared light.

Radio frequency waves often are used for LAN signaling. Radio frequencies can be transmitted across electrical cables (twisted-pair or coaxial) or by using radio broadcast transmission.

Microwave transmissions can be used for tightly focused transmissions between two points. Microwaves are used to communicate between Earth stations and satellites, for example, and they also are used for line-of-sight transmissions on the earth's surface. In addition, microwaves can be used in low-power forms to broadcast signals from a transmitter to many receivers. Cellular phone networks are examples of systems that use low-power microwave signals to broadcast signals.

Infrared light is ideal for many types of network communications. Infrared light can be transmitted across relatively short distances and can be either beamed between two points or broadcast from one point to many receivers. Infrared and higher frequencies of light also can be transmitted through fiber-optic cables.

The next sections examine examples of network transmission media and describe the advantages and disadvantages of each media type.

Characteristics of Transmission Media

Each type of transmission media has special characteristics that make it suitable for a specific type of service. You should be familiar with these characteristics:

▶ Cost

▶ Installation requirements

▶ Bandwidth

▶ Band Usage (Baseband or Broadband)

▶ Attenuation

▶ Immunity from electromagnetic interference

The last four characteristics require some explanation. The following sections introduce you to bandwidth, transmission type, attenuation, and electromagnetic interference.

Bandwidth

In computer networking, the term *bandwidth* refers to the measure of the capacity of a medium to transmit data. A medium that has a high capacity, for example, has a high bandwidth, whereas a medium that has limited capacity has a low bandwidth.

Bandwidth can be best understood by using an analogy to water hoses. If a half-inch garden hose can carry waterflow from a trickle up to two gallons per minute, then that hose can be said to have a bandwidth of two gallons per minute. A four-inch fire hose, however, might have a bandwidth that exceeds 100 gallons per minute.

Data transmission rates frequently are stated in terms of the bits that can be transmitted per second. An Ethernet LAN theoretically can transmit 10 million bits per second and has a bandwidth of 10 megabits per second (Mbps).

The bandwidth that a cable can accommodate is determined in part by the cable's length. A short cable generally can accommodate greater bandwidth than a long cable, which is one reason all cable designs specify maximum lengths for cable runs. Beyond those limits, the highest-frequency signals can deteriorate, and errors begin to occur in data signals.

> The term *bandwidth* also has another meaning. In the communications industry, bandwidth refers to the range of available frequencies between the lower frequency limit and the upper frequency limit. Frequencies are measured in Hertz (Hz), or cycles per second. The bandwidth of a voice telephone line is 400–4,000 Hz, which means that the line can transmit signals with frequencies ranging from 400 to 4,000 cycles per second.

Band Usage (Baseband or Broadband)

The two ways to allocate the capacity of transmission media are with baseband and broadband transmissions. *Baseband* devotes the entire capacity of the medium to one communication channel. *Broadband* enables two or more communication channels to share the bandwidth of the communications medium.

Baseband is the most common mode of operation. Most LANs function in baseband mode, for example. Baseband signaling can be accomplished with both analog and digital signals.

Although you might not realize it, you have a great deal of experience with broadband transmissions. Consider, for example, that the TV cable coming into your house from an antenna or a cable provider is a broadband medium. Many television signals can share the bandwidth of the cable because each signal is modulated using a separately assigned frequency. You can use the television tuner to choose the channel you want to watch by selecting its frequency. This technique of dividing bandwidth into frequency bands is called *frequency-division multiplexing (FDM)* and works only with analog signals. Another technique, called *time-division multiplexing (TDM),* supports digital signals.

Figure 3.2 contrasts the difference between baseband and broadband modes of operation.

Figure 3.2

Baseband and broadband transmission modes.

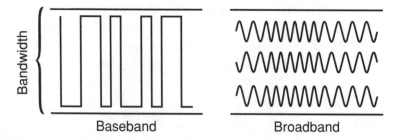

Multiplexing

Multiplexing is a technique that enables broadband media to support multiple data channels. Multiplexing makes sense under a number of circumstances:

▶ **When media bandwidth is costly.** A high-speed leased line, such as a T1 or T3, is expensive to lease. If the leased line has sufficient bandwidth, multiplexing can enable the same line to carry mainframe, LAN, voice, video conferencing, and various other data types.

▶ **When bandwidth is idle.** Many organizations have installed fiber-optic cable that is used only to partial capacity. With the proper equipment, a single fiber can support hundreds of megabits—or even a gigabit or more—of data.

▶ **When large amounts of data must be transmitted through low-capacity channels.** Multiplexing techniques can divide the original data stream into several lower-bandwidth channels, each of which can be transmitted through a lower-capacity medium. The signals then can be recombined at the receiving end.

Multiplexing refers to combining multiple data channels for transmission on a common medium. *Demultiplexing* refers to recovering the original separate channels from a multiplexed signal.

Multiplexing and demultiplexing are performed by a multiplexor (also called a *mux*), which usually has both capabilities.

Frequency-Division Multiplexing

Figure 3.3 illustrates frequency-division multiplexing (FDM). This technique works by converting all data channels to analog form. Each analog signal can be modulated by a separate frequency (called a *carrier frequency*) that makes it possible to recover that signal during the demultiplexing process. At the receiving end, the demultiplexor can select the desired carrier signal and use it to extract the data signal for that channel.

Figure 3.3

Frequency-division multiplexing.

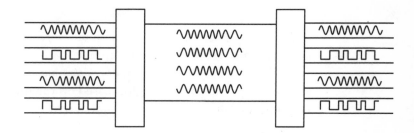

FDM can be used in broadband LANs (a standard for Ethernet also exists). One advantage of FDM is that it supports bidirectional signaling on the same cable.

Time-Division Multiplexing

Time-division multiplexing (TDM) divides a channel into time slots that are allocated to the data streams to be transmitted, as illustrated in figure 3.4. If the sender and receiver agree on the time-slot assignments, the receiver can easily recover and reconstruct the original data streams.

Figure 3.4

Time-division multiplexing creates time slots within the channel for the data streams.

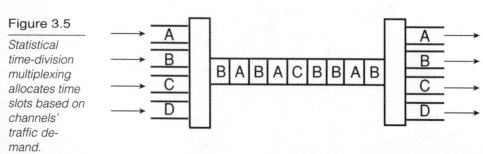

TDM transmits the multiplexed signal in baseband mode. Interestingly, this process makes it possible to multiplex a TDM multiplexed signal as one of the data channels on an FDM system.

Conventional TDM equipment utilizes fixed-time divisions and allocates time to a channel, regardless of that channel's level of activity. If a channel isn't busy, its time slot isn't being fully utilized. Because the time divisions are programmed into the configurations of the multiplexors, this technique often is referred to as *synchronous TDM.*

If using the capacity of the data medium more efficiently is important, a more sophisticated technique, *statistical time-division multiplexing (StatTDM)*, can be used. *A stat-mux* uses the time-slot technique but allocates time slots based on the traffic demand on the individual channels, as illustrated in figure 3.5. Notice that Channel B is allocated more time slots than Channel A, and that Channel C is allocated the fewest time slots. Channel D is idle, so no slots are allocated to it. To make this procedure work, the data transmitted for each time slot includes a control field that identifies the channel to which the data in the time slot should be assigned.

Figure 3.5

Statistical time-division multiplexing allocates time slots based on channels' traffic demand.

Attenuation

Attenuation is a measure of how much a signal weakens as it travels through a medium. This book doesn't discuss attenuation in formal terms, but it does address the impact of attenuation on performance.

Attenuation is a contributing factor to why cable designs must specify limits in the lengths of cable runs. When signal strength falls below certain limits, the electronic equipment that receives the signal can experience difficulty isolating the original signal from the noise present in all electronic transmissions. The effect is exactly like trying to tune in distant radio signals. Even if you can lock on to the signal on your radio, the sound generally still contains more noise than the sound for a local radio station.

Electromagnetic Interference

Electromagnetic interference (EMI) consists of outside electromagnetic noise that distorts the signal in a medium. When you listen to an AM radio, for example, you often hear EMI in the form of noise caused by nearby motors or lightning. Some network media are more susceptible to EMI than others.

Crosstalk is a special kind of interference caused by adjacent wires. Crosstalk is a particularly significant problem with computer networks because large numbers of cables often are located close together with minimal attention to exact placement.

Cable Media

For the Networking Essentials exam, you need to know how to make decisions about network transmission media based on some of the factors described in previous sections of this chapter. The following sections discuss three types of network cabling media, as follows:

▶ Coaxial cable

▶ Twisted-pair cable

▶ Fiber-optic cable

Later in this chapter, you learn about some of the wireless communication forms.

> Some large networks use combinations of media. When you mix and match different types of media, difficulties can arise, largely because mixed media require a greater level of expertise and training on the part of the network support staff. As the number of media types increases, your own responsibilities increase—when a problem arises on the LAN, the number of areas you must investigate increases dramatically when mixed transmission media are involved.

Coaxial Cable

Coaxial cables were the first cable types used in LANs. As shown in figure 3.6, coaxial cable gets its name because two conductors share a common axis; the cable is most frequently referred to as a *coax*.

Figure 3.6

The structure of coaxial cable consists of four main components.

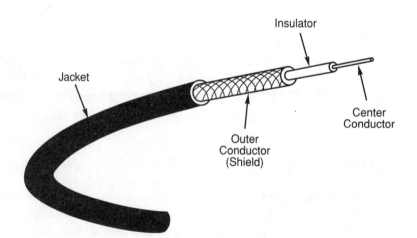

The components of a coaxial cable are as follows:

▶ A *center conductor*, although usually solid copper wire, sometimes is made of stranded wire.

▶ An *outer conductor* forms a tube surrounding the center conductor. This conductor can consist of braided wires, metallic foil, or both. The outer conductor, frequently called the *shield*, serves as a ground and also protects the inner conductor from EMI.

▶ An *insulation layer* keeps the outer conductor spaced evenly from the inner conductor.

▶ A plastic encasement (*jacket*) protects the cable from damage.

Types of Coaxial Cable

The two basic classifications for coaxial cable are as follows:

▶ Thinnet

▶ Thicknet

The following sections discuss thinnet and thicknet coaxial cabling.

Thinnet

Thinnet is a light and flexible cabling medium that is inexpensive and easy to install. Table 3.1 illustrates some Thinnet classifications. Note that Thinnet falls under the RG-58 family, which has a 50-Ohm impedance. Thinnet is approximately .25 inches (6 mm) in thickness.

All coaxial cables have a characteristic measurement called impedance, which is measured in ohms. *Impedance* is a measure of the apparent resistance to an alternating current. You must use a cable that has the proper impedance in any given situation.

Table 3.1

Thinnet Cable Classifications		
Cable	Description	Impedance
RG-58/U	Solid copper center	50-Ohm
RG-58 A/U	Wire strand center	50-Ohm
RG-58 C/U	Military version of RG-58 A/U	50-Ohm

Thinnet cable can reliably transmit a signal for 185 meters (about 610 feet).

Thicknet

Thicknet—big surprise—is thicker than Thinnet. Thicknet coaxial cable is approximately 0.5 inches (13 mm) in diameter. Because it is thicker and does not bend as readily as Thinnet, Thicknet cable is harder to work with. A thicker center core, however, means that Thicknet can carry more signals a longer distance than Thinnet. Thicknet can transmit a signal approximately 500 meters (1650 feet).

Thicknet cable is sometimes called *Standard Ethernet* (although other cabling types described in this chapter are used for Ethernet also). Thicknet can be used to connect two or more small Thinnet LANs into a larger network.

Because of its greater size, Thicknet is also more expensive than Thinnet. Thicknet can be installed safely outside, running from building to building.

Coaxial Characteristics

You should be familiar with the installation, cost, bandwidth, and EMI resistance characteristics of coaxial cable. The following sections discuss some of the characteristics of coaxial cable.

Installation

Coaxial cable typically is installed in two configurations: daisy-chain (from device to device—Ethernet) and star (ARCnet). Both are shown in figure 3.7.

Figure 3.7

Coaxial cable wiring configurations.

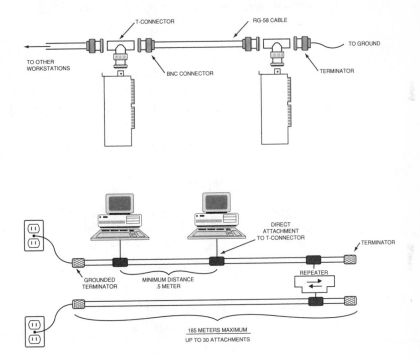

The Ethernet cabling shown in the figure is an example of Thinnet, which uses RG-58 type cable. Devices connect to the cable by means of *T-connectors*. Cables are used to provide connections between *T-connectors*. One characteristic of this type of cabling is that the ends of the cable run must be terminated by a special connector, called a *terminator*. The terminator contains a resistor that is matched to the characteristics of the cable. The resistor prevents signals that reach the end of the cable from bouncing back and causing interference.

Coaxial cable is reasonably easy to install because the cable is robust and difficult to damage. In addition, connectors can be installed with inexpensive tools and a bit of practice. The device-to-device cabling approach can be difficult to reconfigure, however, when new devices cannot be installed near an existing cabling path.

Cost

The coaxial cable used for Thinnet falls at the low end of the cost spectrum, whereas Thicknet is among the more costly options. Detailed cost comparisons are made later in this chapter in the section titled "Summary of Cable Characteristics."

Bandwidth

LANs that employ coaxial cable typically have a bandwidth between 2.5 Mbps (ARCnet) and 10 Mbps (Ethernet). Thicker coaxial cables offer higher bandwidth, and the potential bandwidth of coaxial is much higher than 10 Mbps. Current LAN technologies, however, don't take advantage of this potential.

EMI Characteristics

All copper media are sensitive to EMI, although the shield in coax makes the cable fairly resistant. Coaxial cables, however, do radiate a portion of their signal, and electronic eavesdropping equipment can detect this radiated signal.

Connectors for Coaxial Cable

Two types of connectors are commonly used with coaxial cable. The most common is the *British Naval Connector (BNC)*. Figure 3.8 depicts the following characteristics of BNC connectors and Thinnet cabling:

- ▶ A BNC T-connector connects the network board in the PC to the network. The T-connector attaches directly to the network board.

- ▶ BNC cable connectors attach cable segments to the T-connectors.

- ▶ A BNC barrel connector connects to Thinnet cables.

▶ Both ends of the cable must be terminated. A BNC terminator is a special connector that includes a resistor that is carefully matched to the characteristics of the cable system.

▶ One of the terminators must be grounded. A wire from the
connector is attached to a grounded point, such as the center screw of a grounded electrical outlet.

Figure 3.8

*Thinnet uses
BNC
T-connectors .*

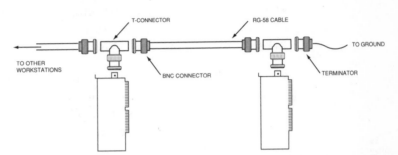

In contrast, Thicknet uses *N-connectors,* which screw on instead of
using a twist-lock (see fig. 3.9). As with Thinnet, both ends of the
cable must be terminated, and one end must be grounded.

Figure 3.9

*Connectors
and cabling
for Thicknet.*

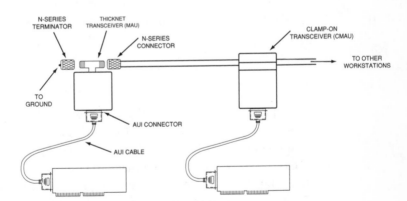

Workstations don't connect directly to the cable with Thicknet. Instead, a connecting device called a *transceiver* is attached to the Thicknet cable. This transceiver has a port for an *AUI connector,* and an *AUI cable* (also called a *transceiver cable* or a *drop cable*) connects the workstation to the Thicknet medium. Transceivers can connect to Thicknet cables in the following two ways:

▶ Transceivers can connect by cutting the cable and using N-connectors and a T-connector on the transceiver. As a result, the original method now is used rather infrequently.

▶ The more common approach is to use a clamp-on transceiver, which has pins that penetrate the cable without the need for cutting it. Because clamp-on transceivers force sharp teeth into the cable, they frequently are referred to as *vampire taps.*

You can use a transceiver to connect a Thinnet LAN to a Thicknet backbone.

AUI port connectors sometimes are called DIX connectors or DB-15 connectors.

Coax and Fire Code Classifications

The space above a drop ceiling (between the ceiling and the floor of a building's next level) is extremely significant to both network administrators and fire marshals. This space (called the *plenum*—see fig. 3.10) is a convenient place to run network cables around a building. The plenum, however, is typically an open space in which air circulates freely, and, consequently, fire marshals pay special attention to it.

Figure 3.10

The plenum—the space between the ceiling of one room and the floor of the level above—is often a convenient spot for network cabling.

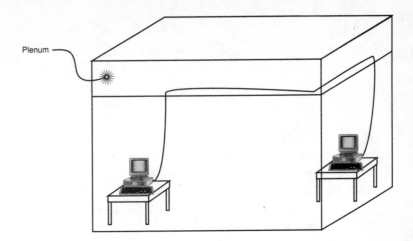

The most common outer covering for coaxial cabling is *polyvinyl chloride (PVC)*. PVC cabling gives off poisonous fumes when it burns. For that reason, fire codes prohibit PVC cabling in the plenum because poisonous fumes in the plenum can circulate freely throughout the building.

Plenum-grade coaxial cabling is specially designed to be used without conduit in plenums, walls, and other areas where fire codes prohibit PVC cabling. Plenum-grade cabling is less flexible and more expensive than PVC cabling, so it is used primarily where PVC cabling can't be used.

Twisted-Pair Cable

Twisted-pair cable has become the dominant cable type for all new network designs that employ copper cable. Among the several reasons for the popularity of twisted-pair cable, the most significant is its low cost. Twisted-pair cable is inexpensive to install and offers the lowest cost per foot of any cable type.

A basic twisted-pair cable consists of two strands of copper wire twisted together (see fig. 3.11). This twisting reduces the sensitivity of the cable to EMI and also reduces the tendency of the cable to radiate radio frequency noise that interferes with nearby cables and electronic components. This is because the radiated signals from the twisted wires tend to cancel each other out. (Antennas, which are purposely designed to radiate radio frequency signals, consist of parallel, not twisted, wires.)

Figure 3.11

Twisted-pair cable.

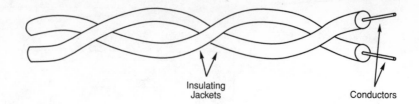

Insulating
Jackets

Conductors

Twisting also controls the tendency of the wires in the pair to cause EMI in each other. Whenever two wires are in close proximity, the signals in each wire tend to produce noise, called crosstalk, in the other. Twisting the wires in the pair reduces crosstalk in much the same way that twisting reduces the tendency of the wires to radiate EMI.

Two types of twisted-pair cable are used in LANs: *shielded* and *unshielded*.

Shielded Twisted-Pair (STP) Cable

Shielded twisted-pair cabling consists of one or more twisted pairs of cables enclosed in a foil wrap and woven copper shielding. Figure 3.12 shows IBM Type 1 cabling, the first cable type used with IBM Token Ring. Early LAN designers used shielded twisted-pair cable because the shield further reduces the tendency of the cable to radiate EMI and thus reduces the cable's sensitivity to outside interference.

Figure 3.12

A shielded twisted-pair cable.

Jacket

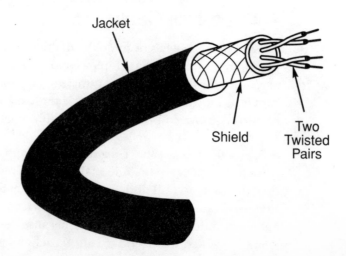

Shield

Two
Twisted
Pairs

Coaxial and STP cables use shields for the same purpose. The shield is connected to the ground portion of the electronic device to which the cable is connected. A *ground* is a portion of the device that serves as an electrical reference point, and usually, it literally is connected to a metal stake driven into the ground. A properly grounded shield prevents signals from getting into or out of the cable.

As shown in figure 3.12, IBM Type 1 cable includes two twisted pairs of wire within a single shield. Various types of STP cable exist, some that shield each pair individually and others that shield several pairs. The engineers who design a network's cabling system choose the exact configuration. IBM designates several twisted-pair cable types to use with their Token Ring network design, and each cable type is appropriate for a given kind of installation. A completely different type of STP is the standard cable for Apple's AppleTalk network.

Because so many different types of STP cable exist, stating precise characteristics is difficult. The following sections, however, offer some general guidelines.

Cost

STP cable costs more than thin coaxial or unshielded twisted-pair cable. STP is less costly, however, than thick coax or fiber-optic cable.

Installation

Naturally, different network types have different installation requirements. One major difference is the connector used. Apple LocalTalk connectors generally must be soldered during installation, a process that requires some practice and skill on the part of the installer. IBM Token Ring uses a so-called unisex data connector (the connectors are both male and female), which can be installed with such common tools as a knife, a wire stripper, and a large pair of pliers.

In many cases, installation can be greatly simplified by using prewired cables. You must learn to install the required connectors, however, when your installation requires the use of bulk cable.

> Most connectors require two connector types to complete a connection. The traditional designation for connector types is male and female. The male connector is the connector with pins, and the female connector has receptacles into which the pins insert. In a standard AC wall outlet, for example, the outlet itself is female and the plug on the line cord is male.
>
> These designations originated when electrical installation was a male province, so the terms male and female gradually are being replaced. A commonly used alternative is "pins and sockets."
>
> The IBM data connector is called a unisex connector because the connector has both pins and sockets. Any IBM data connector can connect to any other IBM data connector.

STP cable tends to be rather bulky. IBM Type 1 cable is approximately $1/2$ inch (13 mm) in diameter. Therefore, it can take little time to fill up cable paths with STP cables.

Capacity

STP cable has a theoretical capacity of 500 Mbps, although few implementations exceed 155 Mbps with 100-meter cable runs. The most common data rate for STP cable is 16 Mbps, which is the top data rate for Token Ring networks.

Attenuation

All varieties of twisted-pair cable have attenuation characteristics that limit the length of cable runs to a few hundred meters, although a 100-meter limit is most common.

EMI Characteristics

The shield in STP cable results in good EMI characteristics for copper cable, comparable to the EMI characteristics of coaxial cable. This is one reason STP might be preferred to unshielded twisted-pair cable in some situations. As with all copper cables, STP is sensitive to interference and vulnerable to electronic eaves-dropping.

Connectors for STP

AppleTalk and Token Ring networks can be cabled using UTP cable and RJ-45 connectors (described later in this chapter), but both networks originated as STP cabling systems. For STP cable, AppleTalk employs a DIN-type connector, shown in figure 3.13. IBM, on the other hand, uses the IBM Data Connector, as shown in figure 3.14.

Figure 3.13

Connectors used with STP cable.

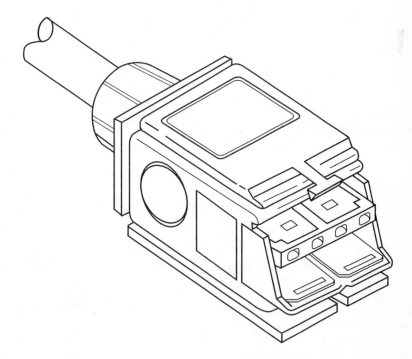

Figure 3.14

A PC ready to connect to a Token Ring network.

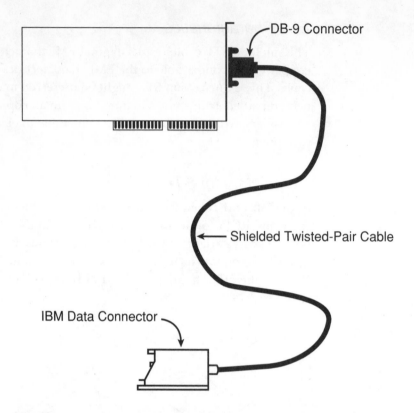

DB-9 Connector

Shielded Twisted-Pair Cable

IBM Data Connector

The IBM Data Connector is unusual because it doesn't come in two gender configurations. Instead, any IBM Data Connector can be snapped to any other IBM Data Connector. The IBM cabling system is discussed later in this chapter.

Unshielded Twisted-Pair (UTP) Cable

Unshielded twisted-pair cable doesn't incorporate a braided shield into its structure. However, the characteristics of UTP are similar in many ways to STP, differing primarily in attenuation and EMI. As shown in figure 3.15, several twisted-pairs can be bundled together in a single cable. These pairs typically are color coded to distinguish them.

Telephone systems commonly use UTP cabling. Network engineers can sometimes use existing UTP telephone cabling (if it is new enough and of a high enough quality to support network communications) for network cabling.

Figure 3.15

*A multipair
UTP cable.*

UTP cable is a latecomer to high-performance LANs because engineers only recently solved the problems of managing radiated noise and susceptibility to EMI. Now, however, a clear trend toward UTP is in operation, and all new copper-based cabling schemes are based on UTP.

UTP cable is available in the following five grades, or categories:

▶ **Categories 1 and 2.** These voice-grade cables are suitable only for voice and for low data rates (below 4 Mbps). Category 1 was once the standard voice-grade cable for telephone systems. The growing need for data-ready cabling systems, however, has caused Categories 1 and 2 cable to be supplanted by Category 3 for new installations.

▶ **Category 3.** As the lowest data-grade cable, this type of cable generally is suited for data rates up to 10 Mbps. Some innovative schemes, however, enable the cable to support data rates up to 100 Mbps. Category 3, which uses four twisted-pairs with three twists per foot, is now the standard cable used for most telephone installations.

▶ **Category 4.** This data-grade cable, which consists of four twisted-pairs, is suitable for data rates up to 16 Mbps.

▶ **Category 5.** This data-grade cable, which also consists of four twisted-pairs, is suitable for data rates up to 100 Mbps. Most new cabling systems for 100 Mbps data rates are designed around Category 5 cable.

> In a UTP cabling system, the cable is only one component of the system. All connecting devices also are graded, and the overall cabling system supports only the data rates permitted by the lowest-grade component in the system. In other words, if you require a Category 5 cabling system, all connectors and connecting devices must be designed for Category 5 operation.
>
> Category 5 cable also requires more stringent installation procedures than the lower cable categories. Installers of Category 5 cable require special training and skills to understand these more rigorous requirements.

UTP cable offers an excellent balance of cost and performance characteristics, as discussed in the following sections.

Cost

UTP cable is the least costly of any cable type, although properly installed Category 5 tends to be fairly expensive. In some cases, existing cable in buildings can be used for LANs, although you should verify the category of the cable and know the length of the cable in the walls. Distance limits for voice cabling are much less stringent than for data-grade cabling.

Installation

UTP cable is easy to install. Some specialized equipment might be required, but the equipment is low in cost and can be mastered with a bit of practice. Properly designed UTP cabling systems easily can be reconfigured to meet changing requirements.

As noted earlier, however, Category 5 cable has stricter installation requirements than lower categories of UTP. Special training is recommended for dealing with Category 5 UTP.

Capacity

The data rates possible with UTP have pushed up from 1 Mbps, past 4 and 16 Mbps, to the point where 100 Mbps data rates are now common.

Attenuation

UTP cable shares similar attenuation characteristics with other copper cables. UTP cable runs are limited to a few hundred meters, with 100 meters as the most frequent limit.

EMI Characteristics

Because UTP cable lacks a shield, it is more sensitive to EMI than coaxial or STP cables. The latest technologies make it possible to use UTP in the vast majority of situations, provided that reasonable care is taken to avoid electrically noisy devices such as motors and fluorescent lights. Nevertheless, UTP might not be suitable for noisy environments such as factories. Crosstalk between nearby unshielded pairs limits the maximum length of cable runs.

Connectors for UTP

The most common connector used with UTP cables is the *RJ-45 connector*, shown in figure 3.16. These connectors are easy to install on cables and are also extremely easy to connect and disconnect. An RJ-45 connector has eight pins and looks like a common RJ-11 telephone jack. They are slightly different sizes and won't fit together: an RJ-11 has only four pins.

Figure 3.16

An RJ-45 connector.

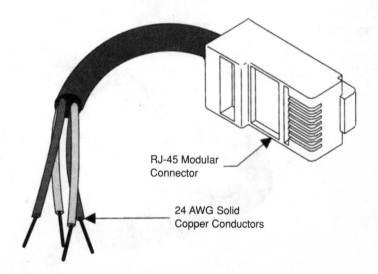

RJ-45 Modular
Connector

24 AWG Solid
Copper Conductors

Distribution racks, shelves, and patch panels are available for
large UTP installations. These accessories enable you to organize
network cabling and also provide a central spot for expansion and
reconfiguration. One necessary accessory, a *jack coupler*, is a small
device that attaches to a wall plate or a patch panel and receives
an RJ-45 connection. Jack couplers can support transmission
speeds of up to 100 Mbps.

Fiber-Optic Cable

In almost every way, fiber-optic cable is the ideal cable for data
transmission. Not only does this type of cable accommodate extremely high bandwidths, but it also presents no problems with
EMI and supports durable cables and cable runs as long as several
kilometers. The two disadvantages of fiber-optic, however, are cost
and installation difficulty.

The center conductor of a fiber-optic cable is a fiber that consists
of highly refined glass or plastic designed to transmit light signals
with little loss. A glass core supports a longer cabling distance, but
a plastic core is typically easier to work with. The fiber is coated
with a cladding that reflects signals back into the fiber to reduce
signal loss. A plastic sheath protects the fiber. See figure 3.17.

Figure 3.17

*A fiber-optic
cable.*

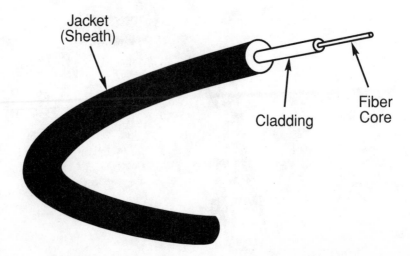

Jacket
(Sheath)

Cladding

Fiber
Core

A fiber-optic network cable consists of two strands separately enclosed in plastic sheaths—one strand sends and the other receives. Two types of cable configurations are available: loose and tight configurations. Loose configurations incorporate a space between the fiber sheath and the outer plastic encasement; this space is filled with a gel or other material. Tight configurations contain strength wires between the conductor and the outer plastic encasement. In both cases, the plastic encasement must supply the strength of the cable, while the gel layer or strength wires protect the delicate fiber from mechanical damage.

Optical fiber cables don't transmit electrical signals. Instead, the data signals must be converted into light signals. Light sources include lasers and light-emitting diodes (LEDs). LEDs are inexpensive but produce a fairly poor quality of light suitable for less-stringent applications.

> A *laser* is a light source that produces an especially pure light that is monochromatic (one color) and coherent (all waves are parallel). The most commonly used source of laser light in LAN devices is called an *injection laser diode (ILD)*. The purity of laser light makes lasers ideally suited to data transmissions because they can work with long distances and high bandwidths. Lasers, however, are expensive light sources used only when their special characteristics are required.

The end of the cable that receives the light signal must convert the signal back to an electrical form. Several types of solid-state components can perform this service.

One of the significant difficulties of installing fiber-optic cable arises when two cables must be joined. The small cores of the two cables (some are as small as 8.3 microns) must be lined up with extreme precision to prevent excessive signal loss.

Fiber-Optic Characteristics

As with all cable types, fiber-optic cables have their share of advantages and disadvantages.

Cost

The cost of the cable and connectors has fallen significantly in recent years. However, the electronic devices required are significantly more expensive than comparable devices for copper cable. Fiber-optic cable is also the most expensive cable type to install.

Installation

Greater skill is required to install fiber-optic cable than to install most copper cables. Improved tools and techniques, however, have reduced the training required. Still, fiber-optic cable requires greater care because the cables must be treated fairly gently during installation. Every cable has a minimum bend radius, for example, and fibers are damaged if the cables are bent too sharply. It also is important not to stretch the cable during installation.

Capacity

Fiber-optic cable can support high data rates (as high as 200,000 Mbps) even with long cable runs. Although UTP cable runs are limited to less than 100 meters with 100 Mbps data rates, fiber-optic cables can transmit 100 Mbps signals for several kilometers.

Attenuation

Attenuation in fiber-optic cables is much lower than in copper cables. Fiber-optic cables are capable of carrying signals for several kilometers.

EMI Characteristics

Because fiber-optic cables don't use electrical signals to transmit data, they are totally immune to electromagnetic interference. The cables also are immune to a variety of electrical effects that must be taken into account when designing copper cabling systems.

When electrical cables are connected between two buildings, the ground potentials (voltages) between the two buildings can differ. When a difference exists (as it frequently does), the current flows through the grounding conductor of the cable, even though the ground is supposed to be electrically neutral and no current should flow. When current flows through the ground conductor of a cable, the condition is called a *ground loop*. Ground loops can result in electrical instability and various other types of anomalies.

Because fiber-optic cable is immune to electrical effects, the best way to connect networks in different buildings is by putting in a fiber-optic link segment.

Because the signals in fiber-optic cable are not electrical in nature, they cannot be detected by the electronic eavesdropping equipment that detects electromagnetic radiation. Therefore, fiber-optic cable is the perfect choice for high-security networks.

Summary of Cable Characteristics

Table 3.2 summarizes the characteristics of the four cable types discussed in this section.

Table 3.2

Comparison of Cable Media

Cable Type	Cost	Installation	Capacity	Range	EMI
Coaxial Thinnet	<STP	Inexpensive/ easy	10 Mbps typical	185 m	<sensitive than UTP
Coaxial Thicknet	>STP <Fiber	Easy	10 Mbps typical	500 m	<sensitive than UTP
Shielded Twisted-Pair (STP)	>UTP <Thicknet	Fairly easy	16 Mbps typical up to 500 Mbps	100 m typical	<sensitive than UTP

Cable Type	Cost	Installation	Capacity	Range	EMI
Unshielded Twisted-Pair (UTP)	Lowest	Inexpensive/ easy	10 Mbps typical up to 100 Mbps	100 m typical	Most sensitive
Fiber-Optic	Highest	Expensive/ difficult	100 Mbps typical	10s of kilometers	Insensitive

When comparing cabling types, remember that the characteristics you observe depend highly on the implementations. Engineers once thought that UTP cable would never reliably support data rates above 4 Mbps, but 100 Mbps data rates now are common.

Some comparisons between cable types are fairly involved. For example, although fiber-optic cable is costly on a per-foot basis, you can construct a fiber-optic cable that is many kilometers in length. To build a copper cable many kilometers in length, you need to install repeaters at several points along the cable to amplify the signal. These repeaters could easily exceed the cost of a fiber-optic cable run.

IBM Cabling

IBM assigns separate names, standards, and specifications for network cabling and cabling components. These IBM cabling types roughly parallel standard forms used elsewhere in the industry, as table 3.3 illustrates. The AWG designation in this table stands for the American Wire Gauge standard, a specification for wire gauges. The higher the gauge, the thinner the wire.

IBM provides a unique connector (mentioned earlier in this chapter) that is of both genders—any two of the same type can be connected together.

Table 3.3

IBM Cabling Types

Cable Type	Description	Comment
Type 1	Shielded twisted-pair (STP)	Two twisted-pairs of 22 AWG wire in braided shield
Type 2	Voice and data	Two twisted-pairs of 22 AWG wire for data and braided shield, and two twisted-pairs of 26 AWG for voice
Type 3	Voice	Four solid UTP pairs; 22 or 24 AWG wire
Type 4	Not defined	
Type 5	Fiber-optic	Two 62.5/125-micron multi-mode fibers
Type 6	Data patch cable	Two twisted-pairs of 26 AWG wire, dual foil, and braided shield
Type 7	Not defined	
Type 8	Carpet grade	Two twisted-pairs of 26 AWG wire with shield for use under carpets
Type 9	Plenum grade	Two twisted-pairs, shielded (See previous discussion of plenum-grade cabling.)

Wireless Media

The extraordinary convenience of wireless communications has placed an increased emphasis on wireless networks in recent years. Technology is expanding rapidly and will continue to expand into the near future, offering more and better options for wireless networks.

Presently, you can subdivide wireless networking technology into three basic types corresponding to three basic networking scenarios:

▶ **Local area networks (LANs).** Occasionally, you will see a fully wireless LAN, but more typically, one or more wireless machines will function as members of a cable-based LAN. A LAN with both wireless and cable-based components is called a *hybrid*.

▶ **Extended local networks.** A wireless connection serves as a backbone between two LANs. For instance, a company with office networks in two nearby but separate buildings could connect those networks using a wireless bridge.

▶ **Mobile computing.** A mobile machine connects to the home network using cellular or satellite technology.

The following sections describe these technologies and some of the networking options available with each.

Wireless point-to-point communications are another facet of wireless LAN technology. Point-to-point wireless technology specifically facilitates communications between a pair of devices (rather than attempting to achieve an integrated networking capability). For instance, a point-to-point connection might transfer data between a laptop and a home-based computer or between a computer and a printer. Point-to-point signals can pass through walls, ceilings, and other obstructions. Point-to-point provides data transfer rates of 1.2 to 38.4 Kbps for a range of up to 200 feet indoors (or one third of a mile for line-of-sight broadcasts).

Reasons for Wireless Networks

Wireless networks are especially useful for the following situations:

▶ **Spaces where cabling would be impossible or inconvenient.** These include open lobbies, inaccessible parts of buildings, older buildings, historical buildings where renovation is prohibited, and outdoor installations.

▶ **People who move around a lot within their work environment.** Network administrators, for instance, must troubleshoot a large office network. Nurses and doctors need to make rounds at a hospital.

▶ **Temporary installations.** These situations include any temporary department set up for a specific purpose that soon will be torn down or relocated.

▶ **People who travel outside of the work environment and need instantaneous access to network resources.**

Wireless Communications with LANs

For some of the reasons described earlier in this chapter, it is often advantageous for a network to include some wireless nodes. Typically, though, the wireless nodes will be part of what is otherwise a traditional, cable-based network.

An *access point* is a stationary transceiver connected to the cable-based LAN that enables the cordless PC to communicate with the network. The access point acts as a conduit for the wireless PC. The process is initiated when the wireless PC sends a signal to the access point; from there, the signal reaches the network. The truly *wireless* communication, therefore, is the communication from the wireless PC to the access point. An access point transceiver is one of several ways to achieve wireless networking. Some of the others are described in later sections.

You can classify wireless LAN communications according to transmission method. The four most common LAN wireless transmission methods are as follows:

▶ Infrared

▶ Laser

▶ Narrow-band radio

▶ Spread-spectrum radio

Characteristics of Radio Transmission

Designing a radio system to have the ideal characteristics for an application requires plenty of design tradeoffs. This is because the characteristics of radio transmissions change dramatically with frequency. Low-frequency radio, for example, supports limited data rates but has the significant advantage that it frequently can communicate past the horizon. Shortwave operators are familiar with this phenomenon, and they commonly can monitor transmissions from the other side of the earth.

As frequency increases, transmissions become increasingly line-of-site. AM radio broadcast frequencies, for example, range from kilohertz to low-megahertz. Perhaps you have picked up an AM radio station from several states away late at night, which can occur because AM radio transmissions can bounce off the atmosphere's ozone layer. Some of the lowest-frequency AM radio transmissions can actually travel along the ground in a phenomenon called *ground waves*. Some transmissions can bounce a considerable distance. Conversely, FM transmissions seldom can be received past the horizon—in fact, you can seldom clearly receive an FM broadcast beyond a range of 100 miles. This is partly a function of power, but the primary cause of the range limitation is the inability of FM frequencies to go beyond the horizon. On a line-of-sight basis, however, high-frequency transmissions attenuate less rapidly than low-frequency transmissions.

Lower-frequency radio waves can penetrate solid materials to a greater degree than higher frequencies. Very low radio frequencies, for example, can be used to communicate with submerged submarines, although the data rates are extremely slow. Penetration capability also is a function of power—higher-power transmissions penetrate building walls more effectively than lower-power transmissions.

The following sections look briefly at these important wireless transmission methods.

Infrared Transmission

You use an infrared communication system every time you control your television with a remote control. The remote control transmits pulses of infrared light that carry coded instructions to a receiver on the TV. This technology also can be adapted to network communication.

Four varieties of infrared communications are as follows:

> ▸ **Broadband optical telepoint.** This method uses broadband technology. Data transfer rates in this high-end option are competitive with those for a cable-based network.

> ▸ **Line-of-sight infrared.** Transmissions must occur over a clear, line-of-sight path between transmitter and receiver.

> ▸ **Reflective infrared.** Wireless PCs transmit toward a common, central unit, which then directs communication to each of the nodes.

> ▸ **Scatter infrared.** Transmissions reflect off floors, walls, and ceilings until (theoretically) they finally reach the receiver. Because of the imprecise trajectory, data transfer rates are slow. The maximum reliable distance is around 100 feet.

Infrared transmissions typically are limited to within 100 feet. Within this range, however, infrared is relatively fast. Infrared's high bandwidth supports transmission speeds of up to 10 Mbps.

Infrared devices are insensitive to radio-frequency interference, but reception can be degraded by bright light. Because transmissions are tightly focused, they are fairly immune to electronic eavesdropping.

Laser Transmission

High-powered laser transmitters can transmit data for several thousand yards when line-of-sight communication is possible. Lasers can be used in many of the same situations as microwave links (described later in this chapter), without requiring an FCC license. On a LAN scale, laser light technology is similar to infrared technology.

Narrow-Band Radio Transmission

In narrow-band radio communications (also called single-frequency radio), transmissions occur at a single radio frequency. The range of narrow-band radio is higher than infrared, effectively enabling mobile computing over a limited area. Neither the receiver nor the transmitter must be placed along a direct line of sight; the signal can bounce off walls, buildings, and even the atmosphere, but heavy walls, such as steel or concrete enclosures, can block the signal.

Spread-Spectrum Radio Transmission

Spread-spectrum radio transmission is a technique originally developed by the military to solve several communication problems. Spread-spectrum improves reliability, reduces sensitivity to interference and jamming, and is less vulnerable to eavesdropping than single-frequency radio.

As its name suggests, spread-spectrum transmission uses multiple frequencies to transmit messages. Two techniques employed are *frequency hopping* and *direct sequence modulation.*

Frequency hopping switches (*hops*) among several available frequencies (see fig. 3.18), staying on each frequency for a specified interval of time. The transmitter and receiver must remain synchronized during a process called a *hopping sequence* in order for this technique to work. Range for this type of transmission is up to two miles outdoors and 400 feet indoors. Frequency hopping typically transmits at up to 250 Kbps, although some versions can reach as high as 2 Mbps.

Figure 3.18

Frequency hopping employs various frequencies for a specific time period.

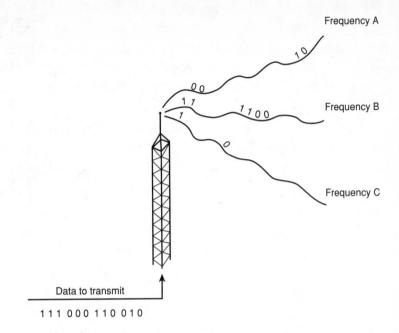

Direct sequence modulation breaks original messages into parts called *chips* (see fig. 3.19), which are transmitted on separate frequencies. To confuse eavesdroppers, decoy data also can be transmitted on other frequencies. The intended receiver knows which frequencies are valid and can isolate the chips and reassemble the message. Eavesdropping is difficult because the correct frequencies are not known, and the eavesdropper cannot isolate the frequencies carrying true data. Because different sets of frequencies can be selected, this technique can operate in environments that support other transmission activity. Direct sequence modulation systems operating at 900 MHz support bandwidths of 2–6 Mbps.

Figure 3.19

Direct sequence modulation.

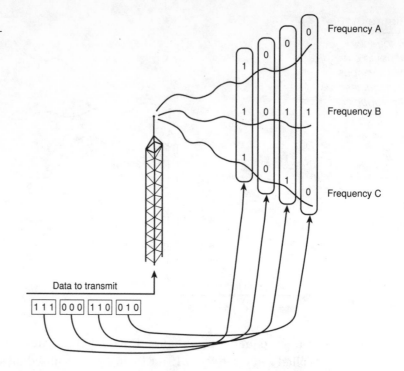

Extended LANs (Wireless Bridging)

Wireless technology can connect LANs in two different buildings into an extended LAN. This capability is, of course, also available through other technologies (such as a T1 line or a leased line from a telephone provider), but depending on the conditions, a wireless solution is sometimes more cost-effective. A wireless connection between two buildings also provides a solution to the ground-potential problem described in a note earlier in this chapter.

A *wireless bridge* acts as a network bridge, merging two local LANs over a wireless connection (see Chapter 2, "Networking Standards," and Chapter 6, "Connectivity Devices," for more information on bridges). Wireless bridges typically use spread-spectrum radio technology to transmit data for up to three miles. (Antennae at each end of the bridge should be placed in an appropriate location, such as a rooftop.) A device called a *long-range wireless bridge* has a range of up to 25 miles.

The Radio Frequency Spectrum

The radio portion of the electromagnetic spectrum extends from 10 KHz to 1 GHz. Within this range are numerous bands, or ranges, of frequencies that are designated for specific purposes. You are probably familiar with the following frequency bands:

▶ Shortwave frequency

▶ Very High Frequency (VHF) (used in television and FM radio)

▶ Ultra High Frequency (UHF) (used in television)

Within the United States, the Federal Communications Commission (FCC) controls the use of radio frequencies. The majority of frequency allocations are licensed; an organization is granted an exclusive license to use a particular range of frequencies within a certain limited geographic area. Thus, you can have only one television Channel 5 within a given area, and Channel 5 allocations are spread out so that they don't interfere with each other. A licensed frequency allocation guarantees the license owner a clear, low-interference communication channel.

A few frequency ranges are unlicensed, which means that they can be used freely for the purpose specified for those frequencies. The FCC has designated three unlicensed frequency bands: 902–928 MHz, 2.4 GHz, and 5.72–5.85 GHz. The 902 MHz range has been available the longest and has been used for everything from cordless telephones to model airplane remote control. Because the 902 MHz range is quite crowded, many vendors are pushing development of devices for the less crowded 2.4 GHz band. Equipment for the 5.72 GHz remains expensive and is used infrequently.

Use of an unlicensed frequency occurs at the user's risk, and a clear communication channel is not guaranteed. Equipment used in these frequency bands, however, must operate at a regulated power level to limit range and reduce the potential for interference.

Mobile Computing

Mobile computing is a growing technology that provides almost unlimited range for traveling computers by using satellite and cellular phone networks to relay the signal to a home network. Mobile computing typically is used with portable PCs or personal digital assistant (PDA) devices.

Three forms of mobile computing are as follows:

▶ **Packet-radio networking.** The mobile device sends and receives network-style packets via satellite. Packets contain a source and destination address, and only the destination device can receive and read the packet.

▶ **Cellular networking.** The mobile device sends and receives cellular digital packet data (CDPD) using cellular phone technology and the cellular phone network. Cellular networking provides very fast communications.

▶ **Satellite station networking.** Satellite mobile networking stations use satellite microwave technology, which is described later in this chapter.

Microwave

Microwave technology has applications in all three of the wireless networking scenarios: LAN, extended LAN, and mobile networking. As shown in figure 3.20, microwave communication can take two forms: terrestrial (ground) links and satellite links. The frequencies and technologies employed by these two forms are similar, but as you'll see, distinct differences exist between them.

Figure 3.20

Terrestrial and satellite microwave links.

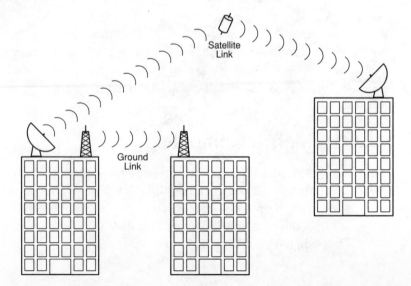

Terrestrial Microwave

Terrestrial microwave communication employs Earth-based transmitters and receivers. The frequencies used are in the low-gigahertz range, which limits all communications to line-of-sight. You probably have seen terrestrial microwave equipment in the form of telephone relay towers, which are placed every few miles to relay telephone signals crosscountry.

Microwave transmissions typically use a parabolic antenna that produces a narrow, highly directional signal. A similar antenna at the receiving site is sensitive to signals only within a narrow focus. Because the transmitter and receiver are highly focused, they must be adjusted carefully so that the transmitted signal is aligned with the receiver.

A microwave link frequently is used to transmit signals in instances in which it would be impractical to run cables. If you need to connect two networks separated by a public road, for example, you might find that regulations restrict you from running cables above or below the road. In such a case, a microwave link is an ideal solution.

Some LANs operate at microwave frequencies at low power and use nondirectional transmitters and receivers. Network hubs can be placed strategically throughout an organization, and workstations can be mobile or fixed. This approach is one way to enable mobile workstations in an office setting.

In many cases, terrestrial microwave uses licensed frequencies. A license must be obtained from the FCC, and equipment must be installed and maintained by licensed technicians.

Terrestrial microwave systems operate in the low-gigahertz range, typically at 4–6 GHz and 21–23 GHz, and costs are highly variable depending on requirements. Long-distance microwave systems can be quite expensive but might be less costly than alternatives. (A leased telephone circuit, for example, represents a costly monthly expense.) When line-of-sight transmission is possible, a microwave link is a one-time expense that can offer greater bandwidth than a leased circuit.

Costs are on the way down for low-power microwave systems for the office. Although these systems don't compete directly in cost with cabled networks, when equipment frequently must be moved, microwave can be a cost-effective technology. Capacity can be extremely high, but most data communication systems operate at data rates between 1 and 10 Mbps. Attenuation characteristics are determined by transmitter power, frequency, and antenna size. Properly designed systems are not affected by attenuation under normal operational conditions—rain and fog, however, can cause attenuation of higher frequencies.

Microwave systems are highly susceptible to atmospheric interference and also can be vulnerable to electronic eavesdropping. For this reason, signals transmitted through microwave are frequently encrypted.

Satellite Microwave

Satellite microwave systems relay transmissions through communication satellites that operate in geosynchronous orbits 22,300 miles above the earth. Satellites orbiting at this distance remain located above a fixed point on earth.

Earth stations use parabolic antennas (satellite dishes) to communicate with satellites. These satellites then can retransmit signals in broad or narrow beams, depending on the locations set to receive the signals. When the destination is on the opposite side of the earth, for example, the first satellite cannot transmit directly to the receiver and thus must relay the signal through another satellite.

Because no cables are required, satellite microwave communication is possible with most remote sites and with mobile devices, which enables transmission with ships at sea and motor vehicles.

The distances involved in satellite communication result in an interesting phenomenon: Because all signals must travel 22,300 miles to the satellite and 22,300 miles when returning to a receiver, the time required to transmit a signal is independent of distance. It takes as long to transmit a signal to a receiver in the same state as it does to a receiver a third of the way around the world. The time required for a signal to arrive at its destination is called *propagation delay.* The delays encountered with satellite transmissions range from 0.5 to 5 seconds.

Unfortunately, satellite communication is extremely expensive. Building and launching a satellite can cost easily in excess of a billion dollars. In most cases, organizations share these costs or purchase services from a commercial provider. AT&T, Hughes Network Services, and Scientific-Atlanta are among the firms that sell satellite-based communication services.

Satellite links operate in the low-gigahertz range, typically at 11–14 GHz. Costs are extremely high and usually are distributed across many users by selling communication services. Bandwidth is related to cost, and firms can purchase almost any required bandwidth. Typical data rates are 1–10 Mbps. Attenuation characteristics depend on frequency, power, and atmospheric conditions. Properly designed systems also take attenuation into account—rain and atmospheric conditions might attenuate higher frequencies. Microwave signals also are sensitive to EMI and electronic eavesdropping, so signals transmitted through microwave frequently are encrypted.

Earth stations can be installed by numerous commercial providers. Transmitters operate on licensed frequencies and require an FCC license.

Summary

This chapter examined the characteristics of some common network transmission media. You learned about some of the advantages and disadvantages of popular transmission media. This chapter looked at characteristics such as cost, distance limitation, ease of installation, EMI characteristics, and common uses for coaxial, UTP, STP, and fiber-optic cable, and wireless communication methods.

Exercises

Exercise 3.1: Shopping for Network Cabling

Objective: Explore the prices and availability of network cabling media in your area. Obtain a real-world view of cabling options.

Estimated time: 15 minutes

This chapter discussed the advantages and disadvantages of common network transmission media. In this exercise, you'll explore how network installation professionals perceive the differences between the cabling types. Remember that the cabling types discussed in this chapter are all tied to particular network topologies and architectures. You may want to read through Chapter 4, "Network Topologies and Architectures," before attempting this exercise.

1. Call a local computer store (preferably a store that provides network installations) and ask for some basic information on network cabling. Ask about coaxial Thinnet and Thicknet, UTP, and STP. Find out which type the store prefers to work with and in what situations they would recommend each of the types. Ask for pricing on Thinnet PVC and Plenum-grade cable. Try to get a feeling for how the real world perceives the cabling types described in this chapter.

Computer vendors generally are busy people, so try to be precise. Don't imply that you're getting ready to buy a whole network (unless you are). Just tell them you're trying to learn more about network cabling—vendors are often happy to share their knowledge. If they're helpful, remember them the next time you need a bid.

Review Questions

The following questions test your knowledge of the information presented in this chapter. For additional exam help, visit Microsoft's site at www.microsoft.com/train_cert/cert/Mcpsteps.htm.

1. Which two of the following are true about coaxial Thinnet:

   A. Thinnet cable is approximately 0.5 in. thick.

   B. Thinnet has 50-ohm impedance.

   C. Thinnet is sometimes called Standard Ethernet.

   D. Thinnet cable includes an insulation layer.

2. Transceivers for Thicknet cables are often connected using _____.

   A. ghost taps

   B. vampire taps

   C. witch widgets

   D. skeleton clamps

3. Which two of the following are true about UTP?

   A. You can use an RJ-11 connector with an RJ-45 socket.

   B. UTP has the lowest cost of any cabling system except Thinnet.

   C. Telephone systems use UTP.

   D. UTP is more sensitive to EMI than Thinnet.

4. Which of the following is not a permissible location for coaxial PVC cabling?

   A. A bathroom

   B. Above a drop ceiling

   C. Outside

   D. Along an exterior wall

5. UTP Category 3 uses _____ twisted-pair(s) of cables.

   A. 1

   B. 2

   C. 3

   D. 8

6. Transmission rates of _____ are typical for fiber-optic cables.

   A. 10 Mbps

   B. 25 Mbps

   C. 100 Mbps

   D. 500 Mbps

7. _____ is a transceiver that connects a wireless node with the LAN.

   A. An access provider

   B. An access point

   C. A Central Access Device (CAD)

   D. A Wireless Access Device (WAD)

8. _____ transmissions are designed to reflect the light beam off walls, floors, and ceilings until it finally reaches the receiver.

   A. Reflective infrared

   B. Scatter infrared

   C. Spread-spectrum infrared

   D. None of the above

9. Which three of the following are forms of mobile network technology?

    A. Cellular

    B. Packet-radio

    C. Wireless bridge

    D. Satellite station

10. Which of the following cable types supports the greatest cable lengths?

    A. Unshielded twisted-pair

    B. Shielded twisted-pair

    C. Thicknet coaxial cable

    D. Thinnet coaxial cable

11. What are two advantages of UTP cable?

    A. Low cost

    B. Easy installation

    C. High resistance to EMI due to twists in cable

    D. Cabling of up to 500 meters

12. What are two benefits of shielding in a cable?

    A. Reduction in signal attenuation

    B. Reduction in EMI radiation

    C. Reduction in sensitivity to outside interference

    D. None of the above

13. What are two disadvantages of fiber-optic cable?

    A. Sensitive to EMI

    B. Expensive hardware

    C. Expensive to install

    D. Limited in bandwidth

14. Which cable type is ideal for connecting between two buildings?

    A. UTP

    B. STP

    C. Coaxial

    D. Fiber-optic

15. As frequency increases, radio transmission becomes increasingly _____.

    A. attenuated

    B. rapid

    C. line-of-sight

    D. sensitive to electromagnetic interference

16. Which two statements are true of microwave systems?

    A. Microwave transmissions do not attenuate under any conditions.

    B. All microwave systems operate in the low-gigahertz range.

    C. Microwave signals are sensitive to EMI and electronic eavesdropping.

    D. Unlike most other types of radio transmitters, micro-wave transmitters don't need to be licensed.

17. DIN Connectors are primarily used for _____.

    A. connecting UTP cables

    B. cabling Macintosh computers to AppleTalk networks

    C. connecting devices with Thick-wire Ethernet

    D. none of the above

18. Which two connectors are frequently used with STP cable?

    A. T-connectors

    B. RJ-45 connectors

    C. IBM unisex connectors

    D. AppleTalk DIN connectors

19. Which two connectors are commonly used with coaxial cable?

    A. DB-25 connectors

    B. N-connectors

    C. ST-connectors

    D. BNC connectors

20. Which two statements are true of Thinnet cabling?

    A. A T-connector must be used to connect the PC's network board to the network.

    B. Either end of the cable can be terminated, but not both ends.

    C. BNC connectors cannot be used.

    D. One terminator must be grounded.

Pretest Answers

1. C (see the section titled "Thicknet")

2. D (see the section titled "Connectors for Coaxial Cable")

3. A (see the section titled "Fiber-Optic Cable")

4. C (see the section titled "Spread-Spectrum Radio Transmission")

Review Answers

1. B, D

2. B

3. C, D

4. B

5. C

6. C

7. B

8. B

9. A, B, D

10. C

11. A, B

12. B, C

13. B, C

14. D

15. C

16. B, C

17. B

18. C, D

19. B, D

20. A, D

Chapter 4

Network Topologies and Architectures

Networks come in a few standard forms, and each form is a complete system of compatible hardware, protocols, transmission media, and topologies. A *topology* is a map of the network. It is a plan for how the cabling will interconnect the nodes and how the nodes will function in relation to one another. Several factors shape the various network topologies, and one of the most important is the choice of an *access method*. An access method is a set of rules for sharing the transmission medium. This chapter describes two of the most important categories of access methods: *contention* and *token passing*. You learn about *CSMA/CD* and *CSMA/CA*, two contention-based access methods, and about some of the fundamental topology archetypes. This chapter then looks at Ethernet and Token Ring networks. Ethernet and Token Ring are network architectures designed around the contention and token-passing access methods, respectively.

Chapter 4 targets the following objective in the Planning section of the Networking Essentials exam:

Test Objectives

▶ Select the appropriate topology for various Token Ring and Ethernet networks

Test Yourself

Stop! Before reading this chapter, test yourself to determine how much study time you will need to devote to this section.

1. In the _____ access method, a computer signals a warning when it is about to transmit data.

    A. CSMA/CD

    B. CSMA/CA

    C. CSMA/BD

    D. Token passing

2. The _____ topology is most often associated with contention-based access methods.

    A. star

    B. mesh

    C. ring

    D. bus

3. Which two of the following are true of 10BASE-T networks?

    A. 10BASE-T uses UTP cable.

    B. 10BASE-T uses STP cable.

    C. 10BASE-T is a physical star but a logical bus.

    D. 10BASE-T is a physical bus but a logical star.

4. IBM specifications call for a maximum cabling distance of _____ for Type 3 cable in Token Ring.

    A. 45 meters

    B. 75 meters

    C. 185 meters

    D. 300 meters

Access Methods

An *access method* is a set of rules governing how the network nodes share the transmission medium. The rules for sharing among computers are similar to the rules for sharing among humans in that they both boil down to a pair of fundamental philosophies: 1) *first come, first serve* and 2) *take turns.* These philosophies are the principles defining the two most important types of media access methods:

▶ **Contention.** In its purest form, *contention* means that the computers are contending for use of the transmission medium. Any computer in the network can transmit at any time (first come, first serve).

▶ **Token passing.** The computers take turns using the transmission medium.

As you can imagine, contention-based access methods can give rise to situations in which two or more of the network nodes try to broadcast at the same time and the signals collide. Specifications for contention-based access methods include procedures for how to avoid collisions and what to do if a collision occurs. This section will introduce the CSMA/CD and CSMA/CA access methods.

On most contention-based networks, the nodes are basically equal. No node has a higher priority than other nodes. A new access method called *demand priority,* however, resolves contention and collisions and in so doing accounts for data type priorities. This section also describes demand priority access.

Contention

In pure contention-based access control, any computer can transmit at any time. This system breaks down when two computers attempt to transmit at the same time, in which case a collision occurs (see fig. 4.1). Eventually, when a network gets busy enough, most attempts to transmit result in collisions and little effective communication can take place.

Figure 4.1

A collision on a contention-based network.

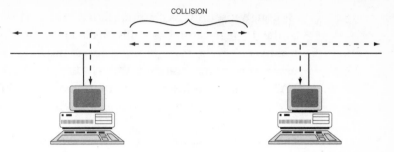

COLLISION

Mechanisms, therefore, usually are put into place to minimize the effects of collisions. One mechanism is *carrier sensing*, whereby each computer listens to the network before attempting to transmit. If the network is busy, the computer refrains from transmitting until the network quiets down. This simple "listen before talking" strategy can significantly reduce collisions.

Another mechanism is *carrier detection*. With this strategy, computers continue to listen to the network as they transmit. If a computer detects another signal that interferes with the signal it's sending, it stops transmitting. Both computers then wait a random amount of time and attempt to retransmit. Unless the network is extremely busy, carrier detection along with carrier sensing can manage a large volume of transmissions.

Carrier detection and carrier sensing used together form the protocol used in all types of Ethernet: *Carrier Sense Multiple Access with Collision Detection (CSMA/CD)*. CSMA/CD limits the size of the network to 2,500 meters. At longer distances, the broadcast-sensing mechanisms don't work—a node at one end can't sense when a node at the other end starts to broadcast.

Apple's LocalTalk network uses the protocol *Carrier Sense Multiple Access with Collision Avoidance (CSMA/CA)*. Collision avoidance uses additional techniques to further reduce the likelihood of collisions. In CSMA/CA, each computer signals a warning that says it is *about* to transmit data, and then the other computers wait for the broadcast. CSMA/CA adds an extra layer of order, thereby reducing collisions, but the warning broadcasts increase network traffic, and the task of constantly listening for warnings increases system load.

Although it sounds as if contention methods are unworkable due to the damage caused by collisions, contention (in particular CSMA/CD in the form of Ethernet) is the most popular media access control method on LANs. (In fact, no currently employed LAN standards utilize pure contention access control without adding some mechanism to reduce the incidence of collisions.)

Contention is a simple protocol that can operate with simple network software and hardware. Unless traffic levels exceed about 30 percent of bandwidth, contention works quite well. Contention-based networks offer good performance at low cost.

Because collisions occur at unpredictable intervals, no computer is guaranteed the capability to transmit at any given time. Contention-based networks are called *probabilistic* because a computer's chance of being permitted to transmit cannot be predicted. Collisions increase in frequency as more computers use the network. When too many computers use the network, collisions dominate network traffic, and few frames are transmitted without error.

All computers on a contention-based network are equal. Consequently, it's impossible to assign certain computers higher priorities and, therefore, greater access to the network.

Contention access control is well-suited for networks that experience bursts in traffic—for instance, from large intermittent file transfers—and have relatively few computers.

Token Passing

Token passing utilizes a frame called a *token*, which circulates around the network. A computer that needs to transmit must wait until it receives the token, at which time the computer is permitted to transmit. When the computer is finished transmitting, it passes the token frame to the next station on the network. Figure 4.2 shows how token passing is implemented on a Token Ring network. Token Ring networks are discussed in greater detail later in this chapter in the section titled "Token Ring."

Figure 4.2

Token passing.

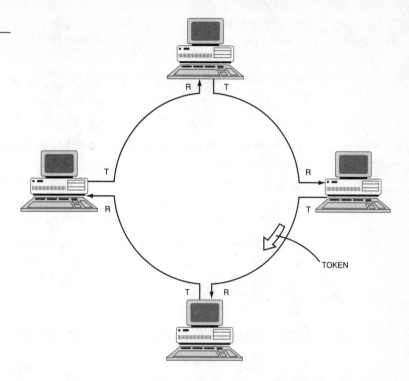

Several network standards employ token passing access control:

- ▶ **Token Ring.** The most common token-passing standard, embodied in IEEE standard 802.5

- ▶ **IEEE standard 802.4.** Implemented infrequently; defines a bus network that also employs token passing

- ▶ **FDDI.** A 100 Mbps fiber-optic network standard that uses token passing and rings in much the same manner as 802.5 Token Ring

Token-passing methods can use station priorities and other methods to prevent any one station from monopolizing the network. Because each computer has a chance to transmit each time the token travels around the network, each station is guaranteed a chance to transmit at some minimum time interval.

Token passing is more appropriate than contention under the following conditions:

▶ **When the network is carrying time-critical data.** Because token passing results in more predictable delivery, token passing is called *deterministic*.

▶ **When the network experiences heavy utilization.** Performance typically falls off more gracefully with a token-passing network than with a contention-based network. Token-passing networks cannot become gridlocked due to excessive numbers of collisions.

▶ **When some stations should have higher priority than others.** Some token-passing schemes support priority assignments.

Comparing Contention and Token Passing

As an access control mechanism, token passing appears to be clearly superior to contention. You find, however, that Ethernet, by far the dominant LAN standard, has achieved its prominence while firmly wedded to contention access control.

Token passing requires a variety of complex control mechanisms for it to work well. The necessary hardware is considerably more expensive than the hardware required to implement the much simpler contention mechanisms. The higher cost of token passing networks is difficult to justify unless the special features are required.

Because token-passing networks are designed for high reliability, building network diagnostic and troubleshooting capabilities into the network hardware is common. These capabilities increase the cost of token-passing networks. Organizations must decide whether this additional reliability is worth the extra cost.

Conversely, although token-passing networks perform better than contention-based networks when traffic levels are high, contention networks exhibit superior performance under lighter loading conditions. Passing the token around (and other maintenance operations) eats into the available bandwidth. As a result, a 10 Mbps Ethernet and a 16 Mbps Token Ring perform comparably well under light loading conditions, but the Ethernet costs considerably less.

Figure 4.3 illustrates the performance characteristics you can expect from each access control method. (This figure implies that token-passing throughput eventually reaches a zero level, which cannot happen, regardless of the loading conditions. Although a station's access to the network might be limited, access is guaranteed with each circuit of the token.)

Figure 4.3

*Comparison of
contention and
token passing.*

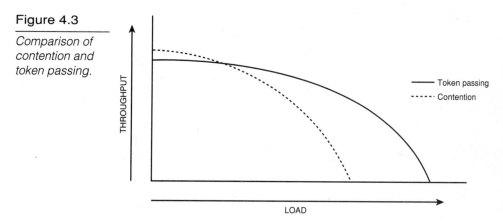

Token passing
Contention

Demand Priority

Demand priority is an access method used with the new 100 Mbps 100VG-AnyLAN standard. Although demand priority is officially considered a contention-based access method, demand priority is considerably different from the basic CSMA/CD Ethernet. In demand priority, network nodes are connected to hubs, and those hubs are connected to other hubs. Contention, therefore, occurs at the hub. (100VG-AnyLAN cables can actually send and receive data at the same time.) Demand priority provides a mechanism for prioritizing data types. If contention occurs, data with a higher priority takes precedence.

> 100VG-AnyLAN cabling uses four twisted-pairs in a scheme called *quartet signaling*.

Physical and Logical Topologies

A topology defines the arrangement of nodes, cables, and connectivity devices that make up the network. Two basic categories form the basis for all discussions of topologies:

► **Physical topology.** Describes the actual layout of the network transmission media

► **Logical topology.** Describes the logical pathway a signal follows as it passes among the network nodes

Another way to think about this distinction is that a physical topology defines the way the network *looks*, and a logical topology defines the way the *data passes* among the nodes. At a glance this distinction may seem nit-picky, but as you learn in this chapter, the physical and logical topologies for a network can be very different. A network with a star physical topology, for example, may actually have a bus or a ring logical topology.

In common usage, the word "topology" applies to a complete network definition, which includes the physical and logical topologies and also specifications for elements such as the transmission medium. The term *topology* as used in Microsoft's test objectives for the Networking Essentials exam applies not to the physical and logical topology archetypes described in this section but to the complete network specifications (such as 10BASE-T or 10BASE5) described in the "Ethernet" and "Token Ring" sections of this chapter.

Physical and logical topologies can take several forms. The most common—and the most important for understanding the Ethernet and Token Ring topologies described later in this chapter—are the following:

▶ Bus topologies

▶ Ring topologies

▶ Star topologies

The following sections discuss each of these important topology types.

Bus Topologies

A *bus physical topology* is one in which all devices connect to a common, shared cable (sometimes called the *backbone*). A bus physical topology is shown in figure 4.4.

Figure 4.4

A bus physical topology.

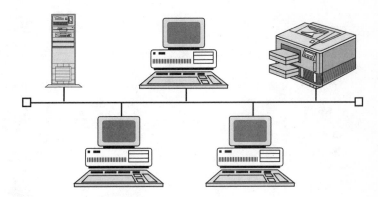

If you think the bus topology seems ideally suited for the networks that use contention-based access methods such as CSMA/CD, you are correct. Ethernet, the most common contention-based network architecture, typically uses bus as a physical topology. 10BASE-T Ethernet networks (described later in this chapter) use bus as a logical topology but are configured in a star physical topology.

Most bus networks broadcast signals in both directions on the backbone cable, enabling all devices to directly receive the signal. Some buses, however, are unidirectional: signals travel in only one direction and can reach only downstream devices. Recall from Chapter 3, "Transmission Media," that a special connector called a *terminator* must be placed at the end of the backbone cable to prevent signals from reflecting back on the cable and causing interference. In the case of a *unidirectional bus,* the cable must be terminated in such a way that signals can reflect back on the cable and reach other devices without causing disruption.

Ring Topologies

Ring topologies are wired in a circle. Each node is connected to its neighbors on either side, and data passes around the ring in one direction only (see fig. 4.5). Each device incorporates a receiver and a transmitter and serves as a repeater that passes the signal on to the next device in the ring. Because the signal is regenerated at each device, signal degeneration is low.

Figure 4.5

A ring topology. (The ring topology is almost always implemented as a logical topology. See fig. 4.6.)

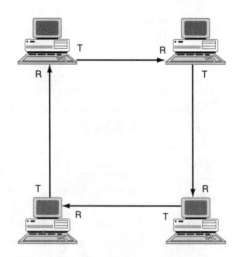

T = TRANSMIT
R = RECEIVE

Ring topologies are ideally suited for token-passing access methods. The token passes around the ring, and only the node that holds the token can transmit data.

Ring physical topologies are quite rare. The ring topology is almost always implemented as a logical topology. Token Ring, for example—the most widespread token-passing network—always arranges the nodes in a physical star (with all nodes connecting to a central hub) but passes data in a logical ring (see fig. 4.6).

Figure 4.6

A logical ring configured in a physical star.

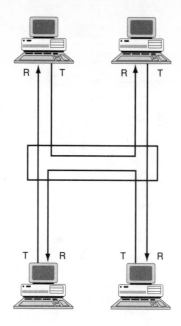

T = TRANSMIT
R = RECEIVE

You get a closer look at Token Ring later in this chapter in the section titled "Token Ring."

Star Topologies

Star topologies require that all devices connect to a central hub (see fig. 4.7). The hub receives signals from other network devices and routes the signals to the proper destinations. Star hubs can be interconnected to form *tree* or *hierarchical* network topologies.

Figure 4.7

A star topology.

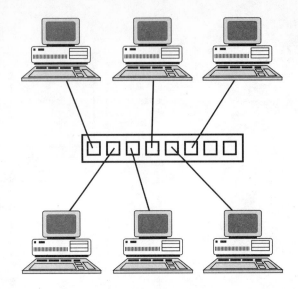

As mentioned earlier, a star physical topology is often used to implement a bus or ring logical topology (refer to fig. 4.6).

A *star physical topology* means that the nodes are all connected to a central hub. The path the data takes among the nodes and through that hub (the logical topology) depends on the design of the hub, the design of the cabling, and the hardware and software configuration of the nodes.

Ethernet

Ethernet is a very popular local area network architecture based on the CSMA/CD access method. The original Ethernet specification was the basis for the IEEE 802.3 specifications (see Chapter 2, "Networking Standards"). In present usage, the term Ethernet refers to original Ethernet (or Ethernet II, the latest version) as well as the IEEE 802.3 standards. The different varieties of Ethernet networks are commonly referred to as *Ethernet topologies*. Typically, Ethernet networks use a bus physical topology, although, as mentioned earlier, some varieties of Ethernet such as 10BASE-T use a star physical topology and a bus logical topology. (Microsoft uses the term "star bus" topology to describe 10BASE-T.)

Ethernet networks, depending on the specification, operate at 10 or 100 Mbps using baseband transmission. Each of the IEEE 802.3 specifications (see Chapter 2) prescribes its own cable types.

The next sections in this chapter examine the following Ethernet topologies:

- ▶ 10BASE2

- ▶ 10BASE5

- ▶ 10BASE-T

- ▶ 10BASE-FL

- ▶ 100VG-AnyLAN

- ▶ 100BASE-X

Note that the name of each Ethernet topology begins with a number (10 or 100). That number specifies the transmission speed for the network. For instance, 10BASE5 is designed to operate at 10 Mbps, and 100BASE-X operates at 100 Mbps.

Ethernet networks transmit data in small units called *frames*. The size of an Ethernet frame can be anywhere between 64 and 1,518 bytes. Eighteen bytes of the total size are taken up by frame overhead, such as the source and destination addresses, protocol information, and error-checking information.

A typical Ethernet II frame has the following sections:

- ▶ **Preamble.** A field that Signifies the beginning of the frame

- ▶ **Addresses.** Source and destination addresses for the frame

- ▶ **Type.** A field that designates the Network layer protocol

- ▶ **Data.** The data being transmitted

- ▶ **CRC.** Cyclical Redundancy Check for error checking

The origins of Ethernet are commemorated in the initials DIX, a 15-pin connector used to interface Ethernet components. The acronym "DIX" derives from the combination of leading letters of the founding Ethernet vendors: Digital, Intel, and Xerox.

The term Ethernet commonly refers to original Ethernet (which has been updated to Ethernet II) as well as the IEEE 802.3 standards. Ethernet and the 802.3 standards differ in ways significant enough to make standards incompatible in terms of packet formats, however. At the Physical layer, Ethernet and 802.3 are generally compatible in terms of cables, connectors, and electronic devices.

Ethernet generally is used on light-to-medium traffic networks and performs best when a network's data traffic transmits in short bursts. Ethernet is the most commonly used network standard. It has become especially popular in many university and government installations.

One advantage of the linear bus topology used by most Ethernet networks (this doesn't apply to star bus networks such as 10BASE-T) is that the required cabling is minimized because each node doesn't require a separate cable run to the hub. One disadvantage is that a break in the cable or a streaming network adapter card can bring down the entire network. Streaming is more frequently referred to as a *broadcast storm*. A broadcast storm occurs when a network card fails and the transmitter floods the cable with traffic, like a faucet stuck open. At this point, the network becomes unusable. See Chapter 13, "Troubleshooting," for more on broadcast storms.

Ethernet Cabling

You can use a variety of cables to implement Ethernet networks. Many of these cable types—Thinnet, Thicknet, UTP—are described in Chapter 3. Ethernet networks traditionally have used coaxial cables of several different types. Fiber-optic cables now are frequently employed to extend the geographic range of Ethernet networks.

The contemporary interest in using twisted-pair wiring has resulted in a scheme for cabling that uses unshielded twisted-pair (UTP): the 10BASE-T cabling standard, which uses UTP in a star physical topology. (10BASE-T is discussed later in this chapter.)

Ethernet remains closely associated with coaxial cable. Two types of coaxial cable still used in small and large environments are Thinnet (10BASE2) and Thicknet (10BASE5). Thinnet and Thicknet Ethernet networks have different limitations that are based on the Thinnet and Thicknet cable specifications. The best way to remember the requirements is to use the 5-4-3 rule of thumb for each cable type.

The 5-4-3 rule (see fig. 4.8) states that the following can appear between any two nodes in the Ethernet network:

▶ Up to 5 segments in a series

▶ Up to 4 concentrators or repeaters

▶ 3 segments of (coaxial only) cable that contain nodes

Figure 4.8

The 5-4-3 rule: 5 segments on a LAN, 4 repeaters, and 3 segments that contain nodes.

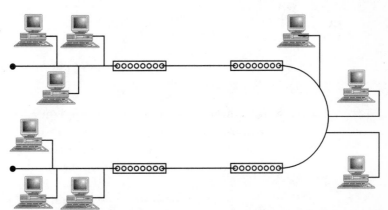

10BASE2

The 10BASE2 cabling topology (Thinnet) generally uses the on-board transceiver of the network interface card to translate the signals to and from the rest of the network. Thinnet cabling, described in Chapter 3, uses BNC T-connectors that directly attach to the network adapter. Each end of the cable should have a terminator, and you must use a grounded terminator on one end.

The main advantage of using 10BASE2 in your network is cost. When any given cable segment on the network doesn't have to be run further than 185 meters (607 feet), 10BASE2 is often the cheapest network cabling option.

10BASE2 is also relatively simple to connect. Each network node connects directly to the network cable by using a T-connector attached to the network adapter. For a successful installation, you must adhere to several rules in 10BASE2 Ethernet environments, including the following:

▶ The minimum cable distance between clients must be 0.5 meters (1.5 feet).

▶ *Pig tails*, also known as *drop cables*, from T-connectors shouldn't be used to connect to the BNC connector on the network adapter. The T-connector must be connected directly to the network adapter.

▶ You may not exceed the maximum network segment limitation of 185 meters (607 feet).

▶ The entire network cabling scheme cannot exceed 925 meters (3,035 feet).

▶ The maximum number of nodes per network segment is 30 (this includes clients and repeaters).

▶ A 50-ohm terminator must be used on each end of the bus with only one of the terminators having either a grounding strap or a grounding wire that attaches it to the screw holding an electrical outlet cover in place.

▶ You may not have more than five segments on a network. These segments may be connected with a maximum of four repeaters, and only three of the five segments may have network nodes.

You should be able to translate cable segment lengths from feet to meters or from meters to feet. A meter is equivalent to 39.37 inches or 3.28 feet.

Figure 4.9 shows two network segments using 10BASE2 cabling. For more on 10BASE2's Thinnet cabling, see Chapter 3.

Figure 4.9

Two segments using 10BASE2 cabling.

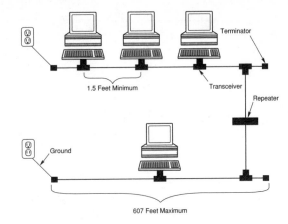

10BASE5

The 10BASE5 cabling topology (Thicknet) uses an external transceiver to attach to the network adapter card (see fig. 4.10). The external transceiver clamps to the Thicknet cable (as described in Chapter 3). An Attachment Universal Interface (AUI) cable runs from the transceiver to a DIX connector on the back of the network adapter card. As with Thinnet, each network segment must be terminated at both ends, with one end using a grounded terminator. The components of a Thicknet network are shown in figure 4.11.

Figure 4.10

Two segments using 10BASE5 cabling.

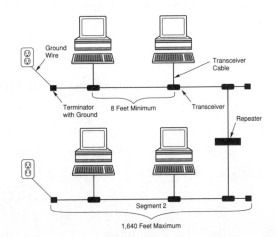

Figure 4.11

*Components of a
Thicknet network.*

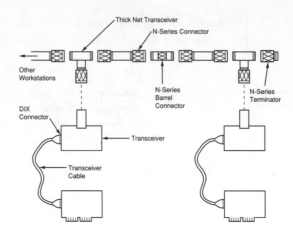

The primary advantage of 10BASE5 is its capability to exceed the cable restrictions that apply to 10BASE2. 10BASE5 does pose restrictions of its own, however, which you should consider when installing or troubleshooting a 10BASE5 network. As with 10BASE2 networks, the first consideration when troubleshooting a 10BASE5 network should be the established cabling rules and guidelines. You must follow several additional guidelines, along with the 5-4-3 rule, when configuring Thicknet networks, such as the following:

▶ The minimum cable distance between transceivers is 2.5 meters (8 feet).

▶ You may not go beyond the maximum network segment length of 500 meters (1,640 feet).

▶ The entire network cabling scheme cannot exceed 2,500 meters (8,200 feet).

▶ One end of the terminated network segment must be grounded.

▶ Drop cables (transceiver cables) can be as short as required but cannot be longer than 50 meters from transceiver to computer.

▶ The maximum number of nodes per network segment is 100. (This includes all repeaters.)

The length of the drop cables (from the transceiver to the computer) is not included in measurements of the network segment length and total network length. Figure 4.12 shows two segments using Thicknet and the appropriate hardware.

As Chapter 3 mentions, Thicknet and Thinnet networks are often combined, with a Thicknet backbone merging smaller Thinnet segments. (See Chapter 3 for more on 10BASE5's Thicknet cabling.)

Figure 4.12

Example of Thicknet network cabling.

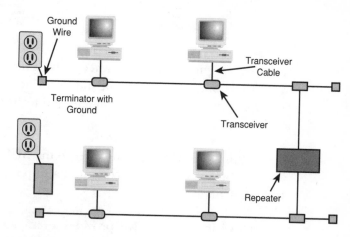

10BASE-T

The trend in wiring Ethernet networks is to use unshielded twisted-pair (UTP) cable. 10BASE-T, which uses UTP cable, is one of the most popular implementations for Ethernet. It is based on the IEEE 802.3 standard. 10BASE-T supports a data rate of 10 Mbps using baseband.

10BASE-T cabling is wired in a star topology. The nodes are wired to a central hub, which serves as a multiport repeater (see fig. 4.13). A 10BASE-T network functions logically as a linear bus. The hub repeats the signal to all nodes, and the nodes contend for access to the transmission medium as if they were connected along a linear bus. The cable uses RJ-45 connectors, and the network adapter card can have RJ-45 jacks built into the back of the card.

Figure 4.13

A 10BASE-T network.

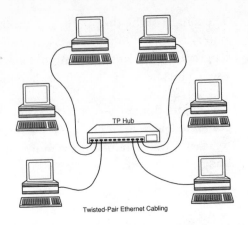

10BASE-T segments can be connected by using coaxial or fiber-optic backbone segments. Some hubs provide connectors for Thinnet and Thicknet cables (in addition to 10BASE-T UTP-type connectors).

By attaching a 10BASE-T transceiver to the AUI port of the network adapter, you can use a computer set up for Thicknet on a 10BASE-T network.

The star wiring of 10BASE-T provides several advantages, particularly in larger networks. First, the network is more reliable and easier to manage because 10BASE-T networks use a concentrator (a centralized wiring hub). These hubs are "intelligent" in that they can detect defective cable segments and route network traffic around them. This capability makes locating and repairing bad cable segments easier.

10BASE-T enables you to design and build your LAN one segment at a time, growing as your network needs to grow. This capability makes 10BASE-T more flexible than other LAN cabling options.

10BASE-T is also relatively inexpensive to use compared to other cabling options. In some cases in which a data-grade phone system already has been used in an existing building, the data-grade phone cable can be used for the LAN.

Networks with star wiring topologies can be significantly easi-er to troubleshoot and repair than bus-wired networks. With a star network, a problem node can be isolated from the rest of the network by disconnecting the cable and directly connect-ing it to the cable hub. If the hub is considered intelligent, management software developed for that hub type, as well as the hub itself, can disconnect the suspect port.

The rules for a 10BASE-T network are as follows:

▶ The maximum number of computers on a LAN is 1,024.

▶ The cabling should be UTP Category 3, 4, or 5. (Shielded twisted-pair cabling, STP, can be used in place of UTP.)

▶ The maximum unshielded cable segment length (hub to transceiver) is 100 meters (328 feet).

▶ The cable distance between computers is 2.5 meters (8 feet).

10BASE-FL

10BASE-FL is a specification for Ethernet over fiber-optic cables. The 10BASE-FL specification calls for a 10 Mbps data rate using baseband.

The advantages of fiber-optic cable (and hence, the advantages of 10BASE-FL) are discussed in Chapter 3. The most important ad-vantages are long cabling runs (10BASE-FL supports a maximum cabling distance of about 2,000 meters) and the elimination of any potential electrical complications.

100VG-AnyLAN

100VG-AnyLAN is defined in the IEEE 802.12 standard. *IEEE 802.12* is a standard for transmitting Ethernet and Token Ring packets (IEEE 802.3 and 802.5) at 100 Mbps. 100VG-AnyLAN is sometimes called 100BASE-VG. The "VG" in the name stands for voice grade.

The section titled "Demand Priority" earlier in this chapter, discussed 100VG-AnyLAN's demand priority access method, which provides for two priority levels when resolving media access conflicts.

100VG-AnyLAN uses a *cascaded star* topology, which calls for a hierarchy of hubs. Computers are attached to *child hubs,* and the child hubs are connected to higher-level hubs called *parent hubs* (see fig. 4.14).

Figure 4.14

Cascaded star topology.

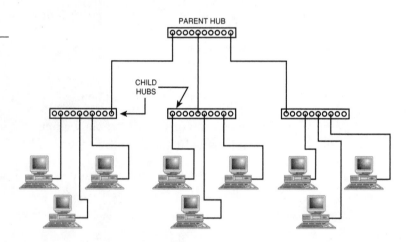

The maximum length for the two longest cables attached to a 100VG-AnyLAN hub is 250 meters (820 ft). The specified cabling is Category 3, 4, or 5 twisted-pair or fiber-optic. 100VG-AnyLAN is compatible with 10BASE-T cabling.

Both 100VG-AnyLAN and 100BASE-X (see the following section) can be installed as a plug-and-play upgrade to a 10BASE-T system.

100BASE-X

100BASE-X uses a star bus topology similar to 10BASE-T's. 100BASE-X provides a data transmission speed of 100 Mbps using baseband.

The 100BASE-X standard provides the following cabling specifications:

- ▶ **100BASE-TX.** Two twisted-pairs of Category 5 UTP or STP

- ▶ **100BASE-FX.** Fiber-optic cabling using 2-strand cable

- ▶ **100BASE-T4.** Four twisted-pairs of Category 3, 4, or 5 UTP

100BASE-X is sometimes referred to as "Fast Ethernet." Like 100VG-AnyLAN, 100BASE-X provides compatibility with existing 10BASE-T systems and thus enables plug-and-play upgrades from 10BASE-T.

Token Ring

Token Ring uses a token-passing architecture that adheres to the IEEE 802.5 standard, as described earlier. The topology is physically a star, but Token Ring uses a logical ring to pass the token from station to station. Each node must be attached to a concentrator called a *multistation access unit (MSAU or MAU)*.

In the earlier discussion of token passing, it may have occurred to you that if one computer crashes, the others will be left waiting forever for the token. MSAUs add fault tolerance to the network, so that a single failure doesn't stop the whole network. The MSAU can determine when the network adapter of a PC fails to transmit and can bypass it.

Token Ring network interface cards can run at 4 Mbps or 16 Mbps. Although 4 Mbps cards can run only at that data rate, 16-Mbps cards can be configured to run at 4 or 16 Mbps. All cards on a given network ring must run at the same rate.

As shown in figure 4.15, each node acts as a repeater that receives tokens and data frames from its nearest active upstream neighbor (NAUN). After the node processes a frame, the frame transmits downstream to the next attached node. Each token makes at least one trip around the entire ring and then returns to the originating node. Workstations that indicate problems send a *beacon* to identify an address of the potential failure.

Figure 4.15

*Operation of a
Token Ring.*

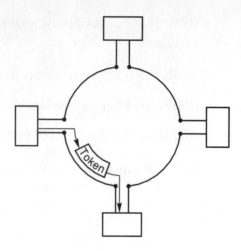

Token Ring Cabling

Traditional Token Ring networks use twisted-pair cable. The following are standard IBM cable types for Token Ring:

▶ **Type 1.** A braided shield surrounds two twisted-pairs of solid copper wire. Type 1 is used to connect terminals and distribution panels or to connect between different wiring closets that are located in the same building. Type 1 uses two STPs of solid-core 22 AWG wire for long, high data-grade transmissions within the building's walls. The maximum cabling distance is 101 meters (331 feet).

▶ **Type 2.** Type 2 uses a total of six twisted-pairs: two are STPs (for networking) and four are UTPs (for telephone systems). This cable is used for the same purposes as Type 1, but enables both voice and data cables to be included in a single cable run. The maximum cabling distance is 100 meters (328 feet).

▶ **Type 3.** Used as an alternative to Type 1 and Type 2 cable because of its reduced cost, Type 3 has unshielded twisted-pair copper with a minimum of two twists per inch. Type 3 has four UTPs of 22 or 24 AWG solid-core wire for networks or telephone systems. Type 3 cannot be used for 16 Mbps Token Ring networks. It is used primarily for long, low data-grade transmissions within walls. Signals don't travel as fast as with Type 1 cable because Type 3 doesn't have the shielding that Type 1 uses. The maximum cabling distance (according to IBM) is 45 meters (about 148 feet). Some vendors specify cabling distances of up to 150 meters (500 feet).

Type 3 cabling (UTP) is the most popular transmission medium for Token Ring. A Token Ring network using Type 3 (UTP) cabling can support up to 72 computers. A Token Ring network using STP cabling can support up to 260 computers.

The minimum distance between computers or between MSAUs is 2.5 meters (8 feet).

A patch cable is a cable that connects MSAUs. Patch cables are typically IBM Type 6 cables that come in standard lengths of 8, 30, 75, or 150 feet. (A Type 6 cable consists of two shielded 26-AWG twisted-pairs.) You can also get patch cables in custom lengths. You can use patch cables to extend the length of Type 3 cables or to connect computers to MSAUs. Patch cables have an IBM connector at each end.

Token Ring adapter cables have an IBM data connector at one end and a nine-pin connector at the other end. Adapter cables connect client and server network adapters to other network components that use IBM data connectors. The type of connectors you'll need for a Token Ring network depends on the type of cabling you're using. Type 3 cabling uses RJ-11 or RJ-45 connectors. (Media filters, if necessary, can convert the network adapter to RJ-11 or RJ-45 format.) Meanwhile, Type 1 and 2 cabling use IBM Type A connectors.

Token Ring networks come in a few sizes and designs. A *small movable* Token Ring system supports up to 12 MSAUs and uses Type 6 cable to attach clients and servers to IBM Model 8228 MSAUs. Type 6 is flexible but has limited distance capabilities. The characteristics of Type 6 cable make it suitable for small networks and for patch cords.

A *large nonmovable* system supports up to 260 clients and file servers with up to 33 MSAUs. This network configuration uses IBM Type 1 or Type 2 cable. The large nonmovable system also involves other wiring needs, such as punch panels or distribution panels, equipment racks for MSAUs, and wiring closets to contain the previously listed components.

The MSAU is the central cabling component for IBM Token Ring networks. The 8228 MSAU was the original wiring hub developed by IBM for Token Ring networks. Figure 4.16 shows 8228 MSAUs. Each 8228 has ten connectors, eight of which accept cables to clients or servers. The other connectors are labeled RI (ring in) and RO (ring out). The RI and RO connectors are used to connect multiple 8228s to form larger networks.

Figure 4.16

An example of Token Ring cabling using MSAUs.

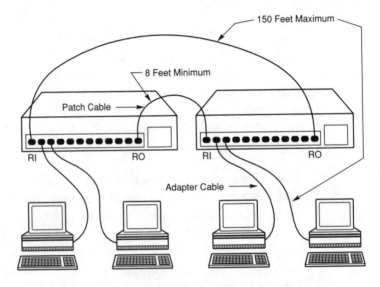

8228s are mechanical devices that consist of relays and connectors. Their purpose is to switch clients in and out of the network. Each port is controlled by a relay powered by a voltage sent to the MSAU from the client. When an 8228 is first set up, each of these relays must be initialized with the setup tool that is shipped with the unit. Insert the setup tool into each port and hold it there until a light indicates that the port is properly initialized.

Figure 4.16 shows an example of a network cabling several clients and MSAUs. The distances noted in the figure are based on the rules for the small movable cabling system.

When you connect a Token Ring network, make sure you do the following:

1. Initialize each port in the 8228 MSAU by using the setup tool shipped with the MSAU.

2. If you're using more than one MSAU, connect the RO port of each MSAU with the RI port of the next MSAU in the loop. Complete the loop so that the MSAUs form a circle or ring.

Passing Data on Token Rings

As this chapter has already described, a frame called a token perpetually circulates around a Token Ring. The computer that holds the token has control of the transmission medium. The actual process is:

1. A computer in the ring captures the token.

2. If the computer has data to transmit, it holds the token and transmits a data frame. A Token Ring data frame contains the fields listed in table 4.1.

3. Each computer in the ring checks to see if it is the intended recipient of the frame.

4. When the frame reaches the destination address, the destination PC copies the frame to a receive buffer, updates the frame status field of the data frame (see step 2), and puts the frame back on the ring.

5. When the computer that originally sent the frame receives it from the ring, it acknowledges a successful transmission, takes the frame off the ring, and places the token back on the ring.

Table 4.1

Token Ring Data Frame Fields	
Field	Description
Start delimiter	Marks the start of the frame
Access control	Specifies priority of the frame; also specifies whether the frame is a token or a data frame
Frame control	Media Access Control information
Destination address	Address of receiving computer
Source address	Address of sending computer
Data	Data being transmitted
Frame check sequence	Error-checking information (CRC)
End delimiter	Marks the end of the frame
Frame status	Tells whether the destination address was located and whether the frame was recognized

The Beaconing Process

Generally, the first station that is powered-up on a Token Ring network automatically becomes what is called the *active monitor* station. The responsibility of the active monitor station is to announce itself to the next active downstream station as the active monitor station and request that station to announce itself to its next active downstream station. The active monitor station sends this beacon announcement every seven seconds.

After each station announces itself to its next active downstream neighbor, the announcing station becomes the nearest active upstream neighbor (NAUN) to the downstream station. Each station on a Token Ring network has an upstream neighbor as well as a downstream neighbor.

After each station becomes aware of its NAUN, the beaconing process continues every seven seconds. If, for some reason, a station doesn't receive one of its expected seven-second beaconed announcements from its upstream neighbor, it attempts to notify the network of the lack of contact from the upstream neighbor. It sends a message out onto the network ring, which includes the following:

▶ The sending station's network address

▶ The receiving NAUN's network address

▶ The beacon type

From this information, the ring can determine which station might be having a problem and then attempt to fix the problem without disrupting the entire network. This process is known as *autoreconfiguration*. If autoreconfiguration proves unsuccessful, manual correction becomes necessary. Figure 4.17 shows a Token Ring network utilizing the beaconing process.

Figure 4.17

Token Ring beaconing.

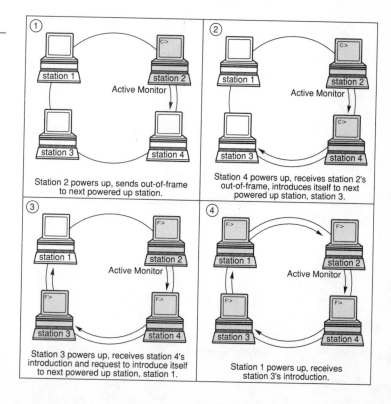

Station 2 powers up, sends out-of-frame to next powered up station.

Station 4 powers up, receives station 2's out-of-frame, introduces itself to next powered up station, station 3.

Station 3 powers up, receives station 4's introduction and request to introduce itself to next powered up station, station 1.

Station 1 powers up, receives station 3's introduction.

Summary

This chapter examined some common network topologies. You learned about the basic access methods, such as contention and token passing. This chapter then described some fundamental topology archetypes (bus, ring, and star) and discussed the differences between physical and logical topologies. Lastly, the chapter described the common varieties of Ethernet and Token Ring networks.

Exercises

Exercise 4.1:   Matching Topologies to Applications

Objective: Practice associating network topologies with appropriate uses.

Time estimate: 10 minutes.

Match the topology to the application. For this exercise, you should be familiar with the material in this chapter and also in Chapter 3.

1. 10BASE2

A. You are looking for an inexpensive network with the maximum flexibility for future expansion. You want to utilize existing data-grade phone lines for some segments.

2. 10BASE5

B. Your network encompasses three buildings. The longest segment length is 450 meters. You want to minimize cost. Differences in electrical ground potential between the buildings is not a problem.

3. 10BASE-T

C. Your company encompasses three buildings. The longest segment length is 1,800 meters. In previous networking attempts, you have experienced problems with the ground potential differences between the buildings.

4. 10BASE-FL

D. You are designing a network for an airline ticket office. Employees query the database constantly, so the network utilization rate is extremely high. The network must be very reliable and capable of self-corrective action to isolate a malfunctioning PC.

5. 100BASE-X

E. You work in a small office with 12 PCs. You are looking for an inexpensive networking

continues

Exercise 4.1:   Continued

solution. The computers are spaced evenly throughout the office (approximately 3–5 meters between workstations). You want to minimize the total amount of cabling.

6. Token Ring   F. Your company colorizes Hollywood movies. Huge, digitized movie files, such as *Bringing Up Baby* or *The Jazz Singer*, must pass quickly through the network so they will arrive with extreme dispatch at colorizing workstations. Very high transmission speeds are required. Your company is reaping huge profits, so the cost of cabling is no concern.

The correct responses are as follows:

1. E

2. B

3. A

4. C

5. F

6. D

Review Questions

The following questions test your knowledge of the information in this chapter. For additional questions, see MCP Endeavor and the Microsoft Roadmap/Assessment Exam on the CD-ROM that accompanies this book.

1. CSMA/CD uses which two of the following techniques to control collisions?

   A. Nodes broadcast a warning before they transmit.

   B. Nodes listen for a clear line before they transmit.

   C. Nodes request and are given control of the medium before transmitting.

   D. Nodes listen while they transmit and stop transmitting if another signal interferes with the transmission.

2. The maximum size of a CSMA/CD network is _____.

   A. 100 meters

   B. 300 meters

   C. 1,500 meters

   D. 2,500 meters

3. CSMA/CA is commonly used by _____.

   A. Microsoft networks

   B. LocalTalk networks

   C. Fast Ethernet networks

   D. 10BASE5 networks.

4. Which three of the following network architectures use the token passing access method?

   A. IEEE 802.4

   B. FDDI

C. Token Ring

D. IEEE 802.3

5. If you see a group of networked computers connected to a central hub, you know that the network has a _____ physical topology.

   A. ring

   B. star

   C. bus

   D. can't tell

6. If you see a group of networked computers connected to a central hub, you know that the network has a _____ logical topology.

   A. ring

   B. star

   C. bus

   D. can't tell

7. The _____ topology uses fiber-optic cable.

   A. 10BASE2

   B. 10BASE5

   C. 10BASE-T

   D. none of the above

8. The _____ topology uses Thicknet cable.

   A. 10BASE2

   B. 10BASE5

   C. 10BASE-T

   D. none of the above

9. The _____ topology uses UTP cable.

    A. 10BASE2

    B. 10BASE5

    C. 10BASE-T

    D. none of the above

10. The _____ topology uses Thinnet cable.

    A. 10BASE2

    B. 10BASE5

    C. 10BASE-T

    D. none of the above

11. 10BASE5 networks cannot exceed a maximum length of
_____.

    A. 185 meters

    B. 300 meters

    C. 500 meters

    D. 1,000 meters

12. Which two of the following are characteristics of a 10BASE-T
network but not a 10BASE2 network?

    A. CSMA/CD

    B. central hub

    C. UTP

    D. BNC

13 _____ is sometimes called "Fast Ethernet."

    A. 10BASE-T

    B. 10BASE5

    C. 100VG-AnyLAN

    D. 100BASE-X

14. A Token Ring network using STP cabling can support
    _____ computers.

    A. 60

    B. 260

    C. 500

    D. 1,024

15. The _____ field of a Token Ring frame is updated by the
    destination PC.

    A. destination address

    B. frame check sequence

    C. end delimiter

    D. frame status

16. Which two of the following statements are true?

    A. Coax Ethernet is a physical bus and a logical bus.

    B. 10BASE-T Ethernet is a physical bus and a logical bus.

    C. Coax Ethernet is a physical star and a logical bus.

    D. 10BASE-T Ethernet is a physical star and a logical bus.

17. What is the main advantage of using 10BASE2 when network
    segments don't have to exceed 185 meters?

    A. It is relatively simple to connect.

    B. Drop cables can be used, making it easier to trouble-
       shoot.

    C. Each node connects directly to the cable.

    D. It is the least expensive of the cabling options.

18. Which two of the Ethernet topologies require that each end of the bus be terminated?

    A. 10BASE2

    B. 10BASE5

    C. 10BASE-T

    D. Thinnet

19. Which of the following isn't an advantage of using 10BASE-T for cabling a network?

    A. It is easier and more reliable to manage.

    B. Centralized hubs make it easier to detect bad cable segments.

    C. Beaconing helps to isolate cable breaks.

    D. It is relatively inexpensive to use.

Pretest Answers

1. B (see the section titled "Contention")

2. D (see the section titled "Bus Topologies")

3. A, C (see the section titled "10BASE-T")

4. A (see the section titled "Token Ring Cabling")

Review Answers

1. B, D

2. D

3. B

4. A, B, C

5. B

6. D

7. D

8. B

9. C

10. A

11. C

12. B, C

13. D

14. B

15. D

16. A, D

17. D

18. B, A

19. C

Chapter 5

Transport Protocols

In Chapter 2, "Networking Standards," you learned that designing network protocols usually is done in pieces, with each piece solving a small part of the overall problem. By convention, these protocols are regarded as layers of an overall set of protocols, called a *protocol suite* or a *protocol stack*.

This chapter examines a variety of actual protocols and protocol suites, such as TCP/IP, IPX/SPX, NetBEUI, AppleTalk, and DLC.

Chapter 5 targets the following objective in the Planning section of the Networking Essentials exam:

Test Objectives

▶ Select the appropriate network and transport protocols for various Token Ring and Ethernet networks. Protocols include the following:

- ▶ DLC
- ▶ AppleTalk
- ▶ IPX
- ▶ TCP/IP
- ▶ NFS
- ▶ SMB

Test Yourself

Stop! Before reading this chapter, test yourself to determine how much study time you will need to devote to this section.

1. NetBEUI operates at the _____ protocol levels.

   A. Application and Presentation

   B. Data Link and Physical

   C. Transport and Network

   D. Session and Transport

2. UDP is part of the _____ protocol suite.

   A. TCP/IP

   B. IPX/SPX

   C. AppleTalk

   D. NetBEUI

3. TCP/IP is _____ than NetBEUI.

   A. faster

   B. slower

   C. easier to install and configure

   D. none of the above

As Chapter 2 describes, the *OSI reference model* is a standard describing the activities at each level of a protocol stack. The OSI reference model is useful as a conceptual tool for understanding protocol layering. Although some protocols have been designed in strict conformance with the OSI reference model, full OSI compliance hasn't become popular. The main influence of the OSI reference model is as a conceptual framework for understanding network communication and comparing various types of protocols.

Protocols are real implementations of the conceptual rules defined in the OSI reference model. Some protocols and protocol suites existed before the OSI reference model was published and can be matched only loosely to the seven-layer model.

Packets and Protocols

Before investigating protocols and protocol stacks, take a moment to quickly review some of the protocol-related issues discussed in previous chapters.

The purpose of a network is to exchange information among computers, and protocols are the rules by which computers communicate. Computers, like humans, can adopt any number of systems for passing messages as long as the sending and receiving computers are using the same (or compatible) rules. Computers, therefore, must agree on common protocols before they can communicate—failing to do so would create a bewildering situation similar to what you'd face if you read a book in Russian to a listener who speaks only Cherokee.

note

The NDIS and ODI standards greatly simplify the task of finding common protocols. NDIS and ODI (described in Chapter 2) enable several protocols to operate simultaneously through the same network adapter card.

You can classify the many tasks that network protocols must oversee into a few basic categories. Think of these categories chronologically, as a series of steps (each step including a collection of related tasks) that must take place before the data can reach the transmission medium. These steps are the layers of a protocol stack, as described in Chapter 2. In one sense, the term *layer* is more than metaphorical. Each layer of the stack (the Application layer, the Presentation layer, and so on) adds a layer of information to the packet, which the corresponding layer of the receiving computer needs in order to process the incoming packet.

The purpose of the layering structure is to enable vendors to adapt to specific hardware and software configurations without recreating the entire stack.

Protocols describe the way in which network data is encapsulated in packets on the source end, sent via the network to a destination, and then reconstructed at the destination into the appropriate file, instruction, or request. Breaking network data into packet-sized chunks provides smoother throughput because the small packets don't tie up the transmission medium as a larger unit of data might. Also, packets simplify the task of error detection and correction. Each file is checked separately for errors, and if an error is discovered, only that packet (instead of a whole file) must be retransmitted.

The exact composition of a network packet depends on the protocols you're using. In general, network packets contain the following:

- ▶ **Header.** The header signifies the start of the packet and contains a bundle of important parameters, such as the source and destination address and time/synchronization information.

- ▶ **Data.** This portion of the packet contains the original data being transmitted.

- ▶ **Trailer.** The trailer marks the end of the packet and typically contains error-checking (Cyclical Redundancy Check, or CRC) information.

As the data passes down through the protocol layers, each layer performs its prescribed function, such as interfacing with an application, converting the data format, or adding addressing and error-checking parameters. (Chapter 2 examines the functions of the OSI protocol layers.) As you learn in this chapter, actual working protocol stacks don't always comply exactly with the OSI model—some, in fact, predate the OSI model—but the concepts and terminology of the OSI model are nevertheless useful for describing protocol functions.

When the packet reaches the transmission medium, the network adapter cards of other computers on the network segment examine the packet, checking the packet's destination address. If the destination address matches the PC's address, the network adapter interrupts the processor, and the protocol layers of the destination PC process the incoming packet (see fig. 5.1).

Figure 5.1

The network adapter card checks if the packet's destination address matches the PC's address.

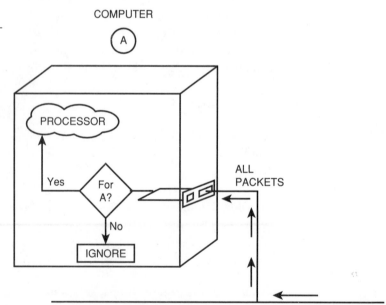

Protocols and Protocol Layers

Many of the addressing, error-checking, retransmission, and acknowledgment services most commonly associated with networking take place at the Network and Transport OSI layers. (Refer to Chapter 2.) Protocol suites are often referred to by the suite's

Transport and Network protocols. In TCP/IP, for instance, TCP is a Transport layer protocol and IP is a Network layer protocol. (Note, however, that TCP/IP predates OSI and diverges from OSI in a number of ways.)

> IPX/SPX is another protocol suite known by its Transport and Network layer protocols, but the order of the protocols is backward from the way the protocols are listed in TCP/IP. IPX is the Network layer protocol; SPX is the Transport layer protocol.

The lower Data Link and Physical layers provide a hardware-specific foundation, addressing items such as the network adapter driver, the media access method, and the transmission medium. Transport and Network layer protocols such as TCP/IP and IPX/SPX rest on that Physical and Data Link layer foundation, and, with the help of the NDIS and ODI standards, multiple protocol stacks can operate simultaneously through a single network adapter. (Refer to the discussion of NDIS and ODI in Chapter 2.)

Upper-level protocols provide compatibility with a particular networking environment. For instance, the so-called *NetBIOS over TCP/IP* stack provides Microsoft clients with TCP/IP.

This chapter describes the common protocol suites and many of the important protocols associated with them. In addition to TCP/IP and IPX/SPX, some of the common Transport and Network layer protocols are the following:

▶ **NWLink.** Microsoft's version of the IPX/SPX protocol essentially spans the Transport and Network layers.

▶ **NetBEUI.** Designed for Microsoft networks, NetBEUI includes functions at the Network and Transport layers. NetBEUI isn't routable and therefore doesn't make full use of Network layer capabilities.

▶ **AppleTalk Transaction Protocol (ATP) and Name Binding Protocol (NBP).** ATP and NBP are AppleTalk Transport layer protocols.

▶ **Datagram Delivery Protocol (DDP).** DDP is the AppleTalk Network layer protocol.

Windows NT Networking

Microsoft describes the Windows NT networking architecture as shown in figure 5.2. Note the importance of NDIS in the Windows NT networking structure. (See Chapter 2 for a description of NDIS.) The NDIS interface, NDIS wrapper, and NDIS-compatible drivers enable the TCP/IP, NWLink, NetBEUI, AppleTalk, and DLC protocols to interact simultaneously with the lower layers. (You learn more about these protocols later in this chapter.)

Figure 5.2

Windows NT networking architecture.

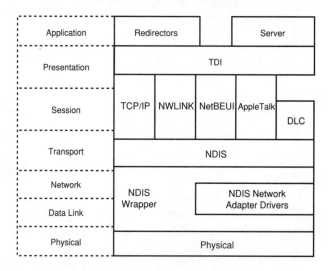

The Transport Driver Interface (TDI) is an interface that enables the server, redirector, and file system drivers to remain independent of the transport protocol.

NWLink is Microsoft's version of IPX/SPX.

Windows NT (like other Microsoft operating systems such as Windows for Workgroups and Windows 95) services client requests by using the Server Message Block (SMB) protocol. *SMB* is an Application layer protocol.

Three stages must take place before a protocol is operational:

1. A model describes the general function of the protocol.

2. The protocol is defined in complete detail.

3. The protocol must be realized by software and hardware designers in real products.

Consider the process of designing a building. The architect first produces sketches that describe the general nature of the building. Then the architect, possibly working with a specialist in particular building trades, develops blueprints that describe every detail of the building. Finally, an actual building is constructed.

Internet Protocols (TCP/IP)

The Internet protocol suite (also commonly called the TCP/IP protocol suite) was originally developed by the United States Department of Defense (DoD) to provide robust service on large internetworks that incorporate a variety of computer types. In recent years, the Internet protocols constitute the most popular network protocols currently in use.

One reason for the popularity of TCP/IP is that no one vendor owns it, unlike the IPX/SPX, DNA, SNA, AppleTalk protocol suites, all of which are controlled by specific companies. TCP/IP evolved in response to input from a wide variety of industry sources. Consequently, TCP/IP is the most open of the protocol suites and is supported by the widest variety of vendors. Virtually every brand of computing equipment now supports TCP/IP.

Much of the popularity of the TCP/IP protocols comes from their early availability on Unix. The protocols were built into the Berkeley Standard Distribution (BSD) Unix implementation. Since then, TCP/IP has achieved universal acceptance in the Unix community and is a standard feature on all versions of Unix.

Figure 5.3 illustrates the relationship of the protocols in the Internet suite to the layers of the OSI reference model. Notice that the suite doesn't include protocols for the Data Link or Physical layers. TCP/IP was designed to work over established standards such as Ethernet. Over time, TCP/IP has been interfaced to the majority of Data Link and Physical layer technologies.

Figure 5.3

The Internet protocol suite (TCP/IP).

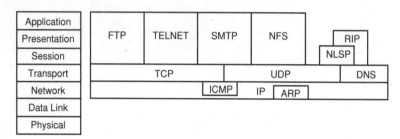

The Internet protocols do not map cleanly to the OSI reference model. The DoD model was, after all, developed long before the OSI model was defined. The model for the Internet protocol suite has four layers (refer to fig. 5.3). From this model, you can see the approximate relationships of the layers. The DoD model's layers function as follows:

▶ The Network Access layer corresponds to the bottom two layers of the OSI model. This correspondence enables the DoD protocols to coexist with existing Data Link and Physical layer standards.

▶ The Internet layer corresponds roughly to the OSI Network layer. Protocols at this layer move data between devices on networks.

▶ The Host-to-Host layer can be compared to the OSI Transport layer. Host-to-Host protocols enable peer communication between hosts on the internetwork. (At the time these protocols were designed, personal computers and workstations didn't exist, and all network computers were host computers. As a result, devices on TCP/IP networks are typically referred to as hosts. The concept of a client/server relationship didn't exist, and all communicating hosts were assumed to be peers.)

▶ The Process/Application layer embraces functions of the OSI Session, Presentation, and Application layers. Protocols at this layer provide network services.

One huge advantage of TCP/IP is that TCP/IP is required for communication over the Internet. One disadvantage is that the size of the protocol stack makes TCP/IP difficult to implement on some older machines. (Present-day PC models should have no problem running TCP/IP.) TCP/IP has traditionally been considered slower than other protocol stacks, but again, the power of the newer machines overcomes much of this difficulty.

A large number of protocols are associated with TCP/IP. Several of these are discussed briefly in the following sections.

Internet Protocol (IP)

The *Internet Protocol (IP)* is a connectionless protocol that provides datagram service, and IP packets are most commonly referred to as IP datagrams. IP is a packet-switching protocol that performs addressing and route selection. An IP header is appended to packets, which are transmitted as frames by lower-level protocols. IP routes packets through internetworks by utilizing dynamic routing tables that are referenced at each hop. Routing determinations are made by consulting logical and physical network device information, as provided by the Address Resolution Protocol (ARP).

IP performs packet disassembly and reassembly as required by packet size limitations defined for the Data Link and Physical layers being implemented. IP also performs error checking on the header data using a checksum, although data from upper layers is not error-checked.

Internet Control Message Protocol (ICMP)

The *Internet Control Message Protocol (ICMP)* enhances the error control provided by IP. Connectionless protocols, such as IP, cannot detect internetwork errors, such as congestion or path failures. ICMP can detect such errors and notify IP and upper-layer protocols.

Routing Information Protocol (RIP)

The *Routing Information Protocol (RIP)* in the TCP/IP suite is not the same protocol as RIP in the NetWare suite, although the two serve similar functions. Internet RIP performs route discovery by using a distance-vector method, calculating the number of hops that must be crossed to route a packet by a particular path.

Although it works well in localized networks, RIP presents many weaknesses that limit its utility on wide-area internetworks. RIP's distance-vector route discovery method, for example, requires more broadcasts and thus causes more network traffic than some other methods. The OSPF protocol, which uses the link-state route discovery method, is gradually replacing RIP. (See Chapter 6, "Connectivity Devices," for more on routing.)

Open Shortest Path First (OSPF)

The *Open Shortest Path First (OSPF)* protocol is a link-state route-discovery protocol that is designed to overcome the limitations of RIP. On large internetworks, OSPF can identify the internetwork topology and improve performance by implementing load balancing and class-of-service routing.

Transmission Control Protocol (TCP)

The *Transmission Control Protocol (TCP)* is an internetwork protocol that corresponds to the OSI Transport layer. TCP provides full-duplex, end-to-end connections. When the overhead of end-to-end communication acknowledgment isn't required, the User Datagram Protocol (UDP) can be substituted for TCP at the Transport (host-to-host) level. TCP and UDP operate at the same layer.

TCP corresponds to SPX in the NetWare environment. TCP maintains a logical connection between the sending and receiving computer systems. In this way, the integrity of the transmission is maintained. TCP detects any problems in the transmission quickly and takes action to correct them. The trade-off is that TCP isn't as fast as UDP.

TCP also provides message fragmentation and reassembly and can accept messages of any length from upper-layer protocols. TCP fragments message streams into segments that can be handled by IP. When used with IP, TCP adds connection-oriented service and performs segment synchronization, adding sequence numbers at the byte level.

In addition to message fragmentation, TCP can maintain multiple conversations with upper-layer protocols and can improve use of network bandwidth by combining multiple messages into the same segment. Each virtual-circuit connection is assigned a connection identifier called a *port*, which identifies the datagrams associated with that connection.

User Datagram Protocol (UDP)

The User Datagram Protocol (UDP) is a connectionless Transport (host-to-host) layer protocol. UDP does not provide message acknowledgments; rather, it simply transports datagrams.

Like TCP, UDP utilizes port addresses to deliver datagrams. These port addresses, however, aren't associated with virtual circuits and merely identify local host processes. UDP is preferred over TCP when high performance or low network overhead is more critical than reliable delivery. Because UDP doesn't need to establish, maintain, and close connections, or control data flow, it generally outperforms TCP.

UDP is the Transport layer protocol used with the *Simple Network Management Protocol (SNMP)*, the standard network management protocol used with TCP/IP networks. UDP enables SNMP to provide network management with a minimum of network overhead.

Address Resolution Protocol (ARP)

Three types of address information are used on TCP/IP internetworks:

▶ **Physical addresses.** Used by the Data Link and Physical layers.

> ▶ **IP addresses.** Provide logical network and host IDs. IP addresses consist of four numbers typically expressed in dotted-decimal form. An example of an IP address is 134.135.100.13.

> ▶ **Logical node names.** Identify specific hosts with alphanumeric identifiers, which are easier for users to recall than the numeric IP addresses. An example of a logical node name is MYHOST.COM.

Given a logical node name, the Address Resolution Protocol (ARP) can determine the IP address associated with that name. ARP maintains tables of address resolution data and can broadcast packets to discover addresses on the internetwork. The IP addresses discovered by ARP can be provided to Data Link layer protocols.

Domain Name System (DNS)

The *Domain Name System (DNS)* protocol provides name and address resolution as a service to client applications. DNS servers enable humans to use logical node names to access network resources.

File Transfer Protocol (FTP)

The *File Transfer Protocol (FTP)* is a protocol for sharing files between networked hosts. FTP enables users to log on to remote hosts. Logged-on users can inspect directories, manipulate files, execute commands, and perform other commands on the host. FTP also has the capability of transferring files between dissimilar hosts by supporting a file request structure that is independent of specific operating systems.

Simple Mail Transfer Protocol (SMTP)

The *Simple Mail Transfer Protocol (SMTP)* is a protocol for routing mail through internetworks. SMTP uses the TCP and IP protocols.

SNMP doesn't provide a mail interface for the user. Creation, management, and delivery of messages to end users must be performed by an e-mail application. (The most popular e-mail application on the Internet is named Eudora.)

Remote Terminal Emulation (TELNET)

TELNET is a terminal emulation protocol. TELNET enables PCs and workstations to function as dumb terminals in sessions with hosts on internetworks. TELNET implementations are available for most end-user platforms, including Unix (of course), DOS, Windows, and Macintosh OS.

Network File System (NFS)

Network File System (NFS), developed by Sun Microsystems, is a family of file-access protocols that are a considerable advancement over FTP and TELNET. Since Sun made the NFS specifications available for public use, NFS has achieved a high level of popularity.

NFS consists of two protocols:

- ▶ **eXternal Data Representation (XDR).** Supports encoding of data in a machine-independent format. C programmers use XDR library routines to describe data structures that are portable between machine environments.

- ▶ **Remote Procedure Calls (RPC).** Function as a service request redirector that determines whether function calls can be satisfied locally or must be redirected to a remote host. Calls to remote hosts are packaged for network delivery and transmitted to RPC servers, which generally have the capability of servicing many remote service requests. RPC servers process the service requests and generate response packets that are returned to the service requester.

NetWare IPX/SPX

The protocols utilized with NetWare are summarized in figure 5.4. The NetWare protocols have been designed with a high degree of modularity. This modularity makes the NetWare protocols adaptable to different hardware and simplifies the task of incorporating other protocols into the suite. Windows NT doesn't use the IPX/SPX suite to communicate with NetWare resources. Microsoft instead developed a clone of IPX/SPX called NWLink IPX/SPX Compatible Transport. IPX/SPX is generally smaller and faster than TCP/IP and, like TCP/IP, it is routable.

Figure 5.4

The NetWare protocol architecture.

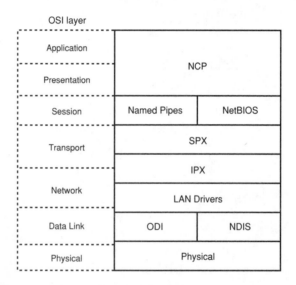

The *Internetwork Packet Exchange Protocol (IPX)* is a Network layer protocol that provides connectionless (datagram) service. (IPX was developed from the XNS protocol originated by Xerox.) As a Network layer protocol, IPX is responsible for internetwork routing and maintaining network logical addresses. Routing uses the RIP protocol (described later in this section) to make route selections.

IPX relies on hardware physical addresses found at lower layers to provide network device addressing. IPX also uses *sockets*, or upper-layer service addresses, to deliver packets to their ultimate destinations. On the client, IPX support is provided as a component of the older DOS shell and the current DOS NetWare requester.

The *Router Information Protocol (RIP)* uses the distance-vector route discover method to determine hop counts to other devices. Like IPX, RIP was developed from a similar protocol in the XNS protocol suite. RIP is implemented as an upper-layer service and is assigned a socket (service address). RIP is based directly on IPX and performs Network layer functions.

Sequenced Packet Exchange (SPX) is a Transport layer protocol that extends IPX to provide connection-oriented service with reliable delivery. Reliable delivery is ensured by retransmitting packets in the event of an error. SPX is derived from a similar SPX protocol in the XNS network protocol suite.

SPX establishes virtual circuits called *connections.* The connection ID for each connection appears in the SPX header. A given upper-layer process can be associated with multiple-connection IDs.

SPX is used in situations where reliable transmission of data is needed. SPX sequences the packets of data. Missing packets or packets that don't arrive in the order in which they were sent are detected immediately. In addition, SPX offers connection multiplexing, which is used in the printing environment. Many accounting programs, for example, call upon the services of SPX to ensure that data is sent accurately. On the client, SPX support is provided as a component of the older DOS shell and of the current NetWare requester.

The *NetWare Core Protocol (NCP)* provides numerous function calls that support network services, such as file service, printing, name management, file locking, and synchronization. NetWare client software interfaces with NCP to access NetWare services.

NCP is a high-level protocol built into the NetWare operating system kernel. NCP covers aspects of the Session, Presentation, and Application layers of the OSI reference model and has its own miniature language that programmers use when writing applications for the NetWare environment. The commands that NCP understands are associated primarily with access to files and directories on a file server.

NetBEUI

NetBEUI is a transport protocol that serves as an extension to Microsoft's Network Basic Input/Output System (NetBIOS). Because NetBEUI was developed for an earlier generation of DOS-based PCs, it is small, easy to implement, and fast—the fastest transport protocol available with Windows NT. Because it was built for small, isolated LANs, however, NetBEUI is non-routable, making it somewhat anachronistic in today's diverse and interconnected networking environment.

Fortunately, the NDIS standard enables NetBEUI to coexist with other routable protocols. For instance, you could use NetBEUI for fast, efficient communications on the LAN segment and use TCP/IP for transmissions that require routing (see exercise 5.2).

AppleTalk

AppleTalk is the computing architecture developed by Apple Computer for the Macintosh family of personal computers. Although AppleTalk originally supported only Apple's proprietary LocalTalk cabling system, the suite has been expanded to incorporate both Ethernet and Token Ring Physical layers.

AppleTalk originally supported networks of limited scope. The *AppleTalk Phase 2* specification issued in 1989, however, extended the scope of AppleTalk to enterprise networks. The Phase 2 specification also enabled AppleTalk to coexist on networks with other protocol suites. Figure 5.5 presents a layered perspective of the AppleTalk protocols.

Figure 5.5

The AppleTalk protocol suite.

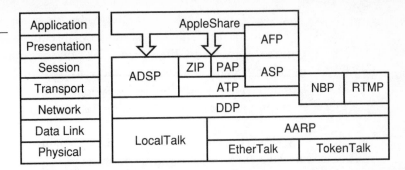

The LocalTalk, EtherTalk, and TokenTalk Link Access Protocols (LLAP, ELAP, and TLAP) integrate AppleTalk upper-layer protocols with the LocalTalk, Ethernet, and Token Ring environments.

Apple's *Datagram Deliver Protocol (DDP)* is a Network layer protocol that provides connectionless service between two sockets. A *socket* is the AppleTalk term for a service address. A combination of a device address, network address, and socket uniquely identifies each process.

DDP performs network routing and consults routing tables maintained by Routing Table Maintenance Protocol (RTMP) to determine routing. Packet delivery is performed by the data link protocol operating on a given destination network.

The *AppleTalk Transaction Protocol (ATP)* is a connectionless Transport layer protocol. Reliable service is provided through a system of acknowledgments and retransmissions. Retransmissions are initiated automatically if an acknowledgment is not received within a specified time interval. ATP reliability is based on transactions. A transaction consists of a request followed by a reply. ATP is responsible for segment development and performs fragmentation and reassembly of packets that exceed the specifications for lower-layer protocols. Packets include sequence numbers that enable message reassembly and retransmission of lost packets. Only damaged or lost packets are retransmitted.

The *AppleTalk File Protocol (AFP)* provides file services and is responsible for translating local file service requests into formats required for network file services. AFP directly translates command syntax and enables applications to perform file format translations. AFP is responsible for file system security and verifies and encrypts logon names and passwords during connection setup.

AppleShare is a client/server system for Macintosh. AppleShare provides three primary application services:

▶ The *AppleShare File Server* uses AFP to enable users to store and access files on the network. It logs in users and associates them with network volumes and directories.

▶ The *AppleShare Print Server* uses NBP and PAP to support network printing. NBP provides name and address information that enables PAP to connect to printers. The AppleShare Print Server performs print spooling and manages printing on networked printers.

▶ The *AppleShare PC* enables PCs running MS-DOS to access AppleShare services by running an AppleShare PC program.

Data Link Control (DLC)

The Data Link Control (DLC) protocol does not provide a fully-functioning protocol stack. (Note in figure 5.2 that DLC is not continuous with the upper layers.) In Windows NT systems, DLC is used primarily to access to Hewlett Packard JetDirect network-interface printers. DLC also provides some connectivity with IBM mainframes.

The Systems Network Architecture (SNA) Protocol Suite

Another important protocol suite is IBM's Systems Network Architecture (SNA). The Microsoft BackOffice suite includes a product called SNA Server that provides connectivity with SNA networks. (The DLC protocol included with Windows NT is also sometimes used as an interface with certain SNA resources such as mainframes.)

SNA evolved when terminals were the devices usually used to interact with centralized computers. Early versions of SNA supported only hierarchical network systems designed for this centralized environment.

In 1984, SNA was updated to support distributed processing environments with a feature called *Advanced Peer-to-Peer Networking (APPN)*. APPN can implement a distributed processing environment that can leverage the processing capabilities of mainframe hosts, minicomputers, and personal computers.

SNA wasn't developed from a preconceived, carefully thought-out model from which protocols were developed. IBM literally was pioneering the development of computer networking, and new protocols were added to meet new needs and design criteria. One result of this is that multiple protocols can be present at any given layer. Each protocol serves a somewhat different purpose in the overall scheme of SNA. As such, SNA doesn't consist of a protocol stack so much as it consists of multiple protocols that work together in different combinations to meet different needs.

SNA was a mature model by the time formulation of the OSI reference model began, and the SNA architecture had a significant influence on the definition of the OSI model. Figure 5.6 compares the layers of the OSI reference model to the layers of the SNA model.

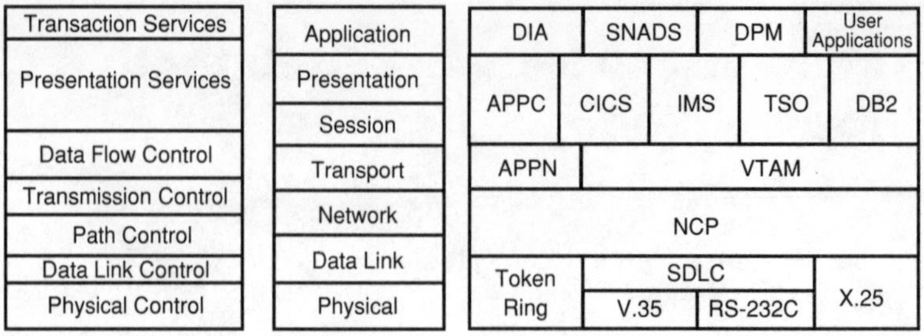

Figure 5.6

SNA protocols and the OSI reference model.

Transaction Services		Application		DIA	SNADS	DPM	User Applications
Presentation Services		Presentation		APPC	CICS	IMS	TSO	DB2
		Session	
Data Flow Control		Transport		APPN		VTAM	
Transmission Control		Network		NCP			
Path Control	
Data Link Control		Data Link		Token Ring	SDLC		X.25
Physical Control		Physical			V.35	RS-232C	

Summary

This chapter examined network protocols and protocol suites. The chapter began with an introduction to protocol stacks. You then learned about some of the most common protocol suites, as follows:

- ▶ **TCP/IP.** The Internet protocol suite

- ▶ **IPX/SPX.** A protocol suite used for Novell NetWare networks

- ▶ **NetBEUI.** A non-routable protocol used on Microsoft networks

- ▶ **AppleTalk.** The Apple Macintosh protocol system

- ▶ **DLC.** A protocol that Windows NT networks use to connect with HP JetDirect printers and IBM mainframes

The NDIS interface standard (discussed in Chapter 2) enables a single computer to bind one network adapter to more than one protocol system. This provides great versatility and interoperability in today's diverse networking environment.

Exercises

Exercise 5.1:   Installing Network Protocols in Windows NT

Objective: Become familiar with the procedure for installing and removing protocols in Windows NT.

Time estimate: 15 minutes

1. You can install, configure, remove, and manage network protocols by using the Network application in Windows NT's Control Panel. Click the Start menu and choose Settings/Control Panel. Then double-click on the Network application icon.

> Another way to reach the Network application is to right-click on the Network Neighborhood icon and choose Properties.

2. In the Network application, choose the Protocols tab (see fig. 5.7). The Network Protocols box displays the protocols currently installed on the system.

Figure 5.7

The Network application's Protocols tab.

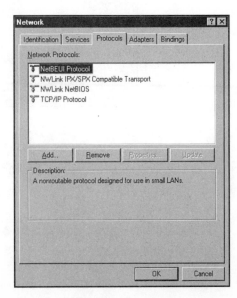

continues

Exercise 5.1: Continued

3. If TCP/IP is installed on your system, select TCP/IP Protocol and choose Properties to invoke the Microsoft TCP/IP Properties dialog box (see fig. 5.8). Note the several tabs that provide various configuration options. Close the Microsoft TCP/IP Properties dialog box and select the NetBEUI

   protocol (if it is installed) in the Network application's Protocols dialog box (refer to fig. 5.7). Note that the Properties button is grayed. Try double-clicking the NetBEUI icon in the box's list of protocols. A message says Cannot configure the software component. Unlike TCP/IP, NetBEUI is not user-configurable.

Figure 5.8

The Microsoft TCP/IP Properties dialog box.

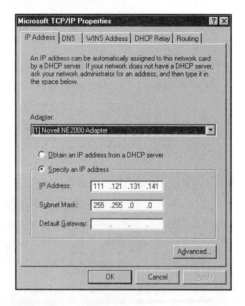

If TCP/IP and NetBEUI aren't installed on your system, you can install them by using the procedure described in steps 4 and 5 of this exercise and then delete them later.

4. To add a protocol, click on the Add button in the Network application's Protocols tab. Select a protocol from the protocol list in the Select Network Protocol dialog box (see fig. 5.9). Click on OK to install the protocol. Windows NT may prompt you for the location of the Windows NT installation

disk. If you are installing a protocol that requires some configuration (such as TCP/IP or NWLink), Windows NT will ask you for the necessary information.

Figure 5.9

The Select Network Protocol dialog box.

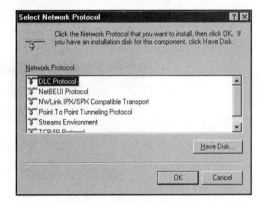

5. Windows NT asks you to restart your system. Shut down your system and restart. Return to the Network application's Protocols tab and see if the protocol is properly installed.

6. To remove a protocol, select the protocol from the Network Protocols list and click on the Remove button (refer to fig. 5.7).

Exercise 5.2: Network Bindings

Objective: Become familiar with the process for enabling and disabling network bindings and changing network access order.

Estimated time: 10 minutes

In Chapter 2, you learned about NDIS and the concept of network bindings. A binding is an association between protocol layers that enables those layers to behave like a protocol stack. By binding a transport protocol such as TCP/IP (which operates at the Transport and Network levels) to a network adapter (which operates at the Data Link and Physical layers) you provide a conduit for the protocol's packets to reach the network and thus enable the protocol to participate in network communications. NDIS lets you bind multiple protocols to a single adapter or multiple adapters to a single protocol.

continues

1. Click on the Start button and choose Settings/Control Panel. In Windows NT's Control Panel, double-click on the Network application icon and choose the Bindings tab (see fig. 5.10).

Figure 5.10

The Network application's Bindings tab.

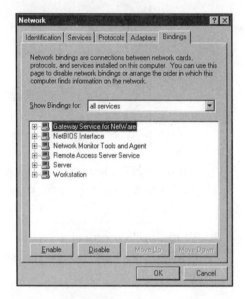

2. Click on the Show Bindings for down arrow to access the drop-down list. Note that you can display bindings for services, protocols, or adapters. A service bound to a protocol bound to an adapter provides a complete pathway from the local system to the network.

3. Click on the plus sign next to the Workstation service. The Workstation service is the Windows NT redirector (refer to Chapter 1, "Networking Terms and Concepts"), which redirects requests from the local system to the network. The protocols currently bound to the Workstation service appear in a list below the Workstation icon. Click on the plus sign next to one of the protocols. The network adapters bound to the protocol now appear in the tree (see fig 5.11).

4. The protocols and their associated adapters represent potential pathways for the Workstation service to access the network. Windows NT prioritizes those pathways according to

the order in which they appear in the Bindings tab. For the configuration shown in figure 5.11, for example, Windows NT attempts to use the NetBEUI protocol with the Workstation service before attempting to use NWLink. The Move Up and Move Down buttons let you change the access order. Select a protocol under the Workstation service. Try the Move Up and Move Down buttons to change the position of the protocol in the access order. (Don't forget to restore the protocol to its original position before leaving the Bindings tab.)

Figure 5.11

Inspect binding information by using the Bindings tab.

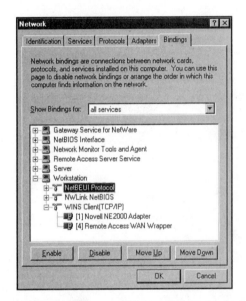

5. The Enable and Disable buttons let you enable or disable a protocol for a given service. Disable a protocol (for instance, NetBEUI) for the Workstation service. Now click the plus sign next to the Server service. Note that although the protocol is disabled for the Workstation service, it is still enabled for the Server service. Re-enable the protocol under the Workstation service and close the Network application.

Review Questions

The following questions test your knowledge of the information in this chapter. For additional exam help, visit Microsoft's site at www.microsoft.com/train_cert/cert/Mcpsteps.htm.

1. Which three of the following are Transport layer protocols?

    A. ATP

    B. IPX

    C. TCP

    D. SPX

2. Which three of the following are Network layer protocols?

    A. NWLink

    B. IPX

    C. TCP

    D. IP

3. SMB operates at the _____ protocol layer.

    A. Application

    B. Transport

    C. Network

    D. Physical

4. Which three of the following protocols are available with Windows NT?

    A. AppleTalk

    B. IPX/SPX

    C. NetBEUI

    D. DLC

5. The best protocol for an isolated LAN with several DOS-based clients is _____.

  A. NWLink

  B. TCP/IP

  C. DLC

  D. NetBEUI

6. The best protocol for a remote PC that interacts with the network via the Internet is _____.

  A. NWLink

  B. TCP/IP

  C. DLC

  D. NetBEUI

7. NCP operates at the _____ protocol level(s).

  A. Application and Presentation

  B. Transport and Network

  C. Network only

  D. Transport only

8. DDP operates at the _____ protocol level(s).

  A. Application and Presentation

  B. Transport and Network

  C. Network only

  D. Transport only

Pretest Answers

1. C (see the section titled "Protocols and Protocol Layers")

2. A (see the section titled "User Datagram Protocol (UDP)")

3. B (see the section titled "NetBEUI")

Review Answers

1. A, C, D

2. A, B, D

3. A

4. A, C, D

5. D

6. B

7. A

8. C

Chapter 6

Connectivity Devices

People sometimes think of a network as a single, local cabling system that enables any device on the network to communicate directly with any other device on the same network. A network by this definition, however, has no connections to other remote networks.

An *internetwork* consists of multiple independent networks that are connected and can share remote resources. These logically separate but physically connected networks can be dissimilar in type. The device that connects the independent networks together may need a degree of "intelligence" because it may need to determine when packets will stay on the local network or when they will be forwarded to a remote network.

This chapter examines some important connectivity devices. In the following sections, you learn about modems, repeaters, bridges, routers, brouters, and gateways. (Some of this material also appears in Chapter 2, "Networking Standards," in the discussion of communication devices and OSI.)

Chapter 6 targets the following objective in the Planning section of the Networking Essentials exam:

Test Objectives

▶ Select the appropriate connectivity devices for various Token Ring and Ethernet networks. Connectivity devices include repeaters, bridges, routers, brouters, and gateways

Test Yourself

Stop! Before reading this chapter, test yourself to determine how much study time you will need to devote to this section.

1. Which of the following connectivity devices is the least expensive?

   A. Repeater

   B. Bridge

   C. Router

   D. Gateway

2. Which of the following connectivity devices uses logical addresses?

   A. Repeater

   B. Bridge

   C. Router

   D. None of the above

3. Which of the following connectivity devices connects dissimilar networking protocol environments?

   A. Repeater

   B. Bridge

   C. Router

   D. Gateway

4. A router that requires a human-configured routing table is called a(n) _____.

   A. explicit router

   B. static router

   C. simple router

   D. bridge

Modems

Standard telephone lines can transmit only analog signals. Computers, however, store and transmit data digitally. Modems can transmit digital computer signals over telephone lines by converting them to analog form.

Converting one signal form to another (digital to analog in this case) is called *modulation.* Recovering the original signal is called *demodulation.* The word "modem" derives from the terms modulation/demodulation.

Modems can be used to connect computer devices or entire networks that are at distant locations. (Before digital telephone lines existed, modems were about the only way to link distant devices.) Some modems operate constantly over dedicated phone lines. Others use standard public switched-telephone network (PSTN) dial-up lines and make a connection only when one is required.

Modems enable networks to exchange e-mail and to perform limited data transfers, but the connectivity made possible is extremely limited. By themselves, modems don't enable remote networks to connect to each other and directly exchange data. In other words, a modem is not an internetwork device. Nevertheless, modems can be used in conjunction with an internetwork device, such as a router, to connect remote networks through the PSTN or through an analog service, such as a 56 KB line.

Modems don't necessarily need to connect through the PSTN. Short-haul modems frequently are used to connect devices in the same building. A standard serial connection is limited to 50 feet, but short-haul modems can be used to extend the range of a serial connection to any required distance.

Many devices are designed to operate with modems. When you want to connect such devices without using modems, you can use a null-modem cable, which connects the transmitter of one device to the receiver of the other device.

Until recently, modem manufacturers used a parameter called *baud rate* to gauge modem performance. The baud rate is the oscillation speed of the sound wave transmitted or received by the modem. Although baud rate is still an important parameter, recent advances in compression technology have made it less meaningful. Some modems now provide a data transfer rate (in bits per second—a more meaningful measure of network performance) that exceeds the baud rate. In other words, you can no longer assume the baud rate and the data transfer rate are equal.

Modems are classified according to the transmission method they use for sending and receiving data. The two basic types of modems are as follows:

▶ Asynchronous modems

▶ Synchronous modems

The following sections describe asynchronous and synchronous transmission.

Asynchronous Transmission

Asynchronous transmission does not use a clocking mechanism to keep the sending and receiving devices synchronized. Instead, this type of transmission uses *bit synchronization* to synchronize the devices for each frame that is transmitted.

In bit synchronization, each frame begins with a start bit that enables the receiving device to adjust to the timing of the transmitted signal. Messages are kept short so that the sending and receiving devices do not drift out of synchronization for the duration of the message. Asynchronous transmission is most frequently used to transmit character data and is ideally suited to environments in which characters are transmitted at irregular intervals, such as when users enter character data.

Figure 6.1 illustrates the structure of a typical frame used to transmit character data. This frame has four components:

- ▶ **A Start bit.** This component signals that a frame is starting and enables the receiving device to synchronize itself with the message.

- ▶ **Data bits.** This component consists of a group of seven or eight bits when character data is being transmitted.

- ▶ **A parity bit.** This component is optionally used as a crude method of detecting transmission errors.

- ▶ **A stop bit or bits.** This component signals the end of the data frame.

Figure 6.1

The structure of an asynchronous frame consists of four key bit components.

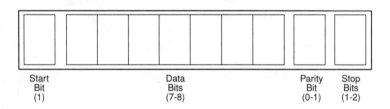

| Start Bit (1) | Data Bits (7-8) | Parity Bit (0-1) | Stop Bits (1-2) |

Asynchronous transmission is a simple, inexpensive technology ideally suited for transmitting small frames at irregular intervals. Because start, stop, and parity bits must be added to each character being transmitted, however, overhead for asynchronous transmission is high—often in the neighborhood of nearly 20 to 30 percent. This high overhead wastes bandwidth and makes asynchronous transmission undesirable for transmitting large amounts of data.

Asynchronous transmission is frequently used for PC-to-PC and terminal-to-host communication. Data in these environments is often of the bursty, character-oriented nature that is ideal for asynchronous communication. Asynchronous transmission generally requires less expensive hardware than synchronous transmission.

Synchronous Transmission

Synchronous transmission eliminates the need for start and stop bits by synchronizing the clocks on the transmitting and receiving devices. This synchronization is accomplished in two ways:

▶ **By transmitting synchronization signals with data.** Some data encoding techniques, by guaranteeing a signal transition with each bit transmitted, are inherently self-clocking.

▶ **By using a separate communication channel to carry clock signals.** This technique can function with any signal-encoding technique.

Figure 6.2 illustrates the two possible structures of messages associated with synchronous transmission.

Figure 6.2

Structures of synchronous transmissions.

Both synchronous transmission methods begin with a series of *synch signals*, which notify the receiver of the beginning of a frame. Synch signals generally utilize a bit pattern that cannot appear elsewhere in messages, ensuring that the signals always are distinct and easily recognizable by the receiver.

A wide variety of data types can be transmitted. Figure 6.2 illustrates both character-oriented and bit-oriented data. Notice that under synchronous transmission, multiple characters or long series of bits can be transmitted in a single data frame. Because the transmitter and receiver remain in synchronization for the duration of the transmission, frames may be very long.

When frames are long, parity is no longer a suitable method for detecting errors. If errors occur, multiple bits are more likely to be affected, and parity techniques are less likely to report an error. A more appropriate error-control technique for synchronous transmission is the *cyclic redundancy check (CRC)*. In this technique, the transmitter uses an algorithm to calculate a CRC value that summarizes the entire value of the data bits. This value is then appended to the data frame. The receiver uses the same algorithm, recalculates the CRC, and compares the CRC in the frame to the CRC value it has calculated. If the values match, the frame almost definitely was transmitted without error.

When synchronous transmission links are idle, communicating devices generally send *fill bits* to the devices synchronized.

Synchronous transmission offers many advantages over asynchronous transmission. The overhead bits (synch, CRC, and end) comprise a smaller portion of the overall data frame, which provides for more efficient use of available bandwidth. Synchronization improves error detection and enables the devices to operate at higher speeds.

The disadvantage of synchronous transmission is that the more complex circuitry necessary for synchronous communication is more expensive.

Hubs

Hubs, also called *wiring concentrators*, provide a central attachment point for network cabling (see fig. 6.3). Coaxial cable Ethernet is the only LAN standard that doesn't use hubs. Hubs come in three types:

▶ Passive

▶ Active

▶ Intelligent

The following sections describe each of these types in more detail.

Figure 6.3

A network wired to a central hub.

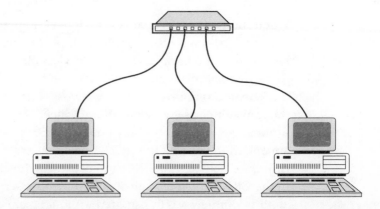

Passive Hubs

Passive hubs do not contain any electronic components and do not process the data signal in any way. The only purpose of a passive hub is to combine the signals from several network cable segments. All devices attached to a passive hub receive all the packets that pass through the hub.

Because the hub doesn't clean up or amplify the signals (in fact, the hub absorbs a small part of the signal), the distance between a computer and the hub can be no more than half the maximum permissible distance between two computers on the network. For example, if the network design limits the distance between two computers to 200 meters, the maximum distance between a computer and the hub is 100 meters.

As you might guess, the limited functionality of passive hubs makes them inexpensive and easy to configure. That limited functionality, however, is also the biggest disadvantage of passive hubs. ARCnet networks commonly use passive hubs. Token Ring networks also can use passive hubs, although the industry trend is to utilize active hubs to obtain the advantages cited in the following section.

Active Hubs

Active hubs incorporate electronic components that can amplify and clean up the electronic signals that flow between devices on the network. This process of cleaning up the signals is called *signal regeneration*. Signal regeneration has the following benefits:

▶ The network is more robust (less sensitive to errors).

▶ Distances between devices can be increased.

These advantages generally outweigh the fact that active hubs cost considerably more than passive hubs.

Later in this chapter, you learn about *repeaters*, devices that amplify and regenerate network signals. Because active hubs function in part as repeaters, they occasionally are called *multiport repeaters*.

Intelligent Hubs

Intelligent hubs are enhanced active hubs. Several functions can add intelligence to a hub:

- ▶ **Hub management.** Hubs now support network management protocols that enable the hub to send packets to a central network console. These protocols also enable the console to control the hub; for example, a network administrator can order the hub to shut down a connection that is generating network errors.

- ▶ **Switching hubs.** The latest development in hubs is the switching hub, which includes circuitry that very quickly routes signals between ports on the hub. Instead of repeating a packet to all ports on the hub, a switching hub repeats a packet only to the port that connects to the destination computer for the packet. Many switching hubs have the capability of switching packets to the fastest of several alternative paths. Switching hubs are replacing bridges and routers on many networks.

Repeaters

As you learned in Chapter 3, "Transmission Media," all media attenuate the signals they carry. Each media type, therefore, has a maximum range that it can reliably carry data. The purpose of a repeater is to extend the maximum range for the network cabling.

A *repeater* is a network device that repeats a signal from one port onto the other ports to which it is connected (see fig. 6.4). Repeaters operate at the OSI Physical layer. (Refer to "The OSI Reference Model" section in Chapter 2.) A repeater does not filter or interpret—it merely repeats (regenerates) a signal, passing all network traffic in all directions.

Figure 6.4

*A repeater regen-
erates a weak
signal.*

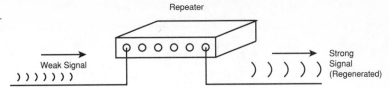

A repeater doesn't require any addressing information from the
data frame because a repeater merely repeats bits of data. This
means that if data is corrupt, a repeater will repeat it anyway. A
repeater will even repeat a broadcast storm caused by a malfunctioning adapter (see Chapter 13, "Troubleshooting").

The advantages of repeaters are that they are inexpensive and
simple. Also, although they cannot connect networks with dissimilar data frames (such as a Token Ring network and an Ethernet
network), some repeaters can connect segments with similar
frame types but dissimilar cabling.

Figure 6.5 shows the use of a repeater to connect two Ethernet
cable segments. The result of adding the repeater is that the potential length of the overall network is doubled.

Figure 6.5

*Using a repeater
to extend an
Ethernet LAN.*

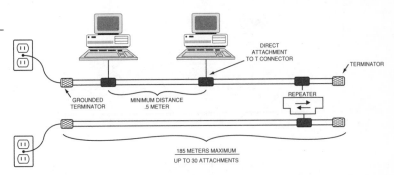

Some repeaters simply amplify signals. Although this increases the
strength of the data signal, it also amplifies any noise on the network. In addition, if the original signal has been distorted in any
way, an amplifying repeater cannot clean up the distortion.

Certainly, it would be nice if repeaters could be used to extend
networks indefinitely, but all network designs limit the size of the
network. The most important reason for this limitation is signal
propagation. Networks must work with reasonable expectations

about the maximum time a signal might be in transit. This is known as *propagation delay*—the time it takes for a signal to reach the farthest point on the network. If this maximum propagation delay interval expires and no signals are encountered, a network error condition is assumed. Given the maximum propagation delay allowed, it is possible to calculate the maximum permissible cable length for the network. Even though repeaters enable signals to travel farther, the maximum propagation delay still sets a limit to the maximum size of the network.

Bridges

Bridges, on the other hand, can extend the maximum size of a network. Although the bridged network in figure 6.6 looks much like the earlier example of a network with a repeater, the bridge is a much more flexible device. Bridges operate at the MAC sublayer of the OSI Data Link layer (see Chapter 2).

Figure 6.6

Extending a network with a bridge.

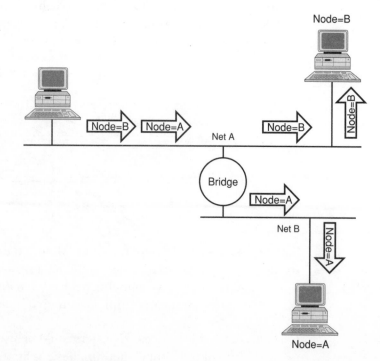

A repeater passes on all signals that it receives. A bridge, on the other hand, is more selective and passes only those signals targeted for a computer on the other side. A bridge can make this determination because each device on the network is identified by a unique address. Each packet that is transmitted bears the address of the device to which it should be delivered. The process works as follows:

1. The bridge receives every packet on LAN A and LAN B.

2. The bridge learns from the packets which device addresses are located on LAN A and which are on LAN B. The bridge then builds a table with this information.

3. Packets on LAN A that are addressed to devices on LAN A are discarded, as are packets on LAN B that are addressed to devices on LAN B. These packets can be delivered without the help of the bridge.

4. Packets on LAN A addressed to devices on LAN B are retransmitted to LAN B for delivery. Similarly, the appropriate packets on LAN B are retransmitted to LAN A.

On older bridges, the network administrator had to manually configure the address tables. Newer bridges are called *learning bridges*. Learning bridges function as described in step 2, automatically updating their address tables as devices are added to or removed from the network.

Bridges accomplish several things. First, they divide busy networks into smaller segments. If the network is designed so that most packets can be delivered without crossing a bridge, traffic on the individual network segments can be reduced. If the Accounting and Sales departments are overloading the LAN, for example, you might divide the network so that Accounting is on one segment and Sales on another. Only when Accounting and Sales must exchange packets does a packet need to cross the bridge between the segments.

Bridges also can extend the physical size of a network. Although the individual segments still are restricted by the maximum size imposed by the network design limits, bridges enable network designers to stretch the distances between segments and extend the overall size of the network.

Bridges, however, cannot join dissimilar types of LANs. This is because bridges depend on the physical addresses of devices. Physical device addresses are functions of the Data Link layer, and different Data Link layer protocols are used for each type of network. A bridge, therefore, cannot be used to join an Ethernet segment to a Token Ring segment.

Bridges sometimes are also used to link a LAN segment through a synchronous modem connection to another LAN segment at a remote location. A so-called *remote bridge* minimizes modem traffic by filtering signals that won't need to cross the modem line (see fig. 6.7).

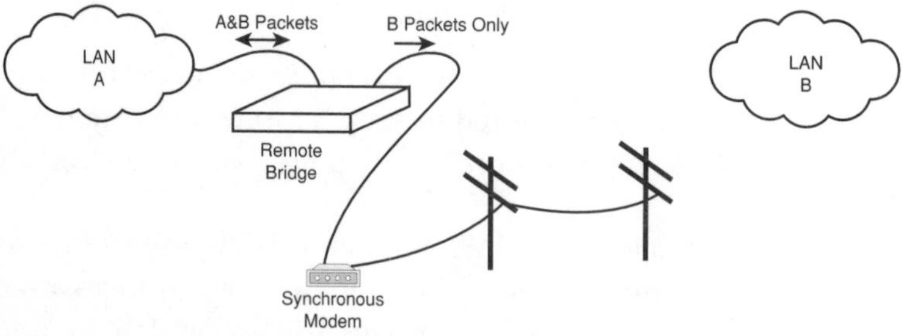

Figure 6.7

A remote bridge acts as a filter for a synchronous modem.

Routing

An internetwork consists of two or more physically connected independent networks that are able to communicate. The networks that make up an internetwork can be of very different types. For example, an internetwork can include Ethernet and Token Ring networks.

Because each network in an internetwork is assigned an address, each network can be considered logically separate; that is, each network functions independently of other networks on the internetwork. Internetwork connectivity devices, such as routers, can use network address information to assist in the efficient delivery of messages. Using network address information to deliver messages is called *routing*. The common feature that unites inter-network connectivity devices (routers and brouters) is that these devices can perform routing. The following list details some common internetwork connectivity devices:

▶ Routers

▶ Brouters

▶ Gateways

Each of these devices is discussed in the following sections.

Routers

Bridges are suitable for relatively simple networks, but bridges have certain limitations that become more significant in complex network situations. One limitation of bridges is that a network with bridges generally cannot include redundant paths. (Redundant paths are desirable because they enable the network to continue functioning when one path goes down.)

Consider the network in figure 6.8. Both bridges are aware of the existence of Node B, and both can pick up the packet from Net A and forward it. At the very least, the same packet can arrive twice at Node B.

A worse case, however, is that these relatively unintelligent bridges can start passing packets around in loops, which results in an ever-increasing number of packets that circulate on the network and never reach their destinations. Ultimately, such activity can (and will) saturate the network.

An algorithm, called the *spanning tree algorithm*, enables complex Ethernet networks to use bridges while redundant routes exist. The algorithm enables the bridges to communicate and construct a logical network without redundant paths. The logical network is reconfigured if one of the paths fails.

Figure 6.8

*A complex net-
work with
bridges.*

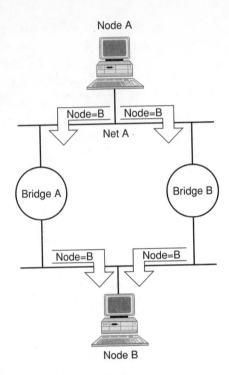

Another problem is that the bridges cannot analyze the network to determine the fastest route over which to forward a packet. When multiple routes exist, this is a desirable capability, particularly in wide area networks (WANs), where some routes are often considerably slower than others.

Routers organize the large network in terms of logical network segments. Each network segment is assigned an address so that every packet has both a destination network address and a destination device address.

Recall that an internetwork consists of two or more logically separate but physically connected networks. By this definition, any network segmented with routers is an internetwork.

Routing in Windows NT

The word "router" evokes the image of a screenless, box-shaped device—and many routers fit that image—but the tasks performed by a router can be (and sometimes are) performed by a PC. Many situations exist in which it is useful to configure a PC for routing functions, and one of the most important is when the PC serves as a remote access server. *Windows NT 4.0 Remote Access Service (RAS)*, for example, is capable of acting as an IP or an IPX router or a NetBIOS Gateway. (More on

the NetBIOS Gateway in the next sidebar.) Modem connections used to enable only point-to-point communications (from one computer to another computer). Under Windows NT, the connection is still a point-to-point connection (from the remote client computer to the RAS server on the local LAN), but the RAS server can route packets to other computers, thus providing the remote client with access to the entire network (see fig. 6.9).

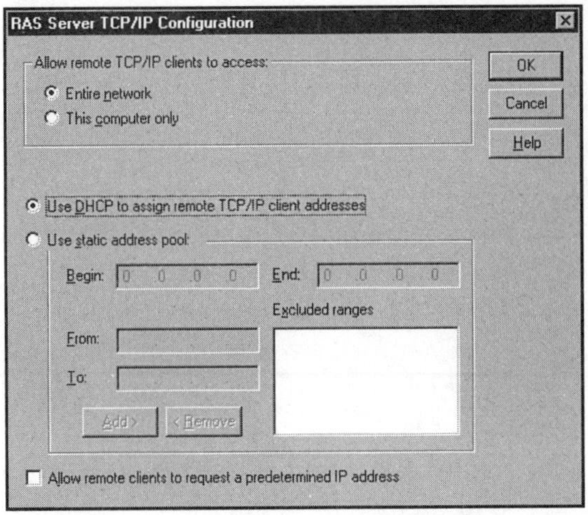

Figure 6.9

In the Windows NT RAS Server TCP/IP Configuration dialog box, you can access to either the entire network or to the RAS server machine only.

Figure 6.10 shows a complex network based on routers.

Figure 6.10

*An internetwork
with routers.*

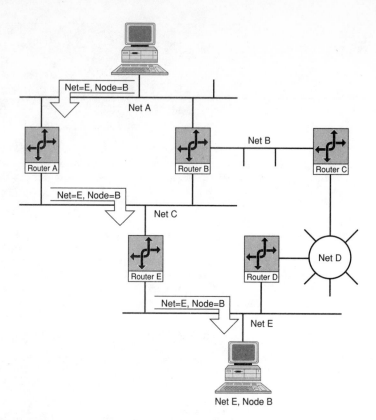

Routers are more "intelligent" than bridges. Not only do routers build tables of network locations, but they also use algorithms to determine the most efficient path for sending a packet to any given network. Even if a particular network segment isn't directly attached to the router, the router knows the best way to send a packet to a device on that network. In figure 6.10, for example, Router A knows that the most efficient step is to send the packet to Router C, not Router B.

Notice that Router B presents a redundant path to the path Router A provides. Routers can cope with this situation because they exchange routing information to ensure that packet loops don't occur. In figure 6.10, if Router A fails, Router B provides a backup message path, thus making this network more robust.

One consequence of all the processing a router performs on a packet is that routers generally are slower than bridges.

You can use routers to divide large, busy LANs into smaller segments, much as you can use bridges. But that's not the only reason to select a router. Routers also can connect different network types. Notice that the network in figure 6.10 includes a Token Ring segment with the Ethernet segments. On such networks, a router is the device of choice.

The protocols used to send data through a router must be specifically designed to support routing functions. IP, IPX, and DDP (the AppleTalk Network-layer protocol) are routable protocols. NetBEUI is a nonroutable protocol.

Because routers can determine route efficiencies, they usually are employed to connect a LAN to a wide area network (WAN). WANs frequently are designed with multiple paths, and routers can ensure that the various paths are used most efficiently.

The Network layer functions independently of the physical cabling system and the cabling system protocols—independently, that is, of the Physical and Data Link layers. This is the reason that routers easily can translate packets between different cabling systems. Bridges, on the other hand, cannot translate packets in this way because they function at the Data Link layer, which is closely tied to physical specifications.

Routers come in two types:

▶ **Static Routers.** These routers do not determine paths. Instead, you must configure the routing table, specifying potential routes for packets.

▶ **Dynamic Routers.** These routers have the capability to determine routes (and to find the optimum path among redundant routes) based on packet information and information obtained from other routers.

To determine the best path for a packet, routers employ some form of routing algorithm. Some common routing algorithms are discussed in the following sections.

Routing Algorithms

Routing refers to the process of forwarding messages through switching networks. In some cases, routing information is programmed into the switching devices. However, preprogrammed switches cannot adjust to changing network conditions. Most routing devices, therefore, are dynamic, which means that they have the capability of discovering routes through the internetwork and then storing the route information in route tables.

Route tables do not store only path information. They also store estimates of the time taken to send a message through a given route. This time estimate is known as the cost of a particular path. Some of the methods of estimating routing costs are as follows:

▶ **Hop count.** This method describes the number of routers that a message might cross before it reaches its destination. If all hops are assumed to take the same amount of time, the optimum path is the path with the smallest hop count.

▶ **Tic count.** This method provides an actual time estimate, where a *tic* is a time unit as defined by the routing implementation.

▶ **Relative expense.** This method calculates any defined measure of the cost (including the monetary cost) to use a given link.

After costs are established, routers can select routes, either statically or dynamically, as follows:

▶ **Static route selection.** This selection method uses routes that have been programmed by the network administrator.

▶ **Dynamic route selection.** Under this selection method, routing cost information is used to select the most cost-effective route for a given packet. As network conditions change and are reflected in routing tables, the router can select different paths to maintain low costs.

Two common methods of discovering routes are *distance vector routing* and *link-state routing*. Both are discussed in the following sections.

Distance Vector Routing

Distance vector routers advertise their presence to other routers on the network. Periodically, each router on the network broadcasts the information in its routing table. Other routers can use this information to update their own router tables.

Figure 6.11 illustrates how the process works. In the figure, Server S3 learns that Server S2 can reach Server S1 in three hops. Because S3 knows that S2 is one hop away, S3 knows that its cost to reach S1 through S2 is two hops.

Figure 6.11

Distance vector routing.

Distance vector routing is an effective algorithm, but it can be fairly inefficient. Because changes must ripple through the network from router to router, it might take a while for a change to become known to all routers on the network. In addition, the frequent broadcasts of routing information produce high levels of network traffic that can hurt performance on larger networks.

Link-State Routing

Link-state routing reduces the network traffic required to update routing tables. Routers that are newly attached to the network can request routing information from a nearby router.

After routers have exchanged routing information about the network, routers broadcast messages only when something changes.

These messages contain information about the state of each link the router maintains with other routers on the network. Because routers keep each other updated, complete network routing updates are not needed often.

Brouters

A *brouter* is a router that also can act as a bridge. A brouter attempts to deliver packets based on network protocol information, but if a particular Network layer protocol isn't supported, the brouter bridges the packet using device addresses.

Gateways

The term "gateway" originally was used in the Internet protocol suite to refer to a router. Today, the term "gateway" more commonly refers to a system functioning at the top levels of the OSI model that enables communication between dissimilar protocol systems. A gateway generally is dedicated to a specific conversion, and the exact functioning of the gateway depends on the protocol translations it must perform. Gateways commonly function at the OSI Application layer.

Gateways connect dissimilar environments by removing the layered protocol information of incoming packets and replacing it with the packet information necessary for the dissimilar environment (see fig. 6.12).

Figure 6.12

Gateways convert packet protocol information to connect dissimilar environments.

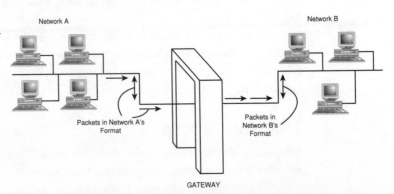

Gateways can be implemented as software, hardware, or a combination of both.

The NetBIOS Gateway

A previous sidebar described how Windows NT 4.0 RAS can act as an IP or an IPX router. RAS's NetBIOS gateway is an even more powerful feature. Not only does the NetBIOS gateway forward remote packets to the LAN, but it also acts as a gateway, providing NetBEUI clients with access to the LAN even if the LAN uses only TCP/IP or IPX/SPX.

The NetBIOS gateway (see fig. 6.13) is very much like the gateways described in this section. The NetBIOS gateway accepts a packet from the remote computer using one protocol (NetBEUI) and converts the packet, stripping incompatible protocol headers and replacing them with the headers the packet will need to circulate under a different protocol.

Figure 6.13

The Windows NT NetBIOS Gateway.

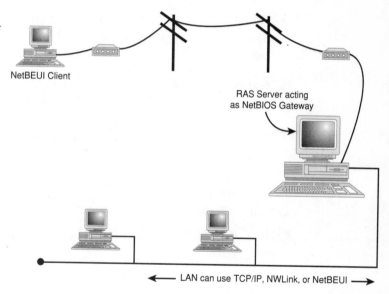

NetBEUI Client

RAS Server acting as NetBIOS Gateway

◄— LAN can use TCP/IP, NWLink, or NetBEUI —►

Summary

This chapter examined some of the connectivity devices that network engineers use to expand, optimize, and interconnect networks. These devices have some similarities, but each is designed for a specific task, as described in the following list:

- ▶ **Repeaters.** Repeaters regenerate a signal and are used to expand LANs beyond cabling limits.

- ▶ **Bridges.** Bridges know the side of the bridge on which a node is located. A bridge passes only packets addressed to computers across the bridge, so a bridge can thus filter traffic, reducing the load on the transmission medium.

- ▶ **Routers.** Routers forward packets based on a logical (as opposed to a physical) address. Some routers can determine the best path for a packet based on routing algorithms.

- ▶ **Gateways.** Gateways function under a process similar to routers except that gateways can connect dissimilar network environments. A gateway replaces the necessary protocol layers of a packet so that the packet can circulate in the destination environment.

You should be familiar with the features of these connectivity devices and with their relative advantages and disadvantages for the Networking Essentials exam.

Exercises

Exercise 6.1: Enabling IPX Routing

Objective: Learn to configure Windows NT Server's NWLink properties so that your Windows NT Server system can act as an IPX router.

Time estimate: 10 minutes

To configure Windows NT Server for IPX routing, you must install the NWLink protocol and add the RIP for NWLink IPX service.

1. Click the Start button and choose Settings/Control Panel.

2. In the Windows NT Control Panel, double-click the Network application and select the Protocols tab (see fig. 6.14).

Figure 6.14

The Network application's Protocols tab.

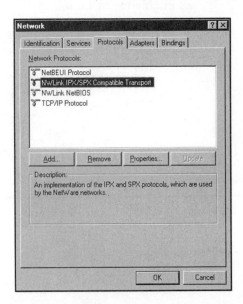

3. Make sure that the NWLink IPX/SPX Compatible Transport is installed. If it isn't, click the Add button and choose NWLink Compatible Transport from the protocols list. Windows NT asks for the Windows NT installation disk and prompts you for NWLink configuration information. (You can let it default if you're just doing this as a test.) Don't shut down your system yet.

continues

Exercise 6.1: Continued

4. Select the Network application's Services tab. Make sure that the RIP for NWLink IPX service is installed. If it isn't, click the Add button and select RIP for NWLink IPX from the Services list. RIP enables routing on IPX/SPX (and NWLink) networks. Windows NT asks for the Windows NT installation disk.

5. Restart your computer. Return to the Network application and select the Protocols tab.

6. Select NWLink IPX/SPX Compatible Transport and click the Properties button.

7. In the NWLink IPX/SPX Properties dialog box, select the Routing tab. A check box lets you enable/disable RIP routing (see fig. 6.15). (If you just installed RIP, RIP routing will be enabled by default.)

Figure 6.15

The Routing tab of the NWLink IPX/SPX Properties dialog box enables you to enable or disable routing.

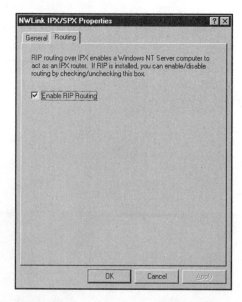

Both the TCP/IP suite and the IPX/SPX suite have protocols called RIP (refer to Chapter 5, "Transport Protocols"). These protocols have similar functions, but they are unrelated. Make sure you install the RIP for NWLink IPX service in this exercise and not the RIP for Internet Protocol service.

Review Questions

The following questions test your knowledge of the information in this chapter. For additional exam help, visit Microsoft's site at www.microsoft.com/train_cert/cert/Mcpsteps.htm.

1. Your LAN includes computers in two rooms at different ends of the company office. The cables connecting the rooms exceed the maximum cabling distance for the transmission medium, and the network is experiencing problems due to signal loss in the long cables. The cheapest and simplest solutions would be to add a _____.

   A. router

   B. repeater

   C. bridge

   D. brouter

2. Your Ethernet LAN is experiencing performance problems due to heavy traffic. A simple solution would be to add a _____.

   A. gateway

   B. repeater

   C. bridge

   D. router

3. The _____ algorithm enables bridges to operate on a network with redundant routes.

   A. distance vector

   B. link-state

   C. spanning tree

   D. learning tree

4. You need to connect a Windows NT LAN with a Unix network. To do so, you will need a _____.

    A. bridge

    B. gateway

    C. brouter

    D. router

5. You need to connect a Token Ring and an Ethernet LAN segment. To do so, you will need a _____.

    A. repeater

    B. bridge

    C. remote bridge

    D. router

6. A _____ uses a routing table to determine where to send a packet.

    A. bridge

    B. router

    C. both A and B

    D. none of the above

7. Which three of the following are advantages of active hubs?

    A. They can regenerate network signals.

    B. LAN ranges can be extended.

    C. They are inexpensive.

    D. They function as repeaters.

8. Which two networks can use passive hubs?

    A. Ethernet

    B. ARCnet

    C. Token Ring

    D. All the above

9. Which two of the following features can add intelligence to a hub?

    A. Signal regeneration

    B. Network-management protocols

    C. Multiport repeaters

    D. Switching circuitry

10. Which two statements are true of repeaters?

    A. Repeaters filter network traffic.

    B. Repeaters extend network distances.

    C. Repeaters regenerate signals.

    D. Repeaters operate at the OSI Data Link layer.

11. Which three statements are true of bridges?

    A. Bridges amplify and regenerate signals.

    B. Bridges can connect logically separate networks.

    C. Bridges use device address tables to route messages.

    D. Bridges divide networks into smaller segments.

Pretest Answers

1. A (see the section titled "Repeaters")

2. C (see the section titled "Routing")

3. D (see the section titled "Gateways")

4. B (see the section titled "Routers")

Review Answers

1. B

2. C

3. C

4. B

5. D

6. C

7. A, B, D

8. B, C

9. B, D

10. B, C

11. A, C, D

Chapter

7

Connection Services

Communication must occur between distant points, but few organizations can justify the costs required to construct a private wide area network. Fortunately, a variety of commercial options are available that enable organizations to pay only for the level of service that they require. This chapter discusses some wide area network (WAN) service options. You also learn about analog and digital lines and dial-up versus dedicated service. This chapter describes some of the available types of digital communication lines and examines some standards for WAN connection services.

Chapter 7 targets the following objective in the Planning section of the Networking Essentials exam:

Test Objectives

▶ List the characteristics, requirements, and appropriate situations for WAN connection services. WAN connection services include: X.25, ISDN, Frame Relay, and ATM

Test Yourself

Stop! Before reading this chapter, test yourself to determine how much study time you will need to devote to this section.

1. A modem uses _____ signaling.

    A. digital

    B. analog

    C. dedicated

    D. none of the above

2. Which three of the following are digital line options?

    A. Switched 16

    B. T1

    C. DDS

    D. Switched 56

3. The _____ service uses a PAD.

    A. X.25

    B. Frame Relay

    C. ATM

    D. ISDN

4. The _____ service transfers data in fixed-length units called cells.

    A. X.25

    B. Frame Relay

    C. ATM

    D. ISDN

Digital and Analog Signaling

Signaling amounts to communicating information. The information being communicated can take one of two forms—analog or digital:

▶ *Analog information* changes continuously and can take on many different values. An analog clock's hands move constantly, displaying time on a continuous scale.

▶ *Digital information* is characterized by discrete states. A light bulb, for example, is on or off. A digital clock represents the time in one-minute intervals and doesn't change its numbers again until the next minute. A digital clock can represent exact minutes but not the seconds that pass in between.

Frequently, information existing as one form must be converted to the other. This conversion often involves the use of some encoding scheme that enables the original information to be recovered from a signal after the signal has been received.

When an analog or a digital signal is altered so that it contains information, the process is called *modulation* or *encoding*. AM radio, for example, transmits information by modulating the radio signal, which increases or decreases the amplitude (signal strength) depending on the information content. Many similar schemes are used to communicate information through different types of signals.

Figure 7.1 illustrates the difference between analog and digital signals. The analog signal constantly changes and takes on values throughout the range of possible values. The digital signal takes on only two (or a few) specific states.

Figure 7.1

Analog and digital signals.

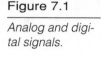

Figure 7.1

Analog and digital signals.

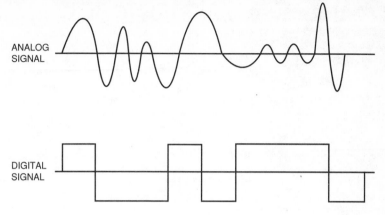

A *modem* is the most common computer connectivity device that transmits an analog signal. (Refer to Chapter 6, "Connectivity Devices," for more on modems.) Modems transmit digital computer signals over telephone lines by converting them to analog form. Modems are wonderfully handy for PC-to-PC communications or for accessing a LAN from a remote location, but modems generally are too slow and too unreliable for the high-tech task of linking busy LAN segments into a WAN. Because computer data is inherently digital, most WANs use some form of digital signaling.

Analog Waveforms

Analog signals constantly vary in one or more values, and these changes in values can be used to represent data. Analog waveforms frequently take the form of sine waves. The two characteristics that define an analog waveform are as follows:

▶ **Frequency.** Indicates the rate at which the waveform changes. Frequency is associated with the wavelength of the waveform, which is a measure of the distance between two similar peaks on adjacent waves. Frequency generally is measured in Hertz (Hz), which indicates the frequency in cycles per second. Frequency is illustrated in figure 7.2.

Figure 7.2

These two analog waveforms differ in frequency.

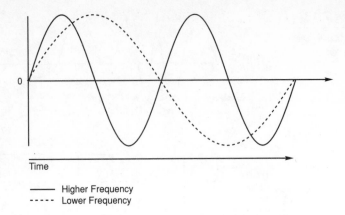

Figure 7.3

These two analog waveforms differ in amplitude.

▶ **Amplitude.** Measures the strength of the waveform. Amplitude is illustrated in figure 7.3.

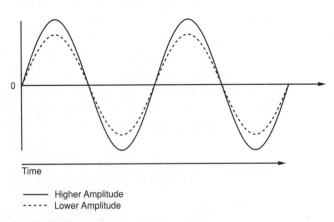

Some analog devices can encode data using a property of waveforms called *phase.* Figure 7.4 illustrates waves that differ in phase. These waveforms have identical frequency and amplitude, but they do not begin their transitions at the same time.

Figure 7.4

These two analog waveforms differ in phase.

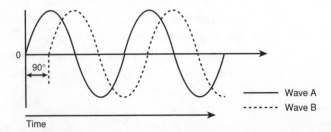

Each of these characteristics—frequency, amplitude, and phase—can be used to encode data.

The Public Telephone Network

Public telephone networks offer two general types of service:

- ▶ **Dial-up services.** The customer pays on a per-use basis.

- ▶ **Leased dedicated services.** The customer is granted exclusive access.

Switched services operate the Public Switched Telephone Network (PSTN), which we know as the telephone system. Voice-grade services have evolved to high levels of sophistication and can be adapted to provide many data services by using devices such as modems. Newer switched options provide higher levels of service while retaining the advantages of switched access.

With dial-up service, subscribers don't have exclusive access to a particular data path. The PSTN maintains large numbers of paths but not nearly enough to service all customers simultaneously. When a customer requests service, a path is switched in to service the customer's needs. When the customer hangs up, the path is reused for other customers. In situations in which the customer doesn't need full-time network access, switched service is extremely cost-effective.

Leased Line Types

When customers require full-time access to a communication path, a dedicated, leased line serves as one option. Several levels of digital lines are available, including those detailed in the following list:

- ▶ T1

- ▶ T3

- ▶ Fractional and multiple T1 or T3

- ▶ Digital data service

- ▶ Switched 56

A very popular digital line, *T1,* provides point-to-point connections and transmits a total of 24 channels across two wire pairs—one pair for sending and one for receiving—for a transmission rate of 1.544 Mbps. *T3* is similar to T1, but T3 has an even higher capacity. In fact, a T3 line can transmit at up to 45 Mbps.

Very few private networks require the capacity of a T3 line, and many do not even need the full capacity of a T1. The channels of a T1 or T3 line thus can be subdivided or combined for *fractional* or *multiple* levels of service. For instance, one channel of a T1's 24-channel bandwidth can transmit at 64 Kbps. This single-channel service is called *DS-0. DS-1* service is a full T1 line. *DS-1C* is two T1 lines, *DS-2* is four T1 lines, and *DS-3* is a full T3 line (equivalent to 28 T1s). A level of service called *T4* is equal to 168 T1 lines.

Microsoft reportedly has three T3 lines going into Redmond.

Digital Data Service (DDS) is a very basic form of digital service. DDS transmits point-to-point at 2.4, 4.8, 9.6, or 56 Kbps. In its most basic form, DDS provides a dedicated line. A special service related to DDS, *Switched 56,* offers a dial-up version of the 56 Kbps DDS. With Switched 56, users can dial other Switched 56 sites and pay only for the connect time.

Packet Routing Services

Many organizations must communicate among several points. Leasing a line between each pair of points can prove too costly. Many services now are available that route packets between different sites. Some of the packet-routing services discussed in this chapter are as follows:

- ▶ X.25

- ▶ Frame Relay

- ▶ ISDN

- ▶ ATM

Figure 7.5

Elements of the Public Switched Telephone Service.

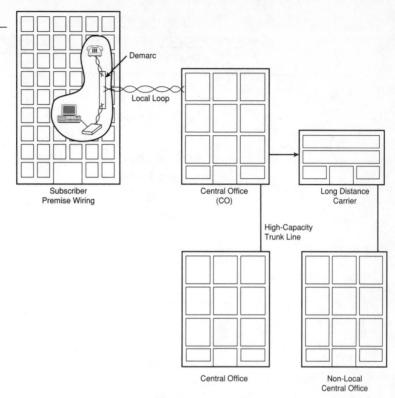

Each of these services has characteristics that suit it to particular uses, and all these services are available on a leased basis from service providers. An organization that must communicate among many sites simply pays to connect each site to the service, and the service assumes the responsibility of routing packets. The expense of operating the network is then shared among all network subscribers. Because the exact switching process is concealed from the subscriber, these networks frequently are depicted as a communication cloud, as shown in figure 7.6.

Figure 7.6

An example of a public network service.

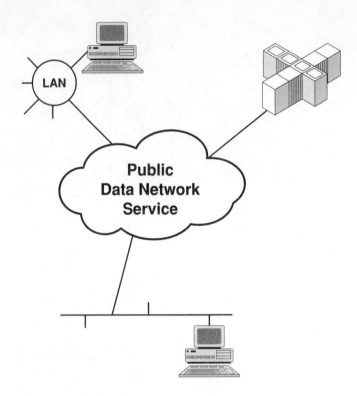

These data rates can be compared to common LAN services such as Ethernet (10 Mbps) and Token Ring (4–16 Mbps).

Many digital transmission methods use a technique called multiplexing. *Multiplexing*, described in Chapter 3, "Transmission Media," enables broadband media to support multiple data channels.

Virtual Circuits

Chapter 2, "Networking Standards," introduces you to packet switching and other routing-related techniques used to send data over WAN links. Packet-switching networks often use virtual circuits to route data from the source to the destination. A virtual circuit is a specific path through the network—a chain of communication links leading from the source to the destination (as opposed to a scheme in which each packet finds its own path). Virtual circuits enable the network to provide better error checking and flow control.

A *switched virtual circuit (SVC)* is created for a specific communication session and then disappears after the session. The next time the computers communicate, a different virtual circuit might be used.

A *permanent virtual circuit (PVC)* is a permanent route through the network that is always available to the customer. With a PVC, charges are still billed on a per-use basis.

X.25

X.25 is a packet-switching network standard developed by the International Telegraph and Telephone Consultative Committee (CCITT), which has been renamed the International Telecommunications Union (ITU). The standard, referred to as *Recommendation X.25*, was introduced in 1974 and is now implemented most commonly in WANs.

As shown in figure 7.7, X.25 is one level of a three-level stack that spans the Network, Data Link, and Physical layers. The middle layer, *Link Access Procedures-Balanced (LAPB),* is a bit-oriented, full-duplex, synchronous Data Link layer LLC protocol. Physical layer connectivity is provided by a variety of standards, including X.21, X.21bis, and V.32.

Figure 7.7

The relationship of X.25 to the OSI reference model.

Application
Presentation
Session
Transport
Network
Data Link
Physical

X.25
LAPB
X.21, etc.

X.25 packet-switching networks provide the options of permanent or switched virtual circuits. Although a datagram (unreliable) protocol was supported until 1984, X.25 now is required to provide reliable service and end-to-end flow control. Because each device on a network can operate more than one virtual circuit, X.25 must provide error and flow control for each virtual circuit.

At the time X.25 was developed, this flow control and error checking was essential because X.25 was developed around relatively unreliable telephone line communications. The drawback is that error checking and flow control slow down X.25. Generally, X.25 networks are implemented with line speeds up to 64 Kbps. These speeds are suitable for the file transfer and terminal activity that comprised the bulk of network traffic when X.25 was defined. Such speeds, however, are inadequate to provide LAN-speed services, which typically require speeds of 1 Mbps or better. X.25 networks, therefore, are poor choices for providing LAN application services in a WAN environment. One advantage of X.25, however, is that it is an established standard that is used internationally.

Figure 7.8 shows a typical X.25 configuration. In X.25 parlance, a computer or terminal is called *data terminal equipment (DTE)*. A DTE could also be a gateway providing access to a local network. *Data communications equipment (DCE)* provides access to the *packet-switched network (PSN)*. A PSE is a packet-switching exchange, also called a *switch* or *switching node*.

Figure 7.8

An X.25 network.

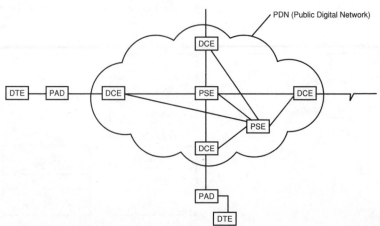

The X.25 protocol oversees the communication between the DTE and the DCE. A device called a *packet assembler/disassembler (PAD)* translates asynchronous input from the DTE into packets suitable for the PDN.

Frame Relay

Frame Relay was designed to support the *Broadband Integrated Services Digital Network (B-ISDN)*, which is discussed in the following section. The specifications for Frame Relay address some of the limitations of X.25. As with X.25, Frame Relay is a packet-switching network service, but Frame Relay was designed around newer, faster fiber-optic networks.

Unlike X.25, Frame Relay assumes a more reliable network. This enables Frame Relay to eliminate much of the X.25 overhead required to provide reliable service on less reliable networks. Frame Relay relies on higher-level protocol layers to provide flow and error control.

Frame Relay typically is implemented as a public data network and, therefore, is regarded as a WAN protocol. The relationship of Frame Relay to the OSI model is shown in figure 7.9. Notice that the scope of Frame Relay is limited to the Physical and Data Link layers.

Figure 7.9

The relationship of Frame Relay to the OSI reference model.

| Application |
| Presentation |
| Session |
| Transport |
| Network |
| Data Link |
| Physical |

| Frame Relay |

Frame Relay provides permanent virtual circuits, which supply permanent virtual pathways for WAN connections. Frame Relay services typically are implemented at line speeds from 56 Kbps up to 1.544 Mbps (T1).

Customers typically purchase access to a specific amount of bandwidth on a frame-relay service. This bandwidth is called the *committed information rate (CIR)*, a data rate for which the customer is guaranteed access. Customers might be permitted to access higher data rates on a pay-per-use, temporary basis. This arrangement enables customers to tailor their network access costs based on their bandwidth requirements.

To use Frame Relay, you must have special, Frame Relay-compatible connectivity devices (such as frame-relay-compatible routers and bridges).

ISDN and B-ISDN

Integrated Services Digital Network (ISDN) is a group of ITU (CCITT) standards designed to provide voice, video, and data-transmission services on digital telephone networks. ISDN uses multiplexing to support multiple channels on high-bandwidth circuits. The relationship of the ISDN protocols to the OSI reference model is shown in figure 7.10.

Figure 7.10

The relationship of ISDN protocols to the OSI reference model.

| Application |
| Presentation |
| Session |
| Transport |
| Network |
| Data Link |
| Physical |

ISDN

LAPD

The original idea behind ISDN was to enable existing phone lines to carry digital communications. Thus, ISDN is more like traditional telephone service than some of the other WAN services discussed in this chapter. ISDN is intended as a dial-up service and not as a permanent, 24-hour connection.

ISDN separates the bandwidth into channels (see the following note for more information). Basic ISDN uses three channels. Two channels (called *B channels*) carry the digital data at 64 Kbps. A third channel (called the *D channel*) provides link and signaling information at 16 Kbps. *Basic Rate ISDN* thus is referred to as *2B+D*. A single PC transmitting through ISDN can use both B channels simultaneously, providing a maximum data rate of 128 Kbps (or higher with compression). The larger-scale *Primary Rate ISDN* supports 23 64 Kbps B channels and one 64 Kbps D channel.

 note

A variety of ISDN channel types are defined. These channel types, often called *bit pipes*, provide different types and levels of service. The following list details the various channels:

- ▶ **A channel.** Provides 4 KHz analog telephone service.

- ▶ **B channels.** Support 64 Kbps digital data.

- ▶ **C channels.** Support 8 or 16 Kbps digital data, generally for out-of-band signaling.

- ▶ **D channels.** Support 16 or 64 Kbps digital data, also for out-of-band signaling. D channels support the following subchannels:

    - ▶ *p subchannels* support low-bandwidth packet data.

    - ▶ *s subchannels* are used for signaling (such as call setup).

    - ▶ *t subchannels* support telemetry data (such as utility meters).

- ▶ **E channels.** Provide 64 Kbps service used for internal ISDN signaling.

- ▶ **H channels.** Provide 384, 1,536, or 1,920 Kbps digital service.

ISDN functions as a data-transmission service only. Acknowledged, connectionless, full-duplex service is provided at the Data Link layer by the LAPD protocol, which operates on the D channel.

Broadband ISDN (B-ISDN) is a refinement of ISDN that is defined to support higher-bandwidth applications, such as video, imaging, and multimedia. Physical layer support for B-ISDN is provided by *Asynchronous Transfer Mode (ATM)* and the *Synchronous Optical Network (SONET)*, discussed later in this chapter. Typical B-ISDN data rates are 51 Mbps, 155 Mbps, and 622 Mbps over fiber-optic media.

Asynchronous Transfer Mode (ATM)

Asynchronous Transfer Mode (ATM) is a high-bandwidth switching technology developed by the ITU Telecommunications Standards Sector (ITU-TSS). An organization called the ATM Forum is responsible for defining ATM implementation characteristics. ATM can be layered on other Physical layer technologies, such as *Fiber Distributed Data Interface* (FDDI) and SONET. The relationships of these protocols to the OSI model are shown in figure 7.11.

Figure 7.11

The relationship of ATM to the OSI reference model.

Application
Presentation
Session
Transport
Network
Data Link
Physical

ATM
SONET/SDH, FDDI, etc.

Several characteristics distinguish ATM from other switching technologies. ATM is based on fixed-length, 53-byte cells, whereas other technologies employ frames that vary in length to accommodate different amounts of data. Because ATM cells are uniform in length, switching mechanisms can operate with a high level of efficiency. This high efficiency results in high data transfer rates. Some ATM systems can operate at an incredible rate of 622 Mbps; a typical working speed for an ATM is around 155 Mbps.

The unit of transmission for ATM is called a *cell*. All cells are 53 bytes long and consist of a 5-byte header and 48 bytes of data. The 48-byte data size was selected by the standards committee as a compromise to suit both audio- and data-transmission needs. Audio information, for instance, must be delivered with little *latency* (delay) to maintain a smooth flow of sound. Audio engineers therefore preferred a small cell so that cells would be more readily available when needed. For data, however, large cells reduce the overhead required to deliver a byte of information.

Asynchronous delivery is another distinguishing feature of ATM. Asynchronous refers to the characteristic of ATM in which transmission time slots don't occur periodically but are granted at irregular intervals. ATM uses a technique called *label multiplexing*, which allocates time slots on demand. Traffic that is time-critical, such as voice or video, can be given priority over data traffic that can be delayed slightly with no ill effect. Channels are identified by cell labels, not by specific time slots. A high-priority transmission need not be held until its next time slot allocation. Instead, it might be required to wait only until the current 53-byte cell has been transmitted.

Other multichannel technologies utilize *time-division* techniques to allocate bandwidth to channels. A T1 (1.544 Mbps) line, for example, might be time-division multiplexed to provide 24 voice channels. With this technique, each channel is assigned a specific time slot in the transmission schedule. The disadvantage of this technique is that an idle channel doesn't yield its bandwidth for the creation of other channels.

Devices communicate on ATM networks by establishing a virtual path, which is identified by a *virtual path identifier (VPI)*. Within this virtual path, virtual circuits can be established, which are in turn associated with *virtual circuit identifiers (VCIs)*. The VPI and VCI together make up a three-byte field included in the cell header.

ATM is relatively new technology, and only a few suppliers provide the equipment necessary to support it. (ATM networks must use ATM-compatible switches, routers, and other connectivity devices.)

Other networks, such as a routed Ethernet, require a six-byte physical address as well as a network address to uniquely identify each device on an internetwork. An ATM can switch cells with three-byte identifiers because VPIs and VCIs apply only to a given device-to-device link. Each ATM switch can assign different VPIs and VCIs for each link, and up to 16 million circuits can be configured for any given device-to-device link.

Although ATM was developed primarily as a WAN technology, it has many characteristics of value for high-performance LANs. An interesting advantage of ATM is that ATM makes it possible to use the same technology for both LANs and WANs. Some disadvantages, however, include the cost, the limited availability of the equipment, and the present lack of expertise regarding ATM due to its recent arrival.

Two other evolving technologies show promise:

▶ **Synchronous Optical Network (SONET).** Bell Communications Research developed SONET, which has been accepted as an ANSI standard. As the "optical" in the name implies, SONET is a standard for communication over fiber-optic networks. Data rates for SONET are organized in a hierarchy based on the *Optical Carrier (OC)* speed and the corresponding *Synchronous Transport Signals (STS)* employed. The basic OC and STS data rate is 51.84 Mbps, but higher data rates are provided in multiples of the basic rate. Thus OC-48 is 48 × 51.84 Mbps or 2488.32 Mbps.

▶ **Switched Multimegabit Digital Service (SMDS).** Developed by Bell Communications Research in 1991, SMDS technology is related to ATM in that it transports data in 53-byte cells. SMDS (see fig. 7.12) is a connectionless Data Link layer service that supports cell switching at data rates of 1.544 to 45 Mbps. IEEE 802.6 (DQDB metropolitan area network) is the primary Physical layer standard employed with SMDS, although other Physical layer standards are supported.

Figure 7.12

The relationship of SMDS to the OSI reference model.

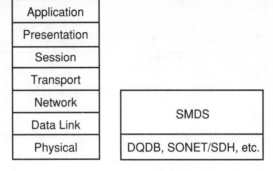

Summary

This chapter examined some basic WAN connectivity concepts, such as analog and digital signaling and dial-up and dedicated service lines. You learned about some types of digital lines, such as the following:

▶ T1

▶ T3

▶ Fractional and multiple T1 and T3 (the DS series)

▶ DDS

▶ Switched 56

This chapter also described the characteristics and appropriate situations for some important WAN connectivity service standards, including the following:

▶ X.25

▶ Frame Relay

▶ ISDN

▶ ATM

Refer to Chapter 2 for more information on packet switching and virtual circuits.

Exercises

Exercise 7.1: Accessing an X.25 Network Through Windows NT Dial-Up Networking

Objective: Learn how to configure Windows NT Dial-Up Networking to connect to an X.25 network provider.

Estimated time: 15 minutes

Windows NT Remote Access Service (RAS) usually is used for modem connections to remote PCs, but you also can use RAS to access an X.25 packet-switching network. RAS supports Packet Assembler/Disassembler (PAD) devices and X.25 smart cards. Alternatively, you can use Windows NT's Dial-Up Networking to connect to a commercial X.25 provider.

1. Click the Start menu and choose Settings/Control Panel. Double-click the Windows NT Control Panel Network application.

2. Choose the Network application's Services tab. Choose Remote Access Service from the Network Services list and click the Properties button to invoke the Remote Access Setup dialog box (see fig. 7.13).

Figure 7.13

The Remote Access Setup dialog box.

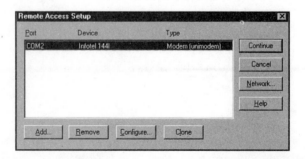

If RAS isn't installed on your system, you might have to install it. To do so, click the Add button and choose Remote Access Service in the Select Network Service dialog box.

3. In the Remote Access Setup dialog box (refer to fig. 7.13), click the Add button. This invokes the Add RAS Device dialog box (see fig. 7.14). You could use this dialog box to install an X.25 PAD for your system. See the button labeled Install X.25 PAD. A port must be available for the Install X.25 PAD dialog box to appear. A number of X.25 PAD options appear in the Install X.25 PAD dialog box (see fig. 7.15).

Figure 7.14

The Add RAS Device dialog box.

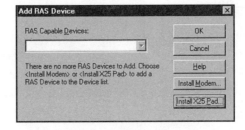

Figure 7.15

The Install X.25 PAD dialog box.

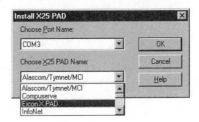

4. Close the Install X.25 PAD dialog box, the Add RAS Device dialog box, and the Network application.

5. Click the Start menu and choose Programs, Accessories, Dial-Up Networking. The Dial-Up Networking main window will appear on your screen. Click the New button.

6. In the New Phonebook Entry dialog box, click the X.25 tab. This tab enables you to specify an X.25 provider and the remote server's X.25 address. The down arrow to the right of the Network box reveals a list of X.25 providers (see fig. 7.16).

continues

Exercise 7.1: Continued

Figure 7.16

The New Phonebook Entry dialog box X.25 tab contains X.25 provider options.

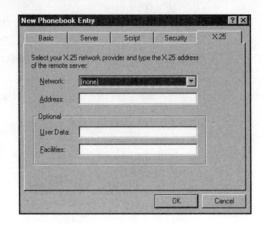

Review Questions

1. _____ signaling is characterized by discrete states.

   A. Analog

   B. Digital

   C. Frequency modulation

   D. None of the above

2. The DS-0 service level provides a transmission rate of _____.

   A. 64 Kbps

   B. 128 Kbps

   C. 1.544 Mbps

   D. 45 Mbps

3. A T3 line provides a transmission rate of _____.

   A. 64 Kbps

   B. 128 Kbps

   C. 1.544 Mbps

   D. 45 Mbps

4. An SVC _____

   A. is a permanent path. Charges are billed on a monthly basis.

   B. is a permanent path. Charges are billed on a per-use basis.

   C. is a temporary path created for a specific communication session.

   D. is none of the above.

5. X.25 is _____ Frame Relay.

    A. faster than

    B. slower than

    C. about the same speed as

    D. nearly identical to

6. _____ was designed to provide digital communications over existing phone lines.

    A. X.25

    B. ISDN

    C. ATM

    D. Frame Relay

7. _____ is sometimes called 2B+D.

    A. Primary rate ISDN

    B. Basic rate X.25

    C. Primary rate Frame Relay

    D. Basic rate ISDN

8. A typical working speed for ATM is _____.

    A. 1.544 Mbps

    B. 45 Mbps

    C. 155 Mbps

    D. 622 Mbps

9. ATM divides data into _____ byte blocks called _____.

    A. 53 / packets

    B. 53 / cells

    C. 56 / frames

    D. 128 / cells

Pretest Answers

1. B (see the section titled "Digital and Analog Signaling")

2. B, C, D (see the section titled "Leased Line Types")

3. A (see the section titled "X.25")

4. C (see the section titled "Asynchronous Transfer Mode (ATM)")

Review Answers

1. B

2. A

3. D

4. C

5. B

6. B

7. D

8. C

9. B

P a r t **3**

Implementation

Chapter 8

Managing and Securing a Microsoft Network

In the preceding chapter, we examined the process of establishing a physical connection between the machines on your network and installing the drivers and services necessary to enable network communication. With these initial considerations out of the way, the next step is to begin organizing and controlling the manner and scope of network usage. This chapter deals with the process of implementing resource sharing on a Microsoft network.

Chapter 8 targets the following objective in the "Implementation" section of the Networking Essentials exam:

Test Objectives

▶ Choose an administrative plan to meet specified needs, including performance management, account management, and security

Stop! Before reading this chapter, test yourself to determine how much study time you will need to devote to this section.

1. This is required for local file-level security.

   A. NTFS

   B. Share-level security

   C. User-level security

   D. FAT

2. What two types of groups can Windows NT networks include?

   A. Local

   B. Domain

   C. Global

   D. Everyone

3. True or False: A single user can be placed in more than one group.

   A. True

   B. False

Resource Sharing Basics

Microsoft uses very specific terms to describe elements of its networking structure, and as such, a good understanding of these terms is essential. The four most basic terms that you must understand are *resources, sharing, rights,* and *permissions.*

Resources

The first concept to be discussed is a *resource.* The two key resources detailed in this chapter are data files and printers, but in theory, a resource can be any information or device relating to the network. Without networking, a resource can be accessed only by physically sitting at the machine on which the resource is installed. This means that you either access a local file or a local printer. The creation of a networking structure grants you the capability to use a server computer to share resources with others at remote client machines.

Remember that the term "server" does not refer exclusively to Windows NT Server. The term is actually a generic reference to any computer that provides resources to other machines on the network. As such, Windows 95, Windows NT Workstation, and Windows for Workgroups all are capable of performing the basic functions of a server.

Sharing

This brings us to the second important concept: *sharing.* Only by specifying that you want to grant others access to a resource—be it a directory, a CD-ROM drive, or a printer—do you make the resource available for use from remote workstations. A shared resource is simply a resource whose owner has leveraged networking to make it available for use by others.

Users

A *user* is anyone who requests network resources. In most cases, you assign a unique username and password to every individual on your network. Users can be created on a number of operating systems, including Windows NT, NetWare, and Unix. Users cannot be created on Windows 95 or Windows for Workgroups because neither of these operating systems have the capability of establishing a user database. Both systems do enable the creation of individualized profiles, but as you see later in the chapter, they must rely on another machine's database to provide true user authentication.

Groups

Groups are administrative units that are comprised of one or more users with similar needs of network resources. Two types of groups exist on Windows NT—Local and Global. These groups are key to efficient security in the Microsoft model.

Permissions

Finally, *permissions* refers specifically to the level of trust that the owner of a resource has in the people with which he shares the resource. Although very subtle permissions structures can be constructed using Windows NT and Windows 95, a resource generally will either be shared as read-only or full-control. By default, both Windows NT and Windows 95 share resources with full-control, which means that others cannot only view your shared resources but also can append, modify, and even delete them. For the less trusting owner, a good compromise is to grant read-only permissions, which enable others to view your files or print to your printer but not to modify those files or change the printer's settings.

Rights

The difference between having rights and receiving permissions might seem like nothing more than a matter of semantics, but this is not the case. In Microsoft terminology, *rights* are general attributes that particular users or groups have. These rights include the capability to log on locally or to load and unload device drivers. These particular user rights make administrators more powerful than users. Permissions refer to the level of control a particular user or group has over a specific resource.

> If a user and an administrator have full-control access to a directory, either of them can read, modify, or even delete that resource. If the directory must be restored from tape, however, only a member of the Administrators, Server Operators, or Backup Operators groups can accomplish this task. By default, only these groups have the right to restore files and directories. To see the different rights available to Windows NT users, select the Policies menu in User Manager for Domains and then select User Rights. Choose the check box in the lower left to view additional Advanced Rights.

All these terms might make network security seem a bit daunting, but this is not necessarily so. Perhaps it is easiest to think of server or workstation resources just as you would think of anything else that you must care for and protect.

For instance, imagine that you have a house. If you want, you can just keep the house to yourself and not admit entrance to anyone else, thus preventing damage to your possessions. Of course, you also can allow others to enter, but then you take the chance that someone might damage your possessions, either maliciously or inadvertently. Because of this, it's a good idea to take some precautions about who you invite to your house. Moreover, you almost certainly will be more watchful of some guests than others, and you will seek to protect certain rooms or possessions more than others. Lastly, because you can't watch everyone all the time, you probably will want to have some good locks on the doors and sufficient insurance against theft or disaster.

Resources on a network deserve the same care. This book has already discussed the insurance (fault tolerance), but has yet to examine how you can grant some network users access to your resources while refusing access to others. The first part of this chapter deals with understanding the underlying security options and examines how different Microsoft operating systems and network configurations operate from a security standpoint.

Managing User Accounts and Groups Using Windows NT

As we saw earlier when looking at the Microsoft networking family, Windows NT is designed to provide far greater security than Windows 95. As such, Windows NT is the centerpiece of any Microsoft network where security is a major issue. An organization might not feel that its everyday documents require security, but most companies have payroll information or other data that they want to guard from access by unauthorized individuals. As you will soon see, Windows NT—both Workstation and Server—can maintain a user database that makes the NT products far more flexible in meeting security needs.

Throughout your MCSE testing, keep in mind a few very basic conceptual frameworks. One of the most important is the interaction of user accounts, Global groups, and Local groups. This chapter defined users and groups in earlier sections, but we now must look more deeply into the actual functional value of each.

User Accounts

In most instances, a user account is created for each individual on the network and is meant for use only by that one person. This account generally is a contracted form of the person's name or some other unique value, and no two users can have the same username in a single user database. At their most basic level, user accounts consist of three required elements:

▶ **A username.** This element distinguishes one account from another.

▶ **A password.** This element confirms the user's identity. Individual passwords should be kept private to avoid unauthorized access.

▶ **The groups of which the user is a member.** These groups determine the user's rights and permissions on the network.

A number of other optional components—such as a home directory (a place where a user can store personal files on the network)—or specific information about the user—such as his full name or description—exist, but none of these is crucial to the functioning of the account in the way that the elements enumerated above are. In exercise 8.1, you create a very basic user account and observe some of the available options.

Remember that if you are on a NetWare network, you will manage users and network resources with either Syscon or NWAdmin. Microsoft does not test you on the usage of these utilities.

Groups

Now that a user has been established, the next step in granting that individual access to resources is to assign proper permissions. This is done by creating a group or a set of groups, assigning permissions to the groups, and then placing the user inside the appropriate groups. By default, Windows NT creates a number of built-in groups that are defined with the rights necessary to perform particular tasks. These groups are task-specific and are inherently different from the type of groups you normally create, which are resource-specific. For instance, the Backup group and the Server Administrators group have capabilities granted to them that are needed to perform backups and server maintenance tasks, respectively. Usually, the default rights will be fine. You create the group and add users to it, at which time the group is ready to be given permissions in the file system, such as Read permissions to a directory or Print permissions to a printer.

Remember that in the creation of user accounts and policies, you must strike a balance between security and user-friendliness. Setting a password expiration date that is too frequent or one that requires too many long, unique passwords is almost certain to result in a less, rather than more, secure environment. If users are unable to remember such a password, they often simply will stick a note to their monitor with their password on it or come up with some other highly insecure way of jogging their memory. If this starts happening, you know that your policies are probably too stringent.

Global and Local Groups

Windows networks can include two types of groups: Global and Local. Each of these has very specific functions.

Global groups are created only on the Primary Domain Controller of a Microsoft Domain, and these groups function as nothing more than containers for user accounts. Global groups cannot contain other groups.

Local groups, on the other hand, can be created on Windows NT Server or Workstation and can include both user accounts and Global groups. Moreover, these groups are assigned permissions in the Microsoft model.

In exercise 8.2, you create both types of groups and explore how they interact with users and resources. Note that this exercise assumes you are using a Windows NT Domain Controller. If this is not the case, you will be unable to complete the steps as written. In that case, you can participate in the creation of the Local group and ignore instructions that deal with Global groups.

Windows NT also creates four special groups, each of which has special uses and access privileges. You cannot delete or rename these groups, but you can give or deny them permissions to resources. The following list details these groups:

▶ **Everyone.** This umbrella group includes all users of the machine, from guests to administrators.

▶ **Creator-owner.** If a user creates or owns a directory, he gains whatever rights are given to this group.

▶ **Interactive.** This group is fluid, in that a user becomes a part of it when he accesses a local resource, and he is excluded from it when accessing a resource over a network connection.

▶ **Network.** This group is exactly the opposite of an Interactive user group. This is another fluid group that includes any user who logs on using a network or modem connection rather than being physically seated at the machine.

Creating groups and users provides the base upon which the rest of your security is built. You should now know what a user is, and how users and groups interact. The next section explores using these groups and users to give or restrict access to network resources.

Implementing Security on Windows NT

After you assign an account to a user in a group, you can begin to give that user access to file-system resources through the Windows Explorer. Keep in mind that resources can be shared only through the machines on which they reside. To set up a shared resource, you simply create or locate a resource that you would like to share and place it into a directory on a local hard drive. For example, if you want to create a share on machine Test leading to files on machine Other, you first must copy those files to a directory on Test and then share that local directory. Setting permissions is a time-consuming process but is not difficult. Nonetheless, as exercise 8.3 shows, the task of assigning permissions does have a number of options and can become confusing if not undertaken with care.

Creating and Assigning Permissions to a Shared Folder on Windows NT

In the exercise 8.3, you create and share a directory called Public. The group Everyone is given Read permissions to the directory, and the group Local Training is given Full Control. Remember that only directories can be shared, and all files and subdirectories within that directory are available over the network through the share. Exercise 8.3 assumes a FAT partition with no NTFS file-level security, or an NTFS partition on which no restrictions have been set. Remember that NTFS is the native Windows NT file system, and that it allows for additional security beyond what FAT can offer.

Rights and permissions also can be given directly to user accounts themselves, but this is not recommended. Not only is such security cumbersome, but it is also difficult to administrate and troubleshoot.

If you have a user who has specific resources that are different than those of anyone else on the network, resist the urge to simply assign that user the needed permissions directly. Rather, create a new set of groups (Local and, if needed, Global), place the user into the proper group or groups, and then assign permissions and rights through the Local groups as needed.

This might seem unnecessarily redundant, but it can be very useful later on, especially if the user leaves your organization and is replaced by a new user who now needs the same permissions. The new user simply can be placed into the needed group(s), and the old account can be removed from them. If, on the other hand, you have assigned file system permissions directly, you then must hunt down all the directories to which the original user had access, remove the old user from each one, and then insert the new user.

Assigning File-Level Permissions on an NTFS Partition

If you are using the standard FAT file system native to DOS, Windows, and Windows 95, your Windows NT security structure will be complete after you assign share-level permissions to your files. In exercise 8.4, however, assume that the partition on which the share is located is formatted with NTFS, Windows NT's native file system. In this case, you can assign additional rights within the share on a per-directory and even per-file basis. The strength of NTFS security is two-fold:

- ▶ NTFS security gives the administrator a wider range of flexibility in assigning rights to files and directories.

- ▶ NTFS security provides security even at the local level, something that a FAT partition does not support. Interactive users are unaffected by share-level security options but still are limited by NTFS file-level security.

In the Public folder shared in exercise 8.3, you see that two share-level permissions exist for this directory:

- ▶ Everyone: Read

- ▶ Administrators: Full Control

In exercise 8.4, you assign a new permission to this directory, this time through NTFS security. The permission to be assigned will be:

- ▶ Everyone: Change

As you always should before altering your permissions structure, consider how this change will affect the permissions of the Everyone and Administrators groups. Remember that Read permissions allow Read (R) and Execute (X) permissions, while Change grants these permissions plus Write (W) and Delete (D). Likewise, Full control offers these permissions plus Take Ownership (O) and Change Permissions (P). Share-level rights and file-level rights are both cumulative within themselves. For instance, an administrator on a Windows NT network will be a member of both Administrators and Everyone—and possibly a number of other groups as well.

In your Public share, the user would gain RX from the Everyone group and RXWDOP from the Administrator group. The user then would have RXWDOP over the share. On the other hand, if you include the NTFS permissions for Everyone, the user has RX-WDOP over the share and only RXWD at the file level. Under NTFS only permissions granted at *both* the share level and the file level will be applied, and the administrative user will have only Change (RXWD) permissions over the share.

> The exception to the principle of additive privilege is the No Access permission, which immediately blocks all other rights. Because of this, the No Access option should be used sparingly and very carefully. Numerous No Access permissions on the network usually point to a poorly implemented security structure. If you don't want users to access a resource, it is sufficient simply to not give them permission—explicitly banning the users access generally is overkill. Also, never implement No Access for the Everyone group—this group includes you, as well as all other administrators and users, none of whom will be able to get to the resource until the No Access is removed, even if they belong to other groups that do have sufficient permissions.

Generally, you will try to use a dedicated server such as NT or NetWare to provide resource access on your network. In some situations, though, you may need to implement a workgroup sharing model or use a Windows 95 machine as a server.

Implementing Security on Windows 95

As noted earlier, Windows 95 also can act as a server, albeit in a less robust capacity. Windows 95 supports two types of security: share-level and user-level. As you read about the application's security models, notice that Windows 95's user-level security is nearly identical to Windows NT's share-level authentication.

Moreover, notice that Windows 95 does not support file-level local security, nor does Windows NT support Windows 95's low-security, password-only share-level option.

Share-Level Security on Windows 95

Under Windows 95's simple share-level security, passwords are assigned to permit access to each directory or printer share. To access the share, a user must supply the correct password.

When creating a shared directory using share-level security, you can grant one of three types of access:

▶ **Read-only access.** After entering the correct password, a remote user can access a directory, its subdirectories, and its files. However, the user cannot delete files or write files to that directory.

▶ **Full access.** A remote user who supplies the correct password has read and write privileges to that directory and all its files and subdirectories.

▶ **Depends on password.** Two different passwords can be created: one allowing read-only access, and one allowing full access. The type of access granted to a user depends on the password that that user has supplied.

If no password is entered, all users have full or read-only access to the directory, depending on which option was specified when the shared directory was created.

In exercise 8.5, you create a directory share using share-level security. Remember that a share is an entry point on your computer from which you can give others access to your local resources.

Print queues also can be shared with other network users using share-level security. If a password is specified for the share, a network user must enter that password to access the print queue and connect to that printer. If a printer is shared with a blank password field—meaning no password was entered—any user can connect to and print to that printer.

Because share-level security relies on access passwords, this form of security has the following disadvantages:

- ▶ To access different shares, a network user must know numerous passwords.

- ▶ Passwords can easily be forgotten. Windows 95 can cache passwords so a user does need to enter them each time. However, if the creator of the share forgets the password, then the password must be changed to enable another user to access the share.

- ▶ Nothing prevents a user from disclosing the password to an unauthorized user.

User-Level Security on Windows 95

User-level security can be used to overcome the shortcomings of share-level security, and where it is available, this type of security is generally the preferred security structure. With user-level security, you can grant specific user accounts or group accounts to a shared directory or printer. Instead of relying on a password that could be used by anyone, the user account accessing a shared resource must be authenticated to ensure that that account has been granted access. User-level security, therefore, provides a level of personal flexibility and accountability that is not available with share-level security.

Windows 95 cannot manage user accounts by itself. Instead, the application must use another authentication database so that Windows NT or a NetWare server can authenticate the user trying to access the resource. In user-level security, Windows 95 must defer to a machine with a user database and present all requests for access to that machine for authentication.

To initiate user-level security, the Windows 95 computer must obtain a copy of the accounts list from one of the following sources:

▶ Windows NT Server 3.5 (or later) computer

▶ Windows NT Workstation 3.5 (or later) computer

▶ NetWare 3.x server

▶ NetWare 4.x server with bindery emulation enabled

When a directory is shared with user-level security, the users or groups to be granted access to the share are assigned privileges. You can grant each user or group one of the following privileges:

▶ **Read-only.** Users can access files and subdirectories in a directory but cannot delete or save files to that share.

▶ **Full access.** Users can read, write, and delete files in the directory.

▶ **Custom.** Any number of the following privileges can be granted:

  ▶ Read Files

  ▶ Write to Files

  ▶ Create Files

  ▶ List Files

  ▶ Delete Files

  ▶ Change File Attributes

  ▶ Change Permissions

When sharing a printer, users or groups can be added to a list of users with access to that printer. More specific information on sharing printers is discussed in exercise 8.8.

Exercise 8.6 demonstrates how to grant a network user access to a directory share. For this exercise, you must be part of a domain that contains a server with a user accounts database. If the user accounts exist on a NetWare server, you will need to install the Client for NetWare Networks, the IPX/SPX-compatible protocol, and File and Printer Sharing for NetWare Networks, and make your selections accordingly throughout the exercise.

You now have learned what a user and a group are, and how they can be used to provide network access and file security. You have seen the way that both Windows 95 and Windows NT handle security issues, and should be able to see some of their major differences. Remember that the same principles that guide file sharing also work for the other major network resource we will look at—printers.

Security for Printer Resources

The second major resource with which you will be expected to be familiar is the printer. For many administrators, printers have been a constant troublespot, and it seems that a disproportionate percentage of network problems are caused by these devices. Because many of these problems are due to improper or modified printer configurations, careful setup and effective security structures can save an administrator considerable time in this area.

Printer Sharing with Windows NT

To connect to a network printer, you first must install and configure the printer on a server. Every network printer, in other words, is just a local printer that has been shared by its owner. This section first examines sharing a printer using Windows NT 4.0 and then discusses the same process with Windows 95. For the most part, the process is the same in Windows NT 4.0 as it is in Windows 95. However, a key difference does exist.

Windows NT has the capability to enable remote users to dynamically download print drivers specific to their own system into RAM each time the users print. This allows for easy driver updates and also enables users to connect to a new printer without having rights to install drivers on their local system. This process is called connecting to a printer.

As you install and assign permissions to the printer in exercise 8.7, observe that many of the processes are very similar to the steps you took in creating, sharing, and securing files and folders.

Printer Sharing with Windows 95

To use Windows 95 as a network print server, the printer must be attached to the Windows 95 machine locally and configured with the proper driver, just as it would be if it were serving only local users. The printer then must be shared to enable other users to access it. To share a printer in Windows 95, the network print server must run a 32-bit, protected-mode client, and a file- and printer-sharing service must be enabled.

Exercise 8.8 demonstrates how to share a network printer from a Windows 95 machine. This exercise assumes that you already have installed and configured a printer.

When the printer has been configured and shared on the network print server, a Windows 95 client can be configured to connect to the print server and print to the printer over the network. This configuration can be established either manually with the Add Printer Wizard or by configuring the network printer for Point and Print setup.

Additional Administrative Tasks

 Besides setting up the network and making sure that your users have access to what they need (and can't get to things they don't) an administrator also has a number of other important day-to-day tasks to fulfill. The remainder of this chapter gives you a brief introduction to the following responsibilities:

- ▶ Auditing

- ▶ Handling data encryption

- ▶ Handling virus protection

- ▶ Securing equipment

Auditing

Another option you might need to consider is *auditing*, which is the process of creating a database that records particular events that occur on your network. Generally, you can decide what events to audit, from application information to security options. Figure 8.1 shows one of many different auditing windows in Windows NT.

Figure 8.1

A Directory Auditing window.

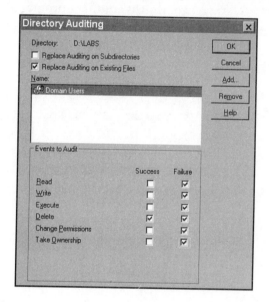

Data Encryption

Usually, the file and share security discussed previously is more than adequate. However, if your network is used for especially sensitive data and you want to prevent anyone from stealing information, you can take an additional security measure by forcing data encryption. *Encryption* codes the information sent on the network using a special algorithm and then decodes it on the other end. This technique offers varying degrees of safety, largely based on the length and complexity of the code used to encrypt the data. With the advent of the Internet, encryption technology is becoming more important and is key in the new "secure transactions" toward which companies on the World Wide Web are now working.

Virus Protection

Much like humans, computers are susceptible to certain types of viruses. Unlike those that strike us, though, computer viruses are created intentionally with the aim of injuring or altering your machines. Viruses can be spread through computer systems in many ways, but the most common is through an executable file. Having a good virus scanning program—none come with any Microsoft program—is a necessity for an administrator. Numerous third-party companies make virus-scanning software, including Norton and MacAffee, to name just two.

> Virus software cannot simply detect any virus; rather, this software generally is designed to look for particular infections. Because of this, scanning software is updated regularly, often at no extra charge. Even if it does cost a bit, though, always keep your virus-checking software as new as possible.

Securing Hardware

You might think that if you have taken care of backup, RAID, shares, NTFS permissions, virus scanning, and encryption, that your data is completely safe. There is, however, one more thing of which you should be sure. Any computer is far more insecure if people can get to its server, so you always should lock your server in a closet or some other inaccessible place. Having the server out in the open provides a security risk and also increases the chance that someone accidentally will shut the machine off—or for that matter, spill coffee on it. Most companies have a "server room"— often a large wiring closet—where all server machines are stored. Make sure this location is neither too cold nor too hot, that it has adequate ventilation, and that only authorized individuals have access to it.

Additionally, whenever you make a change to the network, be certain to document the changes you have made. This can make troubleshooting and maintenance far easier and can save you valuable time. See Chapter 12, "Monitoring the Network," for more information.

Summary

You now have learned to create users and groups and to configure sharing and security for Microsoft resources using either Windows NT or Windows 95. You also can connect to either of these machines to gain access to their shared files and printers. Furthermore, this chapter introduced you to a few optional security measures available for sensitive data.

Knowing how to create network resources through sharing is crucial not only for the Networking Essentials exam, but for an understanding of practical Microsoft networking as well. Make sure that you can implement each of these structures and understand how they work. Experiment with permissions and user rights and make sure that the relationship between groups and users is clear. The review questions test how well you learned this chapter's material.

Exercises

Exercise 8.1: Creating a User Account in Windows NT

Objective: Create a new NT User Account.

Estimated time: 10 minutes

1. Click on Start, Programs, Administrative Tools. Choose either User Manager (Windows NT Workstation) or User Manager for Domains (Windows NT Server).

2. User Manager opens (see fig. 8.2). If this is a new install, only two users appear in the top window. As you might expect, Administrator is the default administrative account for the machine, and Guest is the default account for anonymous access by users who do not have a username and password of their own. The Guest account is disabled by default and must be manually enabled before it is usable.

Figure 8.2

Account administration is done through the Windows NT User Manager for Domains Program.

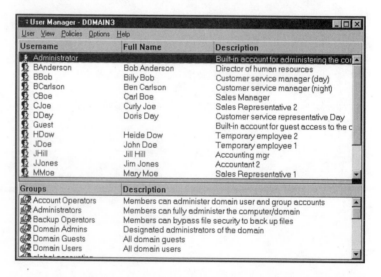

3. Click on Policies, Account to prompt the Account Policy dialog box to appear (see fig. 8.3). Observe that, by default, passwords must be changed every 42 days. In addition, no restrictions are made as to password length or uniqueness. Account Lockout is turned off. Here, you can set some of the default security information for your network. If you are

concerned that someone might try to break into your network by stealing or guessing a user's password, these settings should be set to restrictive levels. Leave the defaults as they are and click Close to return to the User Manager.

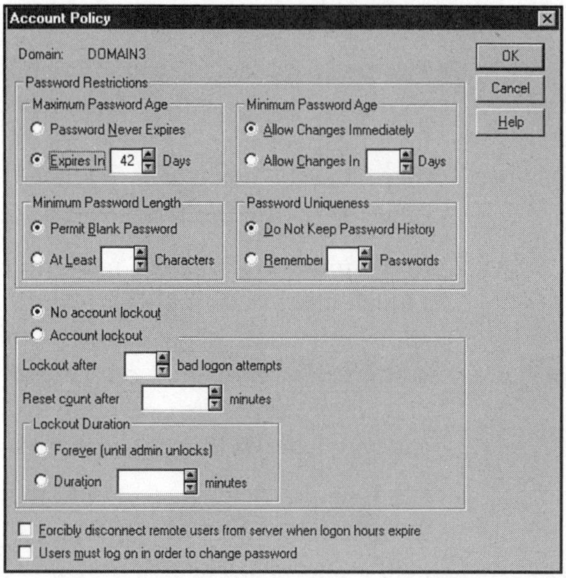

Figure 8.3

The Windows NT Accounts Policy window enables you to set password characteristics.

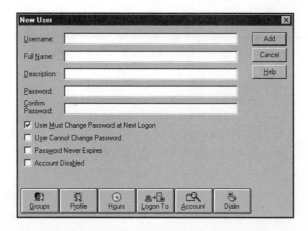

4. Click on File, New User. The New User dialog box appears (see fig. 8.4).

Figure 8.4

The Windows NT New User dialog box enables you to record information about a new user.

5. In the top field, type in a unique username (in this case, **TestUser**) for the new account. This name can be between 1

continues

Exercise 8.1:   Continued

---

and 20 characters and cannot include spaces or any of the following characters:

" / \ [ ] : ; | = , + * ? < >

6. Two text fields enable you to identify the user for which the account is being created. The Full Name field generally defines the person, and the Description field defines the role they fill in the organization. Fill both of these fields with the values **Test User** and **Training Department Manager.**

7. In the password field, you may enter any combination of 1 to 14 characters of your choice, with the same exceptions that apply to the creation of user accounts. Enter **PASSWORD** in both the Password and Confirm Password fields. (Remember that all passwords are case-sensitive, so it matters whether you type PASSWORD or password.)

8. Examine the check boxes below the Confirm Password field. By default, the User Must Change Password at Next Logon field is checked. The first time that New User logs on, he is asked to provide a new password. This enables you to set an initial password but then transfer security over to the user by having him define his own access password.

9. The User Cannot Change Password option generally is used only for guest or multi-user accounts, thereby keeping one guest from changing the password and locking all other guest users out. Leave this box unchecked.

10. The Password Never Expires option is intended for system or guest accounts that require a static password. As you will see, system policies can be set by requiring occasional password changes by network users. This setting overrides such policies. Leave this box unchecked.

11. The Account Disabled option enables you to disable an account temporarily while a user is on vacation or after he no longer is allowed access to the network. Generally, this option is preferable to simply deleting the account, at least until it has been determined that the user definitely will not use the account again. Leave this box unchecked.

12. The row of buttons at the bottom of the window contains additional configuration options. You use the Groups button in the next exercise, but the other buttons contain options beyond the scope of this book. Ignore them for now, but it would be a good idea to return later to click on each of them in turn and investigate the windows they spawn. Close each without making modifications. This idea is good to follow in all exercises because the key to mastering any Windows-based product is to know where to click to find the option you need. You should get used to exploring all the tabs and buttons available, but don't change anything unless you know what will happen.

13. Click the Add button. Notice that although all the fields clear, the Add User window remains open. This enables faster creation of multiple users.

14. Click Close to return to User Manager. You now see a third user, which is the TestUser account you just created.

15. Click User, Exit

Exercise 8.2: Creating Groups on Windows NT

Objective: Create new Global and Local groups and assign accounts to them.

Estimated time: 10 minutes

1. Open User Manager for Domains. Observe the groups in the bottom window pane. Some groups have Globe icons, such as the Domain Admins group. Others, such as the Administrators group, have a Computer icon. As you might suspect, Domain Admins is a Global group, while Administrators is a Local group.

2. Click on the User menu choice and choose New Global Group. The New Global Group dialog box appears (see fig. 8.5).

continues

Exercise 8.2: Continued

Figure 8.5

The New Global Group dialog box enables you to enter members and a description for a Global group.

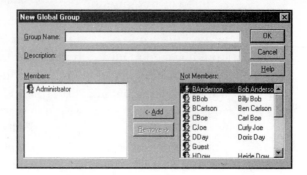

3. Type **Global Training** in the Group Name field. In the Description field, type **Training Department Members**.

4. Note the two boxes at the bottom of the screen. Administrator, Guest, and TestUser are displayed in the Not Members box. Choose TestUser and click the Add button. TestUser moves into the Members box.

5. Click Close to return to User Manager for Domains.

6. Click User and select New Local Group.

7. The New Local Group dialog box appears (see fig. 8.6).

Figure 8.6

The New Local Group dialog box enables you to add users and Global groups, as well as a description of a Local group.

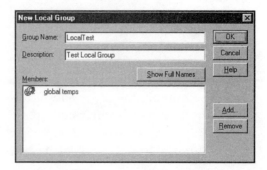

8. Enter **Local Training** in the Group Name field and leave the Description field blank.

9. Observe the members list box, which is empty. Click on Add.

10. The Add Users and Groups dialog box appears. Choose the Global Training group and click Add. Note that you also could have added TestUser to the group directly. In

Windows NT Workstation—which does not support the creation of Global groups—this would have been your only choice. Click Close to return to User Manager for Domains. Click OK to return to the New Local Group dialog box. The members list now includes the Global Training group. Click OK to return to User Manager for Domains.

11. Click User, Exit.

Exercise 8.3: Sharing a Directory on a Windows NT FAT Partition

Objective: Share an NT directory and assign share-level security to it.

Estimated time: 15 minutes

1. Click on Start, Programs. Then click on the Windows NT Explorer icon to bring up the Explorer window.

2. Select the root of the C: drive and then right-click on it to call a context-sensitive menu.

3. Select New, Folder. A folder appears under C:, and you are prompted to enter the name of the folder. Type **Public** and press Enter.

4. Click on the new Public folder (in the left window). The folder is highlighted and the right window is now empty.

5. Right-click in the right window to make a context-sensitive menu appear. Select New, Text Document. Name the document My Shared Doc.

6. Select the Public folder again. Click File, Properties (or use the quick menu and select Sharing from there) to call the Properties dialog box.

7. Click on the Sharing tab. Note that the directory currently is not shared.

8. Click the Shared As option. The Share Name box fills with "Public." You can change or leave this initial name. In this

continues

case, change the share. Replace Public with **My Share** to illustrate the difference between a directory name and a share name.

9. Observe the Maximum Connections option. This option enables you to control the number of concurrent users accessing the folder. Leave the default, which enables unlimited concurrent connections to the share.

10. Click on the Permissions button to call the Access Through Share Permissions dialog box (see fig. 8.7). Observe that, by default, Everyone has Full Control over the new share.

Figure 8.7

The Access Through Share Permissions dialog box enables you to determine the type of access for a particular group.

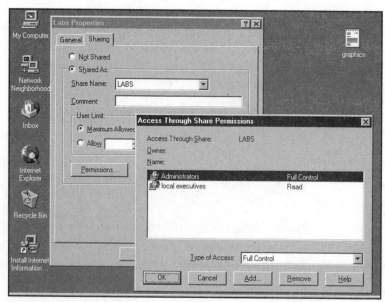

11. Select the Everyone group and click the down arrow in the Type of Access box. The following four selections appear:

   ▶ **No Access.** A member of any group with this permission is banned from the shared resource.

   ▶ **Read.** Members can list, read, and execute files but cannot modify or delete them.

> ▶ **Change.** Members can read, list, execute, and delete files but are not able to change file permissions or assume ownership of the files.

> ▶ **Full Control.** Members have complete control of the resources, assuming that they have sufficient rights to match their permissions.

12. Click on Read in the Type of Access window. Observe that the permissions level for Everyone in the main window reflects the change.

13. Click on Add to call the Add Users and Groups window. Select the Local Training group and click the Add button. The Local Training group appears in the lower window. Click the Type of Access down arrow and select Full Control.

14. Click the OK button and observe that Local Training has been added to the list of groups with permissions to the share.

15. Click OK to close the window and then click OK on the Public Properties application.

16. In a few seconds, a hand appears under the Public folder, indicating that the folder has been shared.

17. Test the share by connecting to it from a Windows 95 or a Windows NT client.

Exercise 8.4: Setting NTFS Permissions on a Shared Folder

Objective: Add NTFS security to the Public share.

Estimated time: 15 minutes

1. Click Start, Programs. Select Windows NT Explorer to open the Explorer window. Choose a directory on an NTFS partition. If you do not have an NTFS partition, you cannot complete this lab.

continues

Exercise 8.4: Continued

2. Create a directory called TestNTFS and then right-click on it. Select the Properties option from the menu to open the TestNTFS Properties window.

3. In the TestNTFS Properties window, click on the Security tab and then click the Permissions button to open the Directory Permissions dialog box (see fig. 8.8).

Figure 8.8

The Directory Permissions dialog box enables you to update or replace permissions for a group.

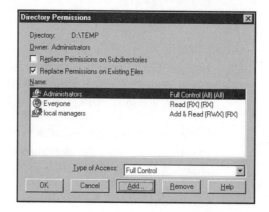

4. Observe that the directory currently has its default permissions list with Everyone—Full Control as the only entry.

5. Select Everyone. Click the down arrow on the Type of Access field and choose Read.

6. Take note of the check boxes near the top of the window. The Replace Permissions on Files option is checked, while the Replace Permissions on Subdirectories option is cleared. If you have subdirectories and want the new access permissions to filter down through them, you must check this box. Because no subdirectories exist in this instance, the point is currently moot, so leave the defaults as they are.

7. If you need to enter additional groups into the list, you can do so by using the Add button. Click this button and observe the Add Users and Groups window. Select the administrators Local group and then click on the down arrow next to the Type of Access drop-down list and observe the expanded choices. Permissions are broken down to more specific

levels, and Special File Access and Special Directory Access enable you to mix and match permissions to suit your needs. In reality, you rarely will grant a group only the List and Delete permissions, but you can if you need to. If, for instance, a user needs to be able to write to a directory, but should not be able to view, read, or modify files in that directory, only Write permission would be given them. Give Administrators Full Control permissions.

8. Click OK to return to the Directory Permissions window. Then click OK to set the new permissions and return to Explorer.

9. Click File, Exit to close Explorer.

10. Share the TestNTFS directory with Everyone—Full Control permissions and log on to the share from a remote machine and observe the permissions available when you log on as an Administrator as opposed to a TestUser. You should be able to modify, create, and delete files across the share if you are logged on as an Administrator, but you should be able to only read and execute while logged on as a TestUser.

Exercise 8.5: Sharing a Directory Using Share-Level Security

Objective: Share a Windows 95 directory using share-level security.

Estimated time: 10 minutes

1. From the Start menu, choose Settings, Control Panel to display the Control Panel.

2. Double-click on the Network icon to display the Network dialog box (see fig. 8.9).

continues

Exercise 8.5: Continued

Figure 8.9

Use the Windows 95 Network application to add and configure networking components.

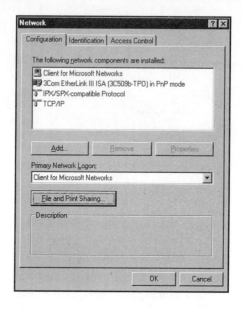

3. Choose the Access Control tab and then choose share-level access control.

4. Select the Configuration tab and choose File, Print Sharing to display the File and Print Sharing dialog box (see fig. 8.10).

Figure 8.10

Windows 95 File and Printer Sharing options offer you the chance to grant access to your files and your printer.

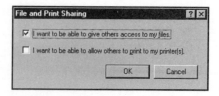

5. Select both the I want to be able to give others access to my files check box and the I want to be able to allow others to print to my printer(s) check box to enable others to access your printers and files. Then choose OK to automatically install File and Printer Sharing for Microsoft Networks.

Share-level security is used by default when File and Printer Sharing for Microsoft Networks is installed. The next exercise demonstrates how this can be changed. Conversely, File and Printer Sharing for NetWare Networks must use user-level security. The share-level security option is unavailable if File and Printer Sharing for NetWare Networks is installed.

6. Choose OK and restart the computer.

7. After Windows 95 has restarted, click Start, Windows Explorer and make a new folder on your C: drive named Password. Choose the Password directory and make a text file within it called Password Test.

8. Right-click on the Password directory to display the context-sensitive menu.

9. Choose Sharing from the context-sensitive menu to open the Sharing tab of the Properties application, as shown in figure 8.11.

Figure 8.11

This Properties application for a shared directory uses share-level security.

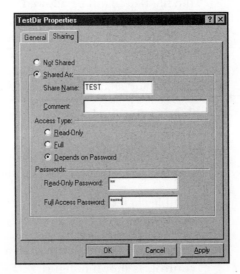

continues

Exercise 8.5: Continued

10. Accept Password as the share name and choose Access Type: Read-Only. Enter a password for Read-only access of **read** and choose OK. The sharing hand symbol replaces the folder symbol for the shared directory.

11. If you have another computer on the network, browse the first computer in Network Neighborhood to display the share name. The share name Password is displayed under the appropriate computer name.

12. Double-click on the share name Password. You are prompted for the password.

13. Enter **read** at the password prompt and choose OK to display the directory contents.

14. Copy the Password Test file from the share to your local hard drive. The file read will be successful.

15. Modify the file and try to copy it back. Then try to delete the original in the shared directory. Neither the file write nor the file delete will be allowed.

Exercise 8.6: Sharing a Directory Using User-Level Security

Objective: Allow Windows 95 to access another machine's user accounts list and share a directory using user-level security.

Estimated time: 15 minutes

1. From the Start menu, choose Settings, Control Panels to display the Control Panels window.

2. Double-click on the Network icon to display the Network dialog box.

3. Choose the Access Control tab and select User-level access control, as shown in figure 8.12.

Figure 8.12

The User-level access control option enables advanced Windows 95 networking security.

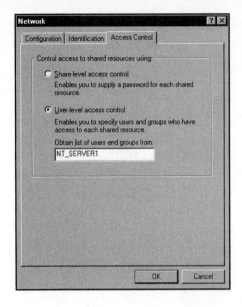

4. Type the name of the server with the user accounts into the Obtain list of users and groups from field. Windows 95 attempts to access the Windows NT or NetWare server to obtain the users list.

5. Select the Configuration tab and choose File, Print Sharing to display the File and Print Sharing dialog box.

6. Select both the I want to be able to give others access to my files check box and the I want to be able to allow others to print to my printer(s) check box to enable others to access your printers and files. Then choose OK to automatically install File and Printer Sharing for Microsoft Networks.

7. Choose OK and restart the computer. Until you have restarted, the new settings will not take effect, and you will not be able to complete the exercise.

8. After Windows 95 restarts, click Start, Windows Explorer. Create a new directory called UserLevel and then create a new text file in the folder named UserTest. Now choose the directory. Observe that the Password folder is no longer shared, as the change to user-level security results in the loss of all existing shares. (This doesn't wipe out the files or folders, but it does eliminate the logical network path to them.)

continues

9. Right-click on the UserLevel directory to display its context-sensitive menu.

10. Select Sharing from the context-sensitive menu to display the Sharing tab of the Properties application.

11. Type **UserLevl** for the share name and give the Local Training group full-access privileges by selecting the group and choosing Full Access. Then choose OK. The folder symbol for the shared directory is replaced with an icon of a folder held by a hand.

Sharing the folder UserLevel with the 8.3 compatible name UserLevl enables DOS workstations on the network to properly understand the name of the share. Remember that if all machines on your network are not capable of long file name support, you should continue to use network file-naming conventions that correspond to your network's lowest common denominator.

12. Log on to another computer on the network using the username to which you gave full-access permissions. Locate the share name UserLevl in the Explorer by browsing the entire network. The share name UserLevl is displayed under the appropriate computer name.

13. Double-click on the share name UserLevl to display the directory contents.

14. Try to copy a file to the shared directory. The file write is allowed.

Exercise 8.7: Creating a Local Printer with Windows NT

Objective: Create a locally installed printer on NT.

Estimated time: 20 minutes

1. Click Start, Settings. Then choose Printers to open the Printers window.

2. Click on Add Printer to display the Add Printer Wizard. As with many other administrative tasks, the process of creating and sharing a printer has been streamlined and simplified by the use of a "wizard," a small program that leads you through a particular task. Choose My Computer and click Next.

3. The wizard asks you to specify the port or ports to which the new printer should print. Choose lpt1: and click Next.

You can define multiple ports because printers in Windows NT and Windows 95 are virtualized. This refers to the fact that a printer in these environments is not a physical machine but rather a collection of settings and configuration information about a particular machine. You can test this by installing a printer—or a modem or a network card—that is not actually physically present in your machine. The device will install perfectly, but you will receive an error if an application attempts to access it, because this device doesn't exist. When a matching physical device is attached, the virtual device will recognize it and forward information as needed. For those of you who have used print queues, it might be easiest to think of a printer as a new name for a print queue. The machine itself is referred to as a printing device.

4. The wizard now asks you to specify the type of physical device to which you are printing or the device type that your printer emulates. Click HP in the left pane and then find and select Color LaserJet. Then click Next.

5. Now you are asked to name your new printer. Remember that each printer on your machine must have a unique name, and that name should be descriptive of its type or function. Type **Color Printer** and click Next.

6. Now you are asked whether the printer will be shared, and if so, what other operating systems will access it. Click Shared, call the new share **MyLaser**, and select Windows 95 from the list of additional operating systems. Note that each supported Windows NT platform requires a different driver. Click Next.

continues

Exercise 8.7: Continued

7. The wizard now has all the information it needs. Leave the Print Test Page option on and click Finish. You will need the source files for both your Windows NT Server or Workstation and for Windows 95. You are prompted for the location of the source files, and the necessary drivers are loaded.

8. The Printer icon for Color Printer is created in the Printers window. Select it and the queue appears. Print a document to the new printer and check the queue again. The document should be waiting to print.

Exercise 8.8: Sharing a Printer on the Network with Windows 95

1. Right-click on the Printer icon and choose Properties to display the Properties sheet.

2. Choose the Sharing tab to display the Sharing configuration settings.

3. Select Shared As and enter a share name and an optional descriptive comment for the printer. Windows 95 does not allow a share name to contain invalid characters, including spaces. In addition, the share name must not exceed 12 characters.

4. You also must grant permissions to access this printer. If share-level permissions are used, you must assign a password to the printer. To access the print queue, users must supply the correct password. If user-level permissions are used, you must add the users who will be granted access to this print queue. For example, to enable everyone to print to the print queue, you would add the Everyone group and grant it the print access right. If you can, assign these permissions from what you have learned. If you have problems, refer back to previous exercises for instructions on setting permissions. Remember that files and printers are shared through the same process with just a few twists.

5. Choose OK to share the printer. The Printer icon now appears as a hand holding or sharing the printer with others. Remote users with the correct permissions now can access the print queue after setting up the correct printer driver on their computers.

Review Questions

The following questions test your knowledge of the information in this chapter. For additional exam help, visit Microsoft's site at www.microsoft.com/train_cert/cert/Mcpsteps.htm.

1. Which type of account is only available on Windows NT domain controllers?

    A. User

    B. Global group

    C. Local group

    D. Global user

2. This group usually is used to assign permissions.

    A. Global

    B. LAN

    C. Local

    D. Either Global or Local

3. Share-level permissions enable which of the following actions?

    A. Defining access levels by user

    B. Controlling file-level access

    C. Providing no access security at all

    D. Defining access levels by password

4. True or False: User-level access is less secure than share-level access.

    A. True

    B. False

5. Which of the following does not add additional security to your network?

   A. Auditing

   B. Virus scanning

   C. Data compression

   D. Data encryption

6. "Log on Locally" is one example of which of the following?

   A. Permissions

   B. Rights

   C. Privileges

   D. Attributes

7. Read and Change are two types of which of the following?

   A. Permissions

   B. Rights

   C. Privileges

   D. Attributes

8. A shared printer is available to whom?

   A. Everyone on the network

   B. Only the person who shared it

   C. Anyone with rights to the share

   D. Anyone with permissions to the share

9. The _____ group includes everyone who uses a resource locally.

   A. Everyone

   B. Interactive

   C. Creator-Owner

   D. Network

10. How many times should each user be created in a single domain?

    A. Once

    B. Once on each domain controller

    C. Once on every Windows NT-based machine

    D. You should avoid creating users and use Global groups instead.

Pretest Answers

1. A (see the section titled "Assigning File-Level Permissions on an NTFS Partition")

2. B (see the section titled "Global and Local Groups")

3. A (see the section titled "Groups" on page 296)

Review Answers

1. B

2. C

3. D

4. B

5. C

6. B

7. A

8. D

9. B

10. A

Chapter

Disaster Recovery

9

One of the major issues that a network administrator must address is the possibility of system failure and associated downtime. The administrator must handle two major issues to guard against the danger of a failed server:

▶ Protecting data

▶ Reducing downtime

This chapter discusses both issues and examines how the use of fault-tolerant disk configurations and a backup strategy can help reduce the danger of lost time and data. This information falls under the "Choose a disaster recovery plan for various situations" job skill in the test preparation guide.

Chapter 9 targets the following objective in the Implementation section of the Networking Essentials exam:

▶ Choose a disaster recovery plan for various situations

Test Objectives

Stop! Before reading this chapter, test yourself to determine how much study time you will need to devote to this section.

1. RAID 5 is a term that describes which of the following?

    A. A weekday backup strategy for enterprise networks

    B. A fault-tolerant disk configuration

    C. An NDIS-compatible SCSI controller

    D. Data backup through directory replication

2. The maximum number of disks in a stripe set is _____.

    A. 2

    B. 16

    C. 32

    D. Limited only by hardware

3. The maximum number of drives in a mirror set is _____.

    A. 2

    B. 4

    C. 16

    D. None of the above

Protecting Data

Natural disasters, equipment failures, power surges, and deliberate vandalism can cause the catastrophic loss of precious network data. Protecting the data is a primary responsibility of the network administrator. Microsoft highlights these important strategies for preventing data loss:

▶ Backup

▶ Uninterruptible Power Supply (UPS)

Both of these strategies are discussed in the following sections.

Backup

A backup schedule is an essential part of any data-protection strategy. You should design a backup system that is right for your situation and the data on your network.

A number of different strategies can be used in backing up files. One way is simply to copy a file to another drive. Operating systems, however, typically have special backup commands that help you with some of the bookkeeping required for maintaining a systematic backup schedule. Most backup commands mark the file with the date and time of the backup so that you (and the backup utility) will know when a copy of the file was saved last. This is the purpose of the FAT file system's Archive attribute. To determine whether this attribute exists, check the properties of any file on a FAT partition. If the Archive attribute is enabled, the file has changed since the last time a backup was done. In this chapter, you will see that some backup techniques reset this attribute, whereas others do not.

Although backups can be accomplished by saving files to a different drive, they typically are performed with some form of tape drive. Commonly called *DAT drives*, these devices are able to store many gigabytes of information quickly and economically. Moreover, the tapes are small and portable. Another important step in your backup plan, therefore, is deciding where to store these backup tapes. Many companies choose to make two copies of each backup tape and store one of the copies off-site, thereby guarding against a catastrophic event such as fire.

In addition to the various types of copy commands, Microsoft identifies the following backup types:

- ▶ **Full backup.** Backs up all specified files.

- ▶ **Incremental backup.** Backs up only those files that have changed since the last backup.

- ▶ **Differential backup.** Backs up the specified files if the files have changed since the last backup. This type doesn't mark the files as having been backed up, however. (A differential backup is somewhat like a copy command. Because the file is not marked as having been backed up, a later differential or incremental backup will back up the file again.)

A typical backup plan includes some combination of these backup types performed at regular intervals. One common practice is to perform an incremental or differential backup each day and a full backup every week. Full backups make the restoration process easier because there is only one set of tapes; however, they also require a lengthy backup process each night, which often means that someone must physically change the tapes.

Incremental backups are much faster because they back up only those files that have been changed since the last backup. The Archive attribute switches on when a file is modified. An incremental backup backs up the file and then removes the attribute so that the file will not be backed up again unless it is changed the next day. A combination of incremental and full backups usually results in four to six incremental tape sets and one full tape set each week. If the drives fail, the administrator must restore the last full backup set, as well as all the incrementals performed since the drive failure. This process obviously is considerably slower than a backup scheme in which a full backup is performed every night.

Differential backups are similar to incrementals except that they do not reset the Archive attribute, which means that each backup during the week backs up all files changed since the last full backup. A full backup once a week (generally Friday or Saturday) and differentials every other day means that only two tapes will be needed in case of failure—the last full backup and the last differential (see fig. 9.1).

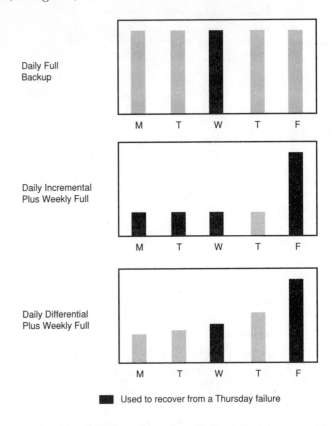

Daily Full Backup

Daily Incremental Plus Weekly Full

Daily Differential Plus Weekly Full

■ Used to recover from a Thursday failure

Keeping a log of all backups is important. Most backup utilities can generate a backup log. Microsoft recommends that you make two copies of the backup log—store one with the backup tapes and keep one at the computer site. Always test your backup system before you trust it. Perform a sample backup, restore the data, and check the data to be sure it is identical to the original.

You can attach a tape drive directly to a single server, or you can back up several servers across the network at once. Backups over the network are convenient for the administrator, but they can produce considerable network traffic. You can reduce the effects of this extra traffic if you place the computer attached to the tape drive on an isolated network segment and connect it directly to secondary network interface cards on each of the servers.

A number of other vendors also offer backup software—such as Arcada's BackupExec or Cheyenne's ArcServe—that include additional features, and in many cases, these are a very wise investment. For the test, though, remember that only the Microsoft Backup utility will be covered.

Uninterruptible Power Supply

An Uninterruptible Power Supply (UPS) is a special battery (or sometimes a generator) that supplies power to an electronic device in the event of a power failure. UPSs commonly are used with network servers to prevent a disorderly shutdown by warning users to log out. After a predetermined waiting period, the UPS software performs an orderly shutdown of the server. Many UPS units also regulate power distribution and serve as protection against power surges. Remember that a UPS generally does not provide for continued network functionality for longer than a few minutes. A UPS is not intended to keep the server running through a long power outage, but rather is designed to give the server time to do what it needs to before shutting down. This can prevent the data loss and system corruption that sometimes results from sudden shutdown.

When purchasing a UPS for a server, note that these come in many varieties (see fig. 9.2). As noted earlier, the UPS is really just a battery backup. Just like a car battery, the more powerful it is, the more expensive it is. Prices run from the hundreds to many thousands of dollars. Before you buy, know how many servers you will be running off the UPS and how much time they need to shutdown properly. One of the most popular UPS manufacturers is APC (American Power Conversion), a company that offers a full line of power supply and UPS products.

Figure 9.2

A large UPS can function in much the same way as a surge protector in that numerous components can be plugged into a single unit.

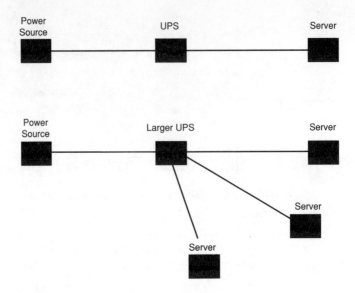

Backups mainly provide a quick method for system recovery. They require a long and tedious restoration process that can cost your company dearly in lost revenue and productivity. Because of this, the following sections examine some methods of minimizing—or even preventing—downtime in case of a drive failure.

Recovering from System Failure

Next to data security, keeping the network up and running properly is the most crucial day-to-day task of an administrator. The loss of a hard drive, even if not disastrous, can be a major inconvenience to your network users and may cost your organization in lost time and money. Procedures for lessening or preventing downtime from single hardware failures should be implemented. Disk configurations that enable this sort of protection are called *fault-tolerant* configurations.

Implementing a Fault-Tolerant Design

Connecting network components into a fault-tolerant configuration ensures that one hardware failure doesn't halt the network. You can achieve network fault-tolerance by providing redundant data paths, redundant hubs, and other such features. Generally, however, the data on the server itself—its hard drives—is the most crucial.

When developing a fault-tolerance scheme, remember that you must balance the need for rapid recovery from a failure against cost. The basic theory behind fault-tolerant design is hardware redundancy, which translates into additional hardware expenses. Also, remember that the greater the level of redundancy, the greater the complexity involved in the implementation.

Using RAID

A vital tool for protecting a network's data is the use of a *Redundant Array of Inexpensive Disks (RAID)*. Using a RAID system enables you to set up the best disk array design to protect your system. A RAID system combines two or more disks to create a large virtual disk structure that enables you to store redundant copies of the data. In a disk array, the drives are coordinated into different levels of RAID, to which the controller card distributes the data.

RAID uses a format of splitting data among drives at the bit, byte, or block level. The term *data striping* refers to the capability of arranging data in different sequences across drives. Demonstrations of data striping are shown in figure 9.3.

Figure 9.3

Data striping arranges data in different sequences across drives.

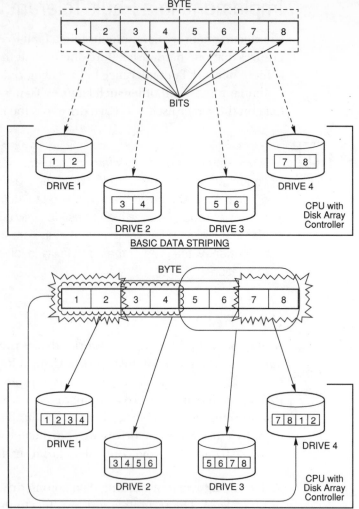

Your input in designing the most reliable drive setup for your network is an important responsibility. You must choose the best RAID implementation level to meet your users' requirements in data integrity and cost. Seven levels of RAID are available on the market today: 0, 1, 2, 3, 4, 5, and 10. A higher number isn't necessarily indicative of a better choice, so you must select the best level for your environment. The following paragraphs present a brief discussion of some of these available levels, notably RAID 0, 1, and 5, which Windows NT Server supports. Windows NT Workstation supports only RAID 0, and Windows 95 is not able to use any RAID levels at all.

A fault-tolerant disk scheme is used only to speed recovery time from a hardware fault. None of these RAID levels is intended to be a replacement for regular tape backups.

RAID 0

Level 0 uses data striping and *block interleaving*, a process that involves distributing the data block by block across the disk array in the same location across each disk. Data can be read or written to these same sectors from either disk, thus improving performance. RAID 0 requires at least two disks, and the striped partitions must be of the same size. Note that redundancy of data is *not* provided in RAID 0, which means that the failure of any single drive in the array can bring down the entire system and result in the loss of all data contained in the array. RAID 0 is supported in Windows NT Server and Windows NT Workstation, but not in Windows 95.

RAID 1

In level 1, drives are paired or mirrored with each byte of information being written to each identical drive. You can duplex these devices by adding a separate drive controller for each drive (duplexing is examined later in this chapter). *Disk mirroring* is defined as two hard drives—one primary, one secondary—that use the same disk channel (controller cards and cable), as illustrated in figure 9.4. Disk mirroring is most commonly configured by using disk drives contained in the server. Duplexing, which is covered later in this chapter, is a form of mirroring that enables you to configure a more robust hardware environment.

Figure 9.4

In disk mirroring, two hard drives use the same disk channel.

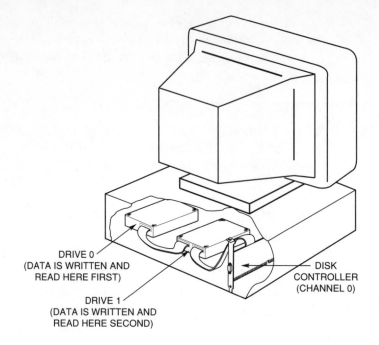

DRIVE 0
(DATA IS WRITTEN AND
READ HERE FIRST)

DRIVE 1
(DATA IS WRITTEN AND
READ HERE SECOND)

DISK
CONTROLLER
(CHANNEL 0)

Mirroring does not provide a performance benefit such as RAID 0 provides. Use mirroring, however, to create two copies of the server's data and operating system, which enables either disk to boot and run the server. If one drive in the pair fails, for instance, the other drive can continue to operate. Disk mirroring can be expensive, though, because it requires 2 GB of disk space for every 1 GB you want to mirror. You also must make sure that your power source has enough wattage to handle the additional devices. Mirroring requires two drives, and the mirrored partitions must be of the same size. Windows NT Server supports mirroring, but Windows NT Workstation and Windows 95 do not.

Remember that mirroring is done for fault-tolerant, not performance reasons. With this said, it should be noted that an NT machine running a mirror set will run at about normal speed on writes to the mirror set, but can have marginal performance gains reading from the set. For the best of both worlds, though, we need to move on to RAID 5.

RAID 2, 3, 4, and 5 are all versions of striping that incorporate similar fault-tolerant designs. Microsoft chose to support only level 5 striping in Windows NT Server. As the numbering scheme would imply, this is the newest revision of the four and is the most popular fault-tolerance scheme in use today. Level 5 requires less disk space than mirroring and has performance gains over other striping methods. As with mirroring, RAID level 5 is not available in Windows NT Workstation or Windows 95.

RAID 5

RAID 5 uses striping with parity information written across multiple drives to enable fault-tolerance with a minimum of wasted disk space. This level also offers the advantage of enabling relatively efficient performance on writes to the drives, as well as excellent read performance.

Striping with parity is based on the principle that all data is written to the hard drive in binary code (ones and zeros). RAID 5 requires at least three drives because this version writes data across two of them and then creates the parity block on the third. If the first byte is 00111000 and the second is 10101001, then the system computes the third by adding the digits together using this system:

$$1+1=0, 0+0=0, 0+1=1, 1+0=1$$

The sum of 00111000 and 10101001 is 10010001, which would be written to the third disk. If any of the disks fail, the process can be reversed and any disk can be reconstructed from the data on the other two. See figure 9.5 for an illustration of the process. Recovery includes replacing the bad disk and then regenerating its data through the Disk Administrator. A maximum of 32 disks can be connected in a RAID 5 array under Windows NT.

Figure 9.5

If Disk 2 fails, the system can re-construct the information on it by using the parity data.

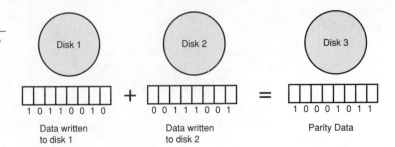

Data written to disk 1   Data written to disk 2   Parity Data

If disk 2 fails, the system is able to reconstruct the information on it by using the parity data...

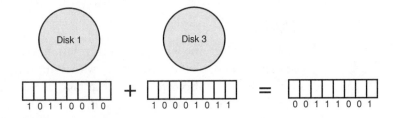

Choosing a RAID Level

When implementing a disk scheme, you have some options to consider. First, you must decide whether you are interested in performance gains (RAID 0) or data redundancy (RAID 1 or 5). Mirroring (RAID 1), for instance, enables the fastest recovery but results in a 50 percent loss of disk space. Likewise, striping with parity (RAID 5) is more economical but requires at least three physical disks and therefore provides more points of potential hardware failure.

Most network administrators prefer the RAID 5 solution, at least on larger servers with multiple drive bays. Because this level is a hybrid of striping and mirroring, it enables greater speed and more redundancy. Mirroring, however, offers the advantage of working well with non-SCSI hardware and is common as a fault-tolerant option on smaller, non-dedicated servers. Striping *without* parity should be reserved for workstations and servers on which speed considerations are paramount and possible downtime is an acceptable risk. See figure 9.6 for a graphical comparison.

Figure 9.6

Different raid levels offer their own unique capabilities.

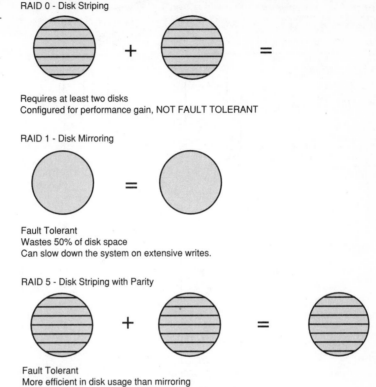

RAID 0 - Disk Striping

Requires at least two disks
Configured for performance gain, NOT FAULT TOLERANT

RAID 1 - Disk Mirroring

Fault Tolerant
Wastes 50% of disk space
Can slow down the system on extensive writes.

RAID 5 - Disk Striping with Parity

Fault Tolerant
More efficient in disk usage than mirroring
Performance aided by striping, slowed by writing parity
End result is moderate write performance, fast reads

Disk Duplexing

In the event of disk channel failure (by a controller card or cable), access to all data on the channel stops and a message appears on the file server console screen (if your users don't let you know about it first). Even though drives can be mirrored, all disk activity on the mirrored pair ceases if the mirrored drives are connected to the same disk controller.

Disk duplexing performs the function of simultaneously writing data to disks located on different channels. As figure 9.7 illustrates, each hard disk in a duplexed pair connects to a separate hard disk controller. This figure shows a configuration in which the drives are housed in separate disk subsystems. Each subsystem also has a separate power supply. Disk duplexing offers a more reliable setup than is possible with mirroring because a failure of one disk drive's power supply doesn't disable the server. Instead, the server continues to work with the system that remains under power.

Figure 9.7

Disk duplexing simultaneously writes data to two disks located on different channels.

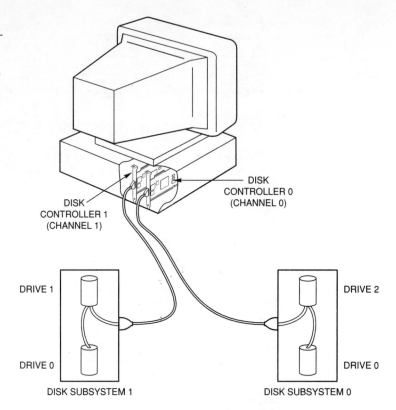

DISK CONTROLLER 0 (CHANNEL 0)

DISK CONTROLLER 1 (CHANNEL 1)

DRIVE 1

DRIVE 2

DRIVE 0

DRIVE 0

DISK SUBSYSTEM 1

DISK SUBSYSTEM 0

Working on the same channel is analogous to going to a baseball game when only one gate into the stadium is open. You can enter or exit through only one gate (channel) at the stadium (file server), and the crowd (data) can get backed up on both sides. If more than one gate (another channel) is open, though, the crowd (data) doesn't become backed up on both sides of the fence (file server or workstation).

Duplexing protects information at the hardware level with duplicate channels (controller cards and cables) and duplicate hard drives (refer to fig. 9.7).

Mirroring uses one controller card and two hard drives (refer to fig. 9.4). The point of failure for this setup is primarily the controller card or the cable connecting the drives to the controller card. Disk duplexing uses two controller cards and a minimum of one drive per controller card. The point of failure is reduced with duplicate hardware.

A number of different vendors also offer RAID protection at the hardware level on their server products. This protection is independent of the operating system, so if you really feel that RAID 5 on your Windows 95 workstation is a necessity, these software vendors might have a solution for you. Third-party products also permit the concept of redundancy to be taken to its logical extreme, resulting in the mirroring of entire Windows NT Server machines. This mirroring protects against the failure of virtually any single piece of hardware you can imagine, from a memory stick to a motherboard. Remember, though, that duplicate servers can get a bit expensive, so they are not recommended for everyone.

The previous sections examined a number of different disk configurations. Exercise 9.1 shows how you implement these RAID levels and other disk configuration options in Windows NT. The primary program for managing disk storage resources is the Disk Administrator, a tool that is usable only by members of the Administrators or Server Operators groups.

Summary

This chapter examined a number of options open to an administrator looking to provide data security and hardware redundancy for the network. Through the use of a regular backup plan, the installation of a UPS, and the implementation of a fault-tolerant disk scheme, you can help to ensure that your network will run as efficiently and safely as possible. Remember that there is no particular formula to use here; rather, you should follow a process of weighing costs against benefits. In the end, you want to provide the highest degree of safety for your critical data that you can achieve given your budget. Now test your knowledge of this chapter's topics by completing the exercise and answering some review questions.

Exercises

Remember that changes made to your disk configuration can have a serious effect on the system. Do not make any changes in Disk Administrator unless you have carefully planned them previously!

Exercise 9.1:   Exploring Windows NT's Disk Administrator

Objective: Explore the options available through Disk Administrator, such as establishing and breaking mirrored drives and creating or regenerating stripe sets with parity.

Estimated time: 10 minutes

To complete exercise 9.1, log on to a Windows NT 4.0 server or workstation with an account that has administrative authority. The server or workstation used can be a production machine—no changes will actually be made to the computer's configuration during this exercise.

1. Click Start, Programs, Administrative Tools. Then choose Disk Administrator.

2. Observe the Disk Administrator window and maximize it if it is not already in this state. The configuration of the disk or disks on your machine displays.

3. Click on one of the partitions on your screen. A dark black line appears around the partition, indicating that the partition is selected. Right-click on the partition and observe the available menu choices in the context-sensitive menu. Note that you can format the partition, change its logical drive letter, or examine its properties. If the disk is removable, the Eject option is also available.

4. Click on Partition in the Menu bar and examine the choices. Most of the choices are unavailable, but they include Create Volume Set and Create Stripe Set. You also can change your active partition in this Menu bar.

5. Click on Fault Tolerance on the Menu bar (Windows NT Server only) and observe that this menu enables you to establish and break mirrored drives, as well as to create or regenerate stripe sets with parity.

6. Feel free to explore further, and when you are finished examining the menus and options, close out of the Disk Administrator by clicking Partition, Exit.

Review Questions

The following questions test your knowledge of the information in this chapter. For additional exam help, visit Microsoft's site at www.microsoft.com/train_cert/cert/Mcpsteps.htm.

1. An incremental backup _____.

   A. backs up parts of the specified file that have changed since the last backup

   B. backs up and marks only those files that have changed since they were last backed up

   C. backs up the files that have changed since they were last backed up but doesn't mark them

   D. backs up the files that have changed over the course of a specified time period

2. A differential backup _____.

   A. backs up files that have changed since the last backup and doesn't mark the files as having been backed up

   B. backs up files that have changed since the last backup and marks the files as having been backed up

   C. copies all files that have been modified within a specific time period and marks them as having been backed up

   D. copies all files that have been modified within a specified time period and doesn't mark them as having been backed up

3. The best way to reduce the effects of extra traffic caused by a network backup is to _____.

   A. attach the tape drive directly to one of the servers

   B. back up each server to a nearby server

    C. place the computer attached to the tape drive on an isolated network segment

    D. back up the servers in ascending order of the size of the backup

4. UPS stands for _____.

    A. Unintentional Packet Switch

    B. Unfamiliar Password Sequence

    C. Unknown Polling Sequence

    D. Uninterruptible Power Supply

5. RAID level 5 _____.

    A. uses bit interleave data striping

    B. uses block interleave data striping

    C. doesn't use data striping

    D. provides parity-checking capabilities

6. RAID level 1 _____.

    A. uses bit interleave data striping

    B. uses block interleave data striping

    C. doesn't use data striping

    D. provides parity-checking capabilities

7. The difference between disk mirroring and disk duplexing is _____.

    A. disk mirroring is more reliable

    B. mirrored disks share the same disk channels

    C. duplexed disks share the same disk channels

    D. nonexistent

8. True or False: Implementing a RAID system eliminates the need for tape backup.

    A. True

    B. False

9. What is the minimum number of disks needed to configure a stripe set with parity on Windows NT Server?

    A. Two

    B. Three

    C. Four

    D. Seven

10. Network documentation should include which of the following?

    A. Hardware installation dates and specifications

    B. Copies of configuration files

    C. Software licensing information

    D. All of the above

Pretest Answers

1. B (see the section titled "RAID 5")

2. C (see the section titled "RAID 5")

3. A (see the section titled "Disk Duplexing")

Review Answers

1. B

2. A

3. C

4. D

5. D

6. C

7. B

8. B

9. B

10. D

Network Adapter Cards

A *network adapter card* is a hardware device that installs in a PC and provides an interface from a PC to the transmission medium. Most PC networks, including Ethernet and Token Ring networks, use network adapter cards. The network adapter card is thus an essential part of networking, and an understanding of network adapter cards is crucial for any networking professional. This chapter examines the role of the network adapter card and describes the processes of installing and configuring network adapter cards. In addition, this chapter discusses how to resolve hardware conflicts related to network adapter cards.

Chapter 10 targets the following objective in the Implementation section of the Networking Essentials exam:

Test Objectives

▶ Given the manufacturer's documentation for the network adapter, to install, configure, and resolve hardware conflicts for multiple adapters in a Token Ring or Ethernet network

Test Yourself

Stop! Before reading this chapter, test yourself to determine how much study time you will need to devote to this section.

1. Three duties of the network adapter card are as follows:

    A. Preparing data

    B. Sending data

    C. Identifying problems with the cabling medium

    D. Controlling the flow of data

2. On Ethernet networks, data flows from the network adapter card to the transmission medium in _____ form.

    A. parallel

    B. serial

    C. either A or B

    D. none of the above

3. A recommended IRQ setting for network adapter cards is _____.

    A. IRQ15

    B. IRQ2

    C. IRQ1

    D. IRQ5

Defining a Network Adapter Card

A network adapter card links a PC with the network cabling system (see fig. 10.1). The network adapter card fits into one of the PC's expansion slots. The card has one or more user-accessible ports to which the network cabling medium is connected.

Figure 10.1

An Ethernet network adapter card.

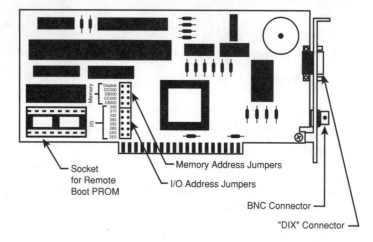

Socket for Remote Boot PROM

Memory Address Jumpers

I/O Address Jumpers

BNC Connector

"DIX" Connector

Like other hardware devices, a network adapter card has a *driver*, a software component that manages the device. The network adapter card driver serves a crucial role in the networking architecture. Adapter card drivers inhabit the Data Link layer of the OSI model (see Chapter 2, "Networking Standards," for more information), or, more specifically, the Media Access Control (MAC) sublayer of the Data Link layer. A network adapter card driver sometimes is also called a MAC driver. As Chapter 2 mentions, the NDIS and ODI standards provide a uniform interface for the adapter card driver, enabling one adapter to support multiple protocols and making one protocol accessible to multiple adapters.

The network adapter card's built-in ROM (read only memory) performs the functions of the Logical Link Control sublayer of the OSI Data Link layer.

The network adapter card and its accompanying software and firmware perform several roles. Microsoft identifies the following roles for the network adapter card:

▶ Preparing data for the transmission medium

▶ Sending data

▶ Controlling the flow of data from the PC to the transmission medium

Of course, the network adapter must also play these roles in reverse, receiving data from the network and converting that data to the form necessary for the local system.

Preparing Data

Data travels on the network in serial form (one bit at a time). Inside the PC, however, data moves along the bus in parallel form (8, 16, or 32 bits at a time). The network adapter card, therefore, must convert the parallel data from the bus into the serial form required for network transmission. If the card receives data from the local system, it can transmit that data to the network. The data then is stored in a memory buffer on the adapter card until the card can catch up.

Because the network adapter card's software and firmware participate in the Data Link layer of the protocol stack, they are responsible for contributing data-link header information, such as the network adapter card's physical address (see Chapter 2).

The *data bus* is a pathway inside your computer that carries data between the hardware components. Four data-bus architectures are used in Intel-based PCs: Industry Standard Architecture (ISA), Extended Industry Standard Architecture (EISA), Micro Channel, and Peripheral Component Interconnect (PCI). In recent models, *PCI* and *EISA* are the most common data-bus architectures. *ISA* is a (more limited) predecessor of EISA. *Micro Channel* is a data bus developed by IBM for the PS/2 series that never caught on—it is, however, still used for some high-end models.

Sending Data

The network adapter card places data on the network and receives data from the network. These tasks require a certain amount of flow control (see the following section). The MAC-layer software also must know *when* to put data on the network.

Chapter 4, "Network Topologies and Architectures," discusses various media-access methods (such as CSMA/CD or token passing) used by the card, as well as how and when each of these methods provides access to the transmission medium.

As Chapter 4 describes, the network adapter card receives packets from the network, checking the destination address of all packets and interrupting the CPU only if the packet is addressed to the local system.

Controlling the Flow of Data

For two computers to exchange data, the computers' network adapter cards must be in agreement on certain transmission parameters. A newer card with a higher maximum transmission rate, for instance, might have the capability to use a lower rate in order to communicate with a slower card. Before sending data, the cards exchange messages and agree on such parameters as a transmission speed and a time interval between packets.

Installing Network Adapter Cards

 The details of how to install a network adapter card might depend on the card, the operating system, or the hardware platform, but the steps are basically the same. To install a network adapter card, you must follow these steps:

1. Physically plug the card into the expansion slot, configuring jumpers and DIP switches as required.

2. Install the network adapter card driver.

3. Configure the operating system so that the network adapter card won't conflict with other devices (see the next section).

4. Bind the network adapter to the required protocols (see Chapter 5, "Transport Protocols," for more information).

5. Attach the network cable to the card.

Depending on the hardware operating system, some of these steps might happen automatically when you plug a card into the slot and start your system. Windows NT is not really plug-and-play capable, so when you install a network adapter card after the operating system is in place, you might have to spend some time with steps 2–4.

To install a network adapter card driver in Windows NT, follow these steps:

1. Click the Start button and choose Settings/Control Panel. Double-click the Control Panel Network application. In the Control Panel Network application, choose the Adapters tab (see fig. 10.2).

Figure 10.2

The Control Panel Network application's Adapters tab.

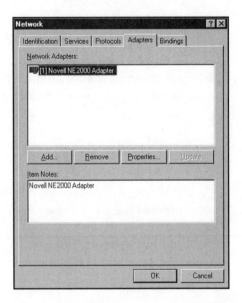

2. In the Adapters tab (refer to fig. 10.2), click the Add button to invoke the Select Network Adapter dialog box (see fig. 10.3). Choose the adapter model from the list or click the Have Disk button to install a driver that isn't listed. Windows NT asks for the location of the Windows NT installation CD-ROM.

Figure 10.3

The Select Net-work Adapter dialog box.

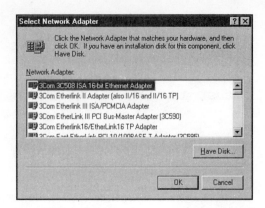

Make sure the adapter is compatible with your version of Windows NT. To do so, check the Windows NT Hardware Compatibility list or consult the manufacturer.

3. Windows NT will attempt to detect the adapter and then might prompt you for additional information (see the section titled "Configuring Network Adapter Cards" later in this chapter).

4. When the installation is complete, shut down Windows NT and Restart.

5. Use the Network application's Bindings tab to check and set protocol bindings for the new adapter (see Chapter 5).

Before you buy a network adapter card, you must make sure it has the correct data-bus architecture for your PC and the correct connector type for your transmission medium.

Almost all PCs use one of four basic data-bus architectures: ISA, EISA, PCI, and Micro Channel. (Refer to the note on data-bus architectures earlier in this chapter.) These architectures are not necessarily compatible—for example, a Micro Channel card won't work on an EISA system and, in fact, won't even fit in the slot—so when you buy a card for an expansion slot, be ready to tell the vendor what type of data-bus architecture you have on your system.

The data-bus architecture is generally independent of the processor type. Two Pentium machines from different vendors might have different (and incompatible) data-bus architectures.

Chapter 3, "Transmission Media," discussed some basic LAN network cabling types. The network adapter is responsible for transmitting in accordance with the specifications of the transmission medium. The adapter card also must supply a connector that is compatible with the cabling system. (See Chapter 3 for more information on Ethernet and token-ring cabling and connectors.) Some boards offer connectors for more than one cabling type, in which case you must configure jumpers or DIP switches to set the active type.

Jumpers are small connectors that bridge across predetermined terminal points on the card itself to hardwire the card for certain user-defined settings, such as the IRQ setting. *DIP (dual inline package) switches* are small switches (usually in groups) that, like jumpers, can configure the card for user-defined settings.

Configuring Network Adapter Cards

You must configure your operating system so that it can communicate with the network adapter card. In many cases, you must manually configure the adapter card (through jumper or DIP switch settings) so that it can communicate with the operating system.

To communicate, the operating system and the network adapter must agree on certain important parameters, called *resource settings.* Some common resource settings for a network adapter are as follows:

- ▶ IRQ

- ▶ Base I/O port address

- ▶ Base memory address

The *IRQ (Interrupt Request Line)* setting reserves an interrupt request line for the adapter to use when contacting the CPU. Devices make requests to the CPU using a signal called an *interrupt.* Each device must send interrupts on a different interrupt request line. Interrupt request lines are part of the system hardware. The IRQ setting (such as IRQ3, IRQ5, or IRQ15) defines which interrupt request line the device will use. By convention, certain IRQ settings are reserved for specific devices. IRQ3 and IRQ5, for instance, typically are used for network adapter cards. Microsoft recommends IRQ5 if it is available; IRQ5 is often the default.

The *base I/O port address* defines a memory address through which data will flow to and from the adapter. The base I/O port address functions more like a port, defining a channel to the adapter (see fig. 10.4).

Figure 10.4

The base I/O port address defines a memory address through which data flows to the adapter.

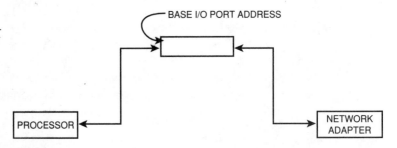

The *base memory address* is a place in the computer's memory that marks the beginning of a buffer area reserved for the network adapter. Not all network adapter cards use the computer's RAM, and therefore not all adapters require a base memory address setting.

Any effort to configure a network adapter card should begin with the card's vendor documentation. The documentation tells you which resources setting you must set, and it might recommend values for some or all of the settings. The documentation also recommends any jumper or DIP switch settings for the card.

The actual process of configuring the operating system to interact with a network adapter card depends on the operating system. A plug-and-play operating system such as Windows 95, when used with a plug-and-play compatible adapter card, may perform much of the configuring automatically. In Windows NT, you can configure adapter card resource settings through the Control Panel

Network application's Adapters tab. The Windows NT Diagnostics application in the Administrative Tools group (see exercise 10.2 at the end of the chapter) indicates the resource settings that are currently available.

Resolving Hardware Conflicts

Hardware conflicts are caused when the devices on the system compete for the same system resources, such as interrupt request lines, base I/O port addresses, and base memory addresses. An improperly configured device can cause a hardware conflict with other devices, so you must make sure that each device has exclusive access to the required system resources.

It is important to note that plug-and-play (sometimes called plug-and-pray) is still relatively new technology for Microsoft-based systems. Ideally, Windows 95 will configure a plug-and-play compatible card without much user intervention, but in some cases, you might still face configuration problems.

In Windows NT, a hardware conflict might invoke a warning message from the system or an entry in the Event Log (see Chapter 13, "Troubleshooting"). If you experience a hardware conflict, use Windows NT Diagnostics (see exercise 10.2) to check resource settings for system devices. Then change the resource settings of any conflicting devices.

In Windows 95, use Device Manager (see the following note) to spot hardware conflicts and track resource settings.

Windows 95 includes a utility called Device Manager that displays system devices by type, looks for resource conflicts, and provides an interface for checking and changing resource settings.

To access Device Manager, follow these steps:

1. Click the Start button and choose Settings/Control Panel.

continues

2. In the Windows 95 Control Panel, double-click the System application.

3. Choose the Device Manager tab in the System Properties dialog box.

4. Device Manager displays system devices in a tree format. Click on the plus sign next to a device type to view the installed devices. Double-click on an installed device (or choose the device and click the Properties button) for a Properties dialog box, such as the one shown in figure 10.5.

Figure 10.5

An adapter card's Properties dialog box in Device Manager.

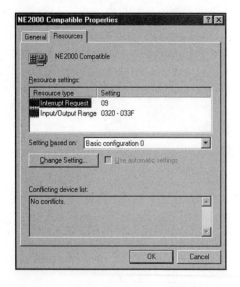

If you can't pinpoint a resource conflict by using Windows NT Diagnostics, Windows 95's Device Manager, or some other diagnostic program, try removing all the cards except the network adapter and then replacing the cards one by one. Check the network with each addition to determine which device is causing the conflict.

Summary

This chapter examined the network adapter card—an essential component in Ethernet and Token Ring networks. The network adapter card performs several functions, including preparing, sending, and controlling the flow of data to the network transmission medium. This chapter also discussed how to install and configure network adapters. Configuration tasks for a network adapter card include setting jumpers and/or DIP switches on the card itself, as well as configuring resource settings (such as IRQ, Base I/O port address, and base memory address) that the operating system must use to communicate with the card.

Exercises

Exercise 10.1: Network Adapter Resource Settings

Objective: Become familiar with the process of configuring network adapter resource settings in Windows NT

Estimated time: 10 minutes

Earlier in this chapter, you learned how to install a network adapter card driver by using the Windows NT Network application. You also can use the Network application to check or change the resource settings for an adapter that is already installed.

1. Click the Start button and choose Settings/Control Panel. Double-click the Windows NT Control Panel Network application.

2. In the Network application, click the Adapters tab (refer to figure 10.2).

3. Select the network adapter that is currently installed on your system and click the Properties button.

4. The Network Card Setup dialog box then appears on your screen (see fig. 10.6).

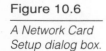

Figure 10.6

A Network Card Setup dialog box.

5. In the Network Card Setup dialog box, you can change the resource settings as required. You might want to use the Windows NT Diagnostics application to look for available settings (see exercise 10.2). Don't change the settings unless you're experiencing problems, though, because you could introduce a hardware conflict with another device.

6. Click Cancel to leave the Network Card Setup dialog box and click Cancel again to leave the Network application.

Exercise 10.2: Windows NT Diagnostics

Objective: Learn to check resource settings through Windows NT Diagnostics

Estimated time: 10 minutes

Windows NT Diagnostics tabulates a number of important system parameters. You can use Windows NT Diagnostics to help resolve resource conflicts for network adapters.

1. Click the Start button and choose Programs/Administrative Tools. Choose Windows NT Diagnostics from the Administrative Tools menu.

2. Windows NT Diagnostics provides several tabs with information on different aspects of the system. Choose the Resources tab (see fig. 10.7).

continues

Exercise 10.2: Continued

Figure 10.7

The Windows NT Diagnostics Resources tab.

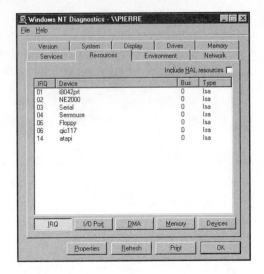

3. Figure 10.7 displays the IRQ settings for system devices. (Note that the network adapter card for which the resource settings were displayed in figure 10.6 is listed here beside IRQ2.) The buttons at the bottom of the screen invoke views of other resource settings. Click on a button to see the associated list. Figure 10.8 shows the I/O Port list.

Figure 10.8

*The Windows NT
Diagnostics
Resources tab—
I/O Port settings.*

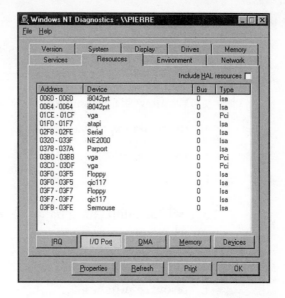

You can't change any values in Windows NT Diagnostics. You
can only view services, devices, statistics, and settings.

Review Questions

1. In Windows NT, you can use _____ to install network adapter card drivers.

   A. Windows NT Diagnostics

   B. the System application

   C. Device Manager

   D. none of the above

2. The user sometimes must hardwire resource settings on a network adapter card using _____.

   A. jumpers

   B. resource switches

   C. needle connectors

   D. none of the above

3. Which two of the following are common data-bus architectures?

   A. EISA

   B. Pentium

   C. Plug-and-Play

   D. PCI

4. Which resource setting gives the device a channel for contacting the CPU?

   A. IRQ

   B. Base I/O port address

   C. Base memory address

   D. None of the above

5. Which resource setting defines a means for passing data to the adapter?

   A. IRQ

   B. Base I/O port address

   C. Base memory address

   D. None of the above

6. Which resource setting specifies a serial communications port for the network adapter?

   A. IRQ

   B. Base I/O port address

   C. Base memory address

   D. None of the above

7. Which resource setting locates a buffer for the adapter in the computer's RAM?

   A. IRQ

   B. Base I/O port address

   C. Base memory address

   D. None of the above

8. A maximum of _____ devices can use the same IRQ simultaneously.

   A. 1

   B. 2

   C. 4

   D. 8

9. Which two of the following enable you to check the resource settings for a network adapter card in Windows NT?

    A. Device Manager

    B. The Network application

    C. Windows NT Diagnostics

    D. The System application

10. Which of the following enables you to change the resource settings for a network adapter card in Windows NT?

    A. Device Manager

    B. The Network application

    C. Windows NT Diagnostics

    D. The System application

Pretest Answers

1. A, B, D (see the section titled "Defining a Network Adapter")

2. B (see the section titled "Preparing Data")

3. D (see the section titled "Configuring Network Adapter Cards")

Review Answers

1. D

2. A

3. A, D

4. A

5. B

6. D

7. C

8. A

9. B, C

10. B

NetBIOS is an interface that provides applications with access to network resources. Every computer on a Windows NT network must have a unique name for it to be accessible through the NetBIOS interface. This unique name is called a computer name or a NetBIOS name.

Chapter 11 targets the following objective in the Implementation section of the Networking Essentials exam:

Test Objectives

▶ Implement a NetBIOS naming scheme for all computers on a given network

Test Yourself

Stop! Before reading this chapter, test yourself to determine how much study time you will need to devote to this section.

1. NetBIOS is used with _____.

    A. NetBEUI

    B. TCP/IP

    C. IPX/SPX

    D. all the above

2. NetBIOS names should be _____ or fewer characters long.

    A. 8

    B. 15

    C. 16

    D. 45

3. Which three of the following elements can be part of a UNC path?

    A. A NetBIOS computer name

    B. A share name

    C. A user name

    D. An MS-DOS–style path

NetBIOS Background

NetBIOS (Network Basic Input/Output System) is an application interface that provides PC-based applications with uniform access to lower protocol layers. NetBIOS was once most closely associated with the NetBEUI protocol—*NetBEUI*, in fact, is an abbreviation for NetBIOS Extended User Interface. In recent years, however, other vendors have recognized the importance of providing compatibility with PC-based applications through NetBIOS, and NetBIOS is now available with many protocol configurations. For instance, such terms as "NetBIOS over IPX" or "NetBIOS over TCP/IP" refer to the protocols used with NetBIOS.

NetBIOS Names

On a NetBIOS network, every computer must have a unique name. The computer name must be 15 characters long or fewer. A NetBIOS name can include alphanumeric characters and any of the following special characters:

!@#$%^&()-_'{}.~

Note that you cannot use a space or an asterisk in a NetBIOS name. Also, NetBIOS names are not case-sensitive.

Within these character limitations, you can choose any name for a PC. The rule of thumb is to choose a name that helps you to identify the computer. Names such as PC1, PC2, and PC3 are difficult to visualize and easy to confuse. Likewise, names such as STUPID-PC or WORTHLESSPC could confuse you in the long run, especially if you have many computers on your network. For these reasons, names that include a hook relating the name of the owner or the location of the computer generally are more effective. Consider the following names, for example:

▶ BILL'S_PC

▶ MARKETINGPC

▶ LUNCHROOM_PC

▶ BILL'SLAPTOP

You must specify a computer name for a Windows NT or Windows 95 computer at installation. The computer name then becomes part of the network configuration. In either Windows NT or Windows 95, you can change the name of the computer through the Control Panel Network application (see the following tip and note).

A NetBIOS computer name must:

▶ Be unique

▶ Consist of 15 characters or fewer

▶ Consist of either alphanumeric characters or the characters !@#$%^&()-_'{}.~

You designate a computer name for your PC when you install the operating system. You can change the computer name later through the Control Panel Network application, but you must have Administrative privileges to change the computer name. To change a NetBIOS computer name, follow these steps:

1. Click the Start button and choose Settings/Control Panel.

2. In Windows NT Control Panel, double-click on the Network application.

3. In the Network application's Identification tab, click on the Change button. The subsequent Identification Changes dialog box is shown in figure 11.1.

4. Change the computer name in the text box labeled Computer Name and click OK.

Figure 11.1

Windows NT's Identification Changes dialog box enables you to change the computer name.

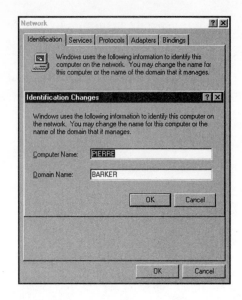

Finding Resources on Microsoft Networks

The Universal Naming Convention is a standard for identifying resources on Microsoft networks. A UNC path consists of the following components:

▶ A NetBIOS computer name preceded with a double backslash (left-leaning slash)

▶ The share name of a shared resource located on the given PC (optional)

▶ The MS-DOS–style path of a file or a directory located on the given share (optional)

Elements of the UNC path are separated with single backslashes. The following list details some legal UNC names:

\\BILL's_PC

\\WEIGHTRM\ACCOUNTS

\\PET_DEPT\CATS\SIAMESE.TXT

Various Windows NT commands use UNC paths to designate network resources. For instance,

net view \\PET_DEPT

enables you to view the shared resources on the computer with the NetBIOS name PET_DEPT. The command

net use G: \\PET_DEPT\CATS

maps the shared directory CATS on the computer PET_DEPT to drive G:.

As with Windows NT, Windows 95 enables you to change the computer name after installation by using the Control Panel Network application. To change the name, follow these steps:

1. Click the Start button and choose Settings/Control Panel.

2. In the Windows 95 Control Panel, double-click on the Network application.

3. In the Network application, choose the Identification tab.

4. To change the computer name, edit the text in the Computer name text box (see fig. 11.2).

Figure 11.2

The Identification tab of the Windows 95 Network dialog box enables you to change the computer name.

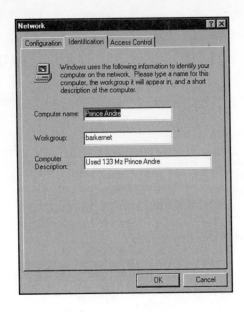

Summary

A computer on a NetBIOS network must have a NetBIOS computer name. The NetBIOS name is configured at installation and, in Windows NT or Windows 95, can be changed later through the Control Panel Network application. Computers use the NetBIOS name (sometimes combined with a share name or a path name) to locate resources on the network.

Exercises

Exercise 11.1: Mapping a Network Drive

Objective: Use the NetBIOS-based UNC path to map a drive letter to a network share.

Estimated time: 10 minutes

1. Double-click Windows NT's Network Neighborhood application. Locate another computer for which network shares have been defined.

> Another useful tool for finding network shares is the Server Manager application in Windows NT Server's Administrative Tools group. To use this tool, click the Start menu and choose Programs, Administrative Tools, Server Manager.

2. Click the Start menu and go to the Windows NT command prompt. (Choose Programs, Command Prompt.)

3. Enter the following command:

   net view

4. The net view command lists the NetBIOS names of computers in your domain. Look for the computer you located using Network Neighborhood in Step 1.

5. Type the following command

   net view \\computername

   where computername is the NetBIOS name of the computer you located in Step 1. This command lists the network shares available on the computer.

6. Locate a directory share in the share list. Then type the following command

   net use * \\computername\sharename

where computername is the NetBIOS name of the computer you located in Step 1, and sharename is the name of the share you located in this step. The asterisk maps the next available drive letter to the share. You could also specify a particular drive letter (followed by a colon) instead of the asterisk. A message will appear on your screen giving you the drive letter that Windows NT used for the connection and indicating whether the command was successful.

7. Now enter the following command

    net view \\computername

    where computername is the name of the computer you chose in Step 1. The drive letter you mapped to the share should appear beside the share name, and the share type in the column should be titled Used as.

8. Enter the drive letter assigned in Step 6 at the command prompt, followed by a colon. For instance, enter **I:**.

9. Enter the command **dir** and press Enter. A directory listing of the shared directory should appear on your screen. You now have accessed the shared directory through the mapped drive letter.

You must have the necessary privileges to access the shared directory. Check with your network administrator for details.

10. To delete the network drive mapping, enter the following command

    net use drive_letter: /delete

    where drive_letter is the drive letter assigned in Step 6.

You also can map drive letters through Windows NT Explorer. To do so, pull down the Tools menu and select Map Network Drive.

Review Questions

1. NetBIOS is an abbreviation for _____.

   A. Network Basic Input/Output System

   B. Network Bilateral Operating System

   C. Network Binary Interchange Operating System

   D. Network Bus Input/Output System

2. Which of the following is a legal NetBIOS computer name?

   A. EAGLES_LODGE_PENT

   B. EAGLES!@#*_PC

   C. 486!!EAGLES_PC

   D. EAGLES LODGE

3. Which of the following UNC paths will lead you to a file called DOUGHNUTS on a PC called FOOD located in the SWEETS directory of the JUNKFOOD share?

   A. \\DOUGHNUTS\FOOD\SWEETS\JUNKFOOD

   B. \\FOOD\JUNKFOOD\SWEETS\DOUGHNUTS

   C. \\FOOD\JUNKFOOD\DOUGHNUTS

   D. \\JUNKFOOD\DOUGHNUTS

4. Which of the following commands produces a list of shared resources on the computer described in Question 3?

   A. Net share \\FOOD

   B. Net view

   C. Net view \\FOOD

   D. Net view \\FOOD /shares

Pretest Answers

1. D (see the section titled "NetBIOS Background")

2. B (see the section titled "NetBIOS Names")

3. A, B, D (see the section titled "Finding Resources on Microsoft Networks")

Review Answers

1. A

2. C

3. B

4. C

Chapter 12

Monitoring the Network

An important part of network management involves monitoring trends on the network. By effectively monitoring network behavior, you can anticipate problems and correct them before they disrupt the network. Monitoring the network also provides you with a *baseline*, a sampling of how the network functions in its equilibrium state. This baseline is beneficial because if you experience a problem later, the changes in certain related parameters could lead you to a possible cause.

Chapter 12 targets the following objective in the Planning section of the Networking Essentials exam:

Test Objectives

▶ Select the appropriate hardware and software tools to monitor trends on a given network

 **Stop! Before reading this chapter, test yourself to determine how much study time you will need to devote to this section.**

1. An enhanced version of Network Monitor is included with _____.

    A. Windows NT

    B. Windows 95

    C. SMS

    D. SNMP

2. _____ keeps a record of the repair histories of network hardware.

    A. Network Monitor

    B. Event log

    C. Client Manager

    D. Nothing—you must do it yourself

Monitoring Network Trends

Monitoring the network is an ongoing task that requires data from several different areas. Some of the monitoring tools that keep watch on the network are discussed in other chapters. The purpose of this chapter is to bring these tools together so that you can view them in the context of an overall network monitoring strategy. The following list details some tools you can use to document network activities:

▶ Pencil and paper (very important in keeping records)

▶ A performance-monitoring tool, such as Windows NT's Performance Monitor

▶ A network-monitoring and protocol-analysis program—such as Windows NT's Network Monitor or the more powerful Network Monitor tool included with Microsoft's BackOffice System Management Server (SMS) package—or a hardware-based protocol analyzer

▶ A system event log, such as the Windows NT event log, which you can access through Windows NT's Event Viewer application.

Keeping Records

A detailed history of changes to the network serves as a tremendous aid in troubleshooting. When a problem occurs, the first thing you want to know is *what* has changed, and you can gather this information from a configuration management database.

The following list details some items your configuration records should include:

▶ Descriptions of all hardware, including installation dates, repair histories, configuration details (such as interrupts and addresses), and backup records for each server

▶ A map of the network showing locations of hardware and cabling details

- ▶ Current copies of workstation configuration files, such as CONFIG.SYS and AUTOEXEC.BAT files

- ▶ Service agreements and important telephone numbers, such as the numbers of vendors, contractors, and software support lines

- ▶ Software licenses to ensure that your network operates within the bounds of the license terms

- ▶ A history of past problems and related solutions

Monitoring Performance

Windows NT's Performance Monitor tool lets you monitor important system parameters for the computers on your network. Performance Monitor can keep an eye on a large number of system parameters, providing a graphical or tabular profile of system and network trends. Performance Monitor also can save performance data in a log for later reference. You can use Performance Monitor to track statistical measurements (called *counters*) for any of several hardware or software components (called *objects*). Some Performance Monitor objects that relate to network behavior are as follows:

- ▶ Network segment

- ▶ Server

- ▶ Server work queues

- ▶ Protocol-related objects, such as NetBEUI, NWLink, and NetBIOS

- ▶ Service-related objects, such as Browser and Gateway Services for NetWare

Of course, any system counter on a server machine—such as those classified under the Processor, Memory, or PhysicalDisk objects—could have implications for the network.

You should use Performance Monitor if you are experiencing problems, but you also should use Performance Monitor to log network activity when things are running smoothly. Logging normal network activity helps you establish a baseline, to which later measurements can be compared.

>
>
> Exercises 12.2 and 12.3 at the end of this chapter provide you with a guided tour of Windows NT's Performance Monitor application.

Monitoring Network Traffic

Protocol analysis tools monitor network traffic by intercepting and decoding frames. Software-based tools, such as Windows NT Server's Network Monitor (see fig. 12.1), analyze frames coming and going from the computer on which they run. Network Monitor records a number of statistics, including the percent of network utilization and the broadcasts per second. In addition, Network Monitor tabulates frame statistics (such as frames sent and received) for each network address.

Figure 12.1

Windows NT Server's Network Monitor main screen.

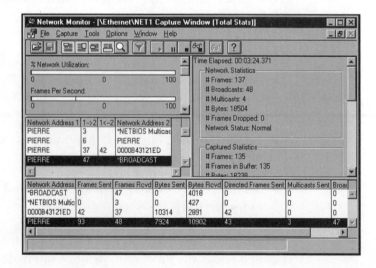

An enhanced version of Network Monitor, which is included with the Microsoft BackOffice System Management Server (SMS) package, monitors traffic not just at the local system but also at other computers on the network.

For large networks, or for networks with complex traffic patterns, you might want to use a hardware-based protocol-analysis tool. A hardware-based protocol analyzer is a portable device that looks like a cross between a portable PC and a suitcase. The advantage of a hardware-based protocol analyzer is that you can carry it to strategic places around the network (such as a network node or a busy cabling intersection) and monitor the traffic at that point.

Some protocol analyzers are quite sophisticated. In addition to keeping network traffic statistics, they can capture bad frames and often isolate the source. They also can help determine the cause of bottlenecks, protocol problems, and connection errors. A hardware-based protocol analyzer is often a good investment for a large network because it concentrates a considerable amount of monitoring and troubleshooting power into a single, portable unit. For a smaller network, however, a hardware-based analyzer might not be worth the initial five-figure expense because less expensive software-based products perform many of the same functions.

Logging Events

Some operating systems, such as Windows NT, have the capability to keep a running log of system events. That log serves as a record of previous errors, warnings, and other messages from the system. Studying the event log can help you find reccurring errors and discover when a problem first appeared.

Windows NT's Event Viewer application provides you with access to the event log. You can use Event Viewer to monitor the following types of events:

▶ **System events.** Warnings, error messages, and other notices describing significant system events. Examples of system log entries include browser elections, service failures, and network connection failures.

▶ **Security events.** Events tracked through Windows NT's auditing features. Refer to Chapter 8, "Managing and Securing a Microsoft Network."

▶ **Application events.** Messages from Win32 applications. If you're having a problem with an application, you can check the application log for an application-related error or warning messages.

Event Viewer is part of the Windows NT Server Administrative Tools group. To start Event Viewer, click on the Start button and choose Programs, Administrative Tools, Event Viewer. Figure 12.2 shows the Event Viewer main screen. Click on the Log menu to select the System, Security, or Application log.

Figure 12.2

The Event Viewer main screen.

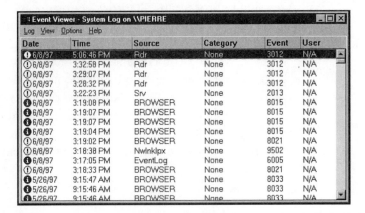

If you double-click on a log entry in Event Viewer, an Event Detail dialog box will appear on your screen (see fig. 12.3). An Event Detail provides detailed description of the event.

Figure 12.3

Event detail describing a system event.

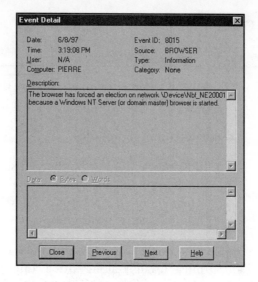

Summary

This chapter reviewed some of the tools you can use to monitor network trends, including the following:

- ▶ Performance-monitoring devices

- ▶ Hardware- and software-based network-monitoring and protocol-analysis tools

- ▶ Event logs

This chapter also discussed the importance of keeping detailed written records of important network installations, configurations, and changes.

Exercises

Objective: Examine the main window display of Windows NT Server 4.0's Network Monitor application.

Estimated time: 15 minutes

1. If Network Monitor has been installed on your system, click the Start menu and choose Programs/Administrative Tools. Then choose the Network Monitor application from the Administrative Tools group and proceed to Step 4.

2. If Network Monitor hasn't been installed on your system, you must install it, along with a component called the Network Monitor Agent. Network Monitor and the Network Monitor Agent can be installed together by using the Control Panel Network application. Click the Start menu and choose Settings/Control Panel. Double-click the Network application and choose the Services tab.

3. In the Network application Services tab, click on the Add button. Choose Network Monitor and Agent from the Network Service list and click OK. Windows NT prompts you for the Windows NT installation disk. When the installation is complete, click OK to shut down your system and restart Windows NT. Then start the Network Monitor application, as described in Step 1.

4. Examine the four panes of the Network Monitor main screen (refer to fig. 12.1). The following list describes the four panes:

   ▶ The Graph pane is located in the upper-left corner of the display. The Graph section includes five bar graphs describing network activity. Only two of the graphs are visible, as in figure 12.1; use the scroll bar to view the other three graphs.

   ▶ The Session Statistics pane, which appears below the Graph pane, tracks network activity by session, showing the two computers in the session and the frames sent each way.

▶ The Total Statistics pane, which appears to the right of the Graph pane, lists such important statistics as the number of frames and the number of broadcasts. You can use the scroll bar to reach other entries that are not visible.

▶ The Station Statistics pane, which sits at the bottom of the window, shows statistics for frames listed by network address.

5. Pull down the Capture menu and choose Start. Network Monitor then starts monitoring the network.

6. Ping the Network Monitor PC from another computer on the network. (Go to the command prompt and type **Ping**, followed by the IP address on the Network Monitor computer—for example, ping 111.121.131.141.) Watch the Station Statistics pane at the bottom of the screen to see if any new information appears.

7. Experiment with sending files or other requests to or from the Network Monitor PC. Study the effect of network activity on the values displayed in the four panes of the Network Monitor main window.

8. When you are finished, pull down the Capture menu and click Stop to stop capturing data. Then exit Network Monitor.

Exercise 12.2:   Creating a Chart in Performance Monitor

Objectives: Become familiar with the process of creating and reading a Performance Monitor chart. Understand the basic components of the Performance Monitor main window and the Add to Chart dialog box. Learn how to turn on disk performance counters using the *diskperf* command.

Estimated time: 25 minutes

1. From the Start menu, select Programs. Choose the Administrative Tools group and click Performance Monitor. The Performance Monitor main window appears on your screen.

continues

Exercise 12.2: Continued

2. Pull down the Edit menu and choose Add to Chart (see fig. 12.4.). The Add to Chart dialog box appears (see fig. 12.5). You can also invoke the Add to Chart dialog box by clicking the plus sign in the tool bar of the Performance Monitor main window.

Figure 12.4

The Performance Monitor main window.

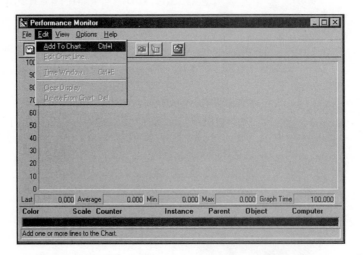

Figure 12.5

The Add to Chart dialog box.

3.a. The box labeled Computer at the top of the Add to Chart dialog box tells Performance Monitor which computer you want to monitor. The default is the local system. Click the ellipsis button to the right of the box for a list of computers on the network.

3.b. The box labeled Object tells Performance Monitor which object you want to monitor. As you learned earlier in this chapter, an object is a hardware or software component of your system. You can think of an object as a *category* of system statistics. Pull down the Object menu. Scroll through the list of objects and look for the Processor, Memory, PhysicalDisk, LogicalDisk, Server, and Network Segment objects described earlier in this chapter. Choose the PhysicalDisk object. If you have more than one physical disk on your system, a list of your physical disks will appear in the Instance box to the right of the Object box. The Instance box lists all instances of the object selected in the Object box. If necessary, choose a physical disk instance.

3.c. The box labeled Counter displays the counters (the statistical measurements) that are available for the object displayed in the object box. Scroll through the list of counters for the PhysicalDisk object. If you feel like experimenting, select a different object in the Object box. Notice that the new object is accompanied by a different set of counters. Switch back to the PhysicalDisk object and choose the %Disk Time counter. Click the Explain button on the right side of the Add to Chart dialog box. Notice that a description of the %Disk Time counter appears at the bottom of the dialog box.

3.d. Click the Done button in the Add to Chart dialog box. The dialog box disappears, and you see the Performance Monitor main window.

4. In the Performance Monitor main window, a vertical line sweeps across the chart from left to right. You may also see a faint colored line at the bottom of the chart recording a %Disk Time value of 0. If so, you haven't enabled the disk performance counters for your system. (If the disk performance monitors are enabled on your system, you should see a spikey line that looks like the readout from an electrocardiogram. You're done with this step. Go on to step 5.)

If you need to enable the disk performance counters, click the Start button and go to the command prompt. Enter the command: **diskperf -y**. Then reboot your system and repeat Steps 1-4. (You don't have to browse through the object and counter menus this time.)

continues

Exercise 12.2: Continued

5. You should now see a spikey line representing the percent of time that the physical disk is busy reading or writing. Select Add to Chart from the Edit menu. Select the PhysicalDisk object and choose the counter Avg. Disk Queue Length. Click the Add button. Then choose the counter Avg. Disk Bytes/Read. Click the Add button and then click the Done button.

6. Examine the Performance Monitor main window. All three of the counters you selected should be tracing out spikey lines on the chart (see fig. 12.6). Each line is a different color. At the bottom of the window is a table showing which counter goes with which color. The table also gives the scale of the output, the instance, the object, and the computer.

Figure 12.6

Displaying performance data.

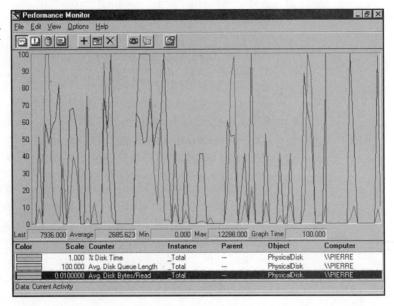

7. Below the chart (but above the table of counters) is a row of statistical parameters labeled: Last, Average, Min, Max, and Graph Time. These parameters pertain to the counter that is selected in the table at the bottom of the window. Select a different counter and you see that some of these values change. The Last value is the counter value over the last

second. Graph time is the time it takes (in seconds) for the vertical line that draws the chart to sweep across the window.

8. Start Windows Explorer. Select a file (a graphics file or a word processing document) and choose Copy from Explorer's Edit menu. (This copies the file you selected to the clipboard.) Go to another directory and select Paste from the Edit menu. (This creates a copy of the file in the second directory.) Minimize Explorer and return to the Performance Monitor main screen. The disk activity caused by your Explorer session is now reflected in the spikes of the counter lines.

9. Pull down the Options menu and select Chart. The Chart Options dialog box appears on your screen (see fig. 12.7). The Chart Options dialog box provides a number of options governing the chart display. The Update Time section enables you to choose an update interval. The update interval tells Performance Monitor how frequently it should update the chart with new values. (If you choose the Manual Update option, the chart will update only when you press Ctrl+U or click Update Now in the Options menu.) Experiment with the Chart Options or click the Cancel button to return to the main window.

Figure 12.7

The Chart Options dialog box.

10. Pull down the File menu. Choose Exit to exit Performance Monitor. Note that the Save Chart Settings and Save Chart Settings As options in the File menu enable you to save the collection of objects and counters you're using now so you can monitor the same counters later and avoid setting them

continues

Exercise 12.2: Continued

> up again. The Export Chart option enables you to export the data to a file that you can then open with a spreadsheet or database application. The Save Workspace option saves the settings for your chart, as well as any settings for alerts, logs, or reports specified in this session. Learn more about alerts, logs, and reports in exercise 12.3.

Exercise 12.3: Performance Monitor Alerts, Logs, and Reports

> Objectives: Become familiar with the alternative views (Alert view, Log view, and Report view) available through the Performance Monitor View menu. Log performance data to a log file.
>
> Estimated time: 25 minutes
>
> 1. Click Programs in the Start menu and choose Performance Monitor from the Administrative Tools group. The Performance Monitor main window appears on-screen (refer to fig. 12.4).
>
> 2. Pull down the View menu. You'll see four options, as follows:
>
>   ▶ The Chart option plots the counters you select in a continuous chart (refer to exercise 12.1).
>
>   ▶ The Alert option automatically alerts a network official if the predetermined counter threshold is surpassed.
>
>   ▶ The Log option saves your system performance data to a log file.
>
>   ▶ The Report option displays system performance data in a report format.
>
> The setup is similar for each of these view formats. All use some form of the Add to Chart dialog box (refer to exercise 12.1). All have options that are configured through the first command at the top of the Options menu. (The first command at the top of the Options menu changes its name depending on the active view. It was the Chart option in exercise 12.1.)

3.a. Click the Alert option in the View menu.

3.b. Click the plus sign in the toolbar or choose Add to Alert from the Edit menu. The Add to Alert dialog box (see figure 12.8) is similar to the Add to Chart dialog box in figure 12.5 except for two additional items at the bottom of the screen. The Alert If box enables you to type in a threshold for the counter. The Over/Under radio buttons specify whether you want to receive an alert if the counter value is over or under the threshold value. The Run Program on Alert box lets you specify a command line that will execute if the counter value reaches the threshold you specify in the Alert If box. You can ask Performance Monitor to send a message to your beeper, to send you an e-mail message, or to notify your paging service.

Figure 12.8

The Add to Alert dialog box.

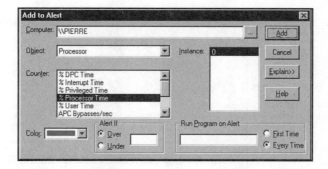

Don't specify a batch file in the Run Program on Alert box. Performance Monitor uses Unicode format, which can confuse the command-prompt interpreter. (The < and > symbols, which are used in Unicode format, are interpreted as a redirection of input or output.)

3.c. The default object in the Add to Alert dialog box should be the Processor object. The default counter should be %Processor Time. Enter the value **5%** in the Alert If box and make sure the Alert If radio button is set to Over. In the Run Program on Alert box, type **SOL**. Set the Run Program on Alert radio button to First Time. This configuration tells Performance Monitor to execute Windows NT's Solitaire program when the %Processor Time exceeds 5%.

continues

Exercise 12.3: Continued

If the Run Program on Alert radio button is not set to First Time, Performance Monitor will execute a new instance of Solitaire every time the %Processor Time exceeds 5%, which happens every time it executes a new instance of Solitaire. You'll probably have to close Performance Monitor using the X button or reboot to stop the incessant shuffling and dealing.

3.d. Click the Add button and then click the Done button. The Alert Legend at the bottom of the Alert window describes the active alert parameters. The Alert Log shows every instance of an alert (see fig. 12.9).

Figure 12.9

The Performance Monitor alert log.

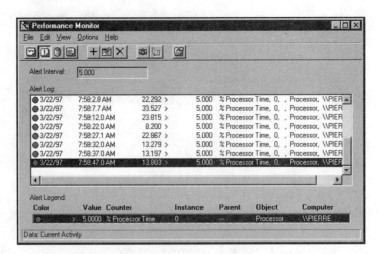

3.e. Make some changes to your desktop. (Hide or reveal the task bar, change the size of the Performance Monitor window—anything that will cause a 5% utilization of the processor.) The Solitaire program should miraculously appear on your screen. In a real alert situation, Performance Monitor would execute an alert application instead of starting a card game.

3.f. Pull down the Edit menu and select Delete Alert.

4.a. Pull down the View menu and select Log. Performance Monitor's Log view saves performance data to a log file rather than displaying it on the screen.

4.b. Pull down the Edit menu and select Add to Log. Notice that only the objects appear in the Add to Log dialog box. The counters and instances boxes don't appear because Performance Monitor automatically logs all counters and all instances of the object to the log file. Select the Memory Object and click Add. If you want, you can select another object, such as the Paging File object, and click Add again. When you are finished adding objects, click Done.

4.c. Pull down the Options menu and select Log. The Log Options dialog box appears on your screen (see fig. 12.10). The Log Options dialog box enables you to designate a log file that Performance Monitor will use to log the data. In the File name box, enter the name **exer2**. You also can specify an update interval. The update interval is the interval at which Performance Monitor records performance data to the log. The Manual Update radio button specifies that the file won't be updated unless you press Ctrl+U or select Update Now from the Options menu. Click the Start Log button to start saving data to the log. Wait a few minutes and then return to the Log Options dialog box and click the Stop Log button.

Figure 12.10

The Log Options dialog box.

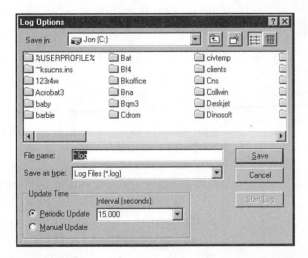

4.d. Pull down the View menu and switch to Chart view.

4.e. Pull down the Options menu and select Data From. The Data From dialog box enables you to specify a source for the

continues

performance data that appears in the Chart. Note that the default source is Current Activity. (That is why the chart you created in exercise 12.1 took its data from current system activity.) The alternative to the Current Activity option is to use data from a log file. Click the Log File radio button. Click the ellipsis button to the right of the log file window and select the exer2 file you created in step 4.c. Click OK.

4.f.   Pull down the Edit menu and click Add to Chart. Click the down arrow to the right of the Object menu. Notice that your only object choices are the Memory object and any other objects you selected in step 4.b. Select the Memory object. Browse through the counter list and select Pages/sec. Click the Add button. Select any other memory counters you want to display and click the Add button. Click Done.

4.g.   The log file's record of the counters you selected in 4.f appears in the chart in the Performance Monitor's main window. Notice that, unlike the chart you created in exercise 12.1, this chart does not continuously sweep out new data. That is because this chart represents static data from a previous, finite monitoring session.

4.h.   Pull down the Edit menu and select Time Window. The Time Window enables you to focus on a particular time interval within the log file (see fig. 12.11). In this example (because you only collected data for a few minutes), the Time Window may seem unnecessary. If you collected data for a longer period, however, and you want to zero in on a particular event, the Time Window can be very useful. Set the beginning and end points of your time window by adjusting the gray start and stop sliders on the Time Window slide bar. The Bookmark section at the bottom of the dialog box enables you to specify a log file bookmark as a start or stop point. (You can create a bookmark by selecting the Bookmark option from the Options menu while you are collecting data to the log file or by clicking the book in the Performance Monitor tool bar.) Click OK to view the data for the time interval.

Figure 12.11

The Performance Monitor Input Log File Timeframe dialog box, invoked by the Edit menu Time Window command.

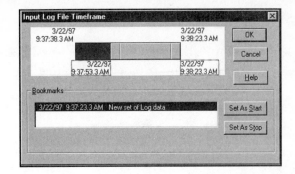

5.a. Pull down the View menu and switch to Report view. Pull down the Options menu and select Data From. Switch the Data From setting back to Current Activity. Report view displays the performance data in a report rather than in a graphics format.

5.b. Select Add to Report from the Edit menu. Select the processor object and choose the %Processor Time, %Interrupt Time, and Interrupts/sec counters. (Hold down the Ctrl key to select all three and then click Add. Select the PhysicalDisk object and choose the %Disk Time, Avg. Disk Queue Length, and Current Disk Queue Length counters. Click the Add button. Select the Memory object and choose the Pages/sec, Page Faults/sec, and Available Bytes counters. Click the Add button. Click Done.

5.c. Examine the main report window. Performance Monitor displays a report of the performance data you specified in a hierarchical format, with counters listed under the appropriate object.

6. Select Exit in the File menu to exit Performance Monitor.

Review Questions

1. An advantage of hardware-based network monitoring tools over software-based tools is that _____.

   A. they are less expensive

   B. they are easier to use

   C. a hardware-based tool can also serve as a PC

   D. none of the above

2. Which tool would you use to determine if a Windows NT Server system displayed the same error message at the same time every day?

   A. Network Monitor

   B. Performance Monitor

   C. Event Viewer

   D. None of the above

3. Which tool would you use to determine if a Windows NT Server machine has enough RAM?

   A. Network Monitor

   B. Performance Monitor

   C. Event Viewer

   D. None of the above

Pretest Answers

1. C (see the section titled "Keeping Records")

2. D (see the section titled "Monitoring Network Traffic")

Review Answers

1. D

2. C

3. B

P a r t **4**

Troubleshooting

Chapter 13

Troubleshooting

Troubleshooting is the art of seeking out the cause of a problem and eliminating the problem by managing or eliminating the cause. With something as complex as a computer network, the list of possible problems and causes is nearly endless. In real life, however, a large number of network problems fall into a few well-defined categories. In this chapter, you learn about some of these categories. You also learn about some of the strategies and tools you can use to troubleshoot network problems.

Of course, no matter how effective you are at problem-solving, it almost always is better to avoid problems than to solve them. Chapter 8, "Managing and Securing a Microsoft Network," discusses administration strategies that minimize the need for troubleshooting. Chapter 12, "Monitoring the Network," discusses monitoring and record-keeping strategies that can help you identify problems when they appear. This chapter looks specifically at troubleshooting techniques for solving problems related to network cabling, adapter cards, modems, and other important connectivity components. In addition, you learn some guidelines for troubleshooting network performance problems, and you can glance over a quick summary of sources for troubleshooting information.

Chapter 13 targets the following objectives in the Troubleshooting section of the Networking Essentials exam:

Test Objectives

▶ Identify common errors associated with components required for communications

▶ Diagnose and resolve common connectivity problems with cards, cables, and related hardware

▶ Resolve broadcast storms

▶ Identify and resolve network performance problems

Stop! Before reading this chapter, test yourself to determine how much study time you will need to devote to this section.

1. _____ send sound waves down the cable to look for imperfections.

    A. DVMs

    B. Oscilloscopes

    C. TDRs

    D. None of the above

2. Which three of the following could degrade network performance?

    A. A generator or mechanical device near the network

    B. A computer game

    C. Sudden, disorderly shutdown of a workstation

    D. New hardware

3. Which two of the following are possible problems with Token Ring network adapters?

    A. Broadcast messages from the card are not timed properly.

    B. The card is not bound to a network service.

    C. The card removed itself from the network.

    D. A 16 Mbps card exists on a 4 Mbps ring.

Initiating the Troubleshooting Process

Microsoft recommends the following five-step approach to network troubleshooting:

1. **Set the problem's priority.** Ask yourself a few questions: How serious is this problem? Will the network still function if I attend to other matters first? Can I quantify the loss of work time or productivity the problem is causing? These will help you determine the severity of the problem relative to the other pressing problems you might face.

2. **Collect information to identify the symptoms.** Collecting information can be as simple as asking users to describe the problem in detail. A user's description of the problem can lead to further questions, which can lead to a deeper description. If you keep a documented history of your network (see Chapter 12, "Monitoring the Network"), you can compare the present behavior of the network with the baseline behavior. You also can look for possible previous occurrences of the problem.

3. **Develop a list of possible causes.** Again, ask yourself a few questions: Was the problem a result of connectivity devices? Cabling? Protocols? A faltering workstation? What do past occurrences have in common with the present occurrence? List all possibilities.

4. **Test to isolate the cause.** Develop tests that will prove or disprove each of the possible causes. The tests could be as simple as checking a setup parameter or as complicated as studying network traffic with a protocol analyzer. You learn about some of the hardware and software network testing tools in the section titled "Using Troubleshooting Tools" later in this chapter.

5. **Study the results of the test to identify a solution.** Your tests will (ideally) point you to the real problem; after you know the problem, you can determine a solution.

These five steps are sufficient to guide you through a myriad of network problems. Similar approaches appear in the documentation of other network vendors.

Part of the challenge of network troubleshooting is to determine how you can apply these five troubleshooting steps to your own situation.

Using Troubleshooting Tools

Network administrators use a number of tools for searching out network problems. The following list details some of these tools:

- ▶ **Protocol Analyzers.** These hardware or combined hardware and software products are used to monitor network traffic, track network performance, and analyze packets. Protocol analyzers can identify bottlenecks, protocol problems, and malfunctioning network components (see Chapter 12, "Monitoring the Network").

- ▶ **Network Monitors.** These software-based tools monitor network traffic, displaying packet information and keeping statistics on network usage (see Chapter 12).

- ▶ **Digital Volt Meter (DVM).** This hand-held electronic measuring tool enables you to check the voltage of network cables. You can use a DVM to help you find a break or a short in a network cable.

- ▶ **Time-Domain Reflectometer (TDM).** TDMs send sound waves along a cable and look for imperfections that might be caused by a break or a short in the line.

- ▶ **Oscilloscope.** This device measures fluctuations in signal voltage and can help find faulty or damaged cabling.

Several diagnostic software tools provide information on virtually any type of network hardware, as well. A considerable number of diagnostic software packages are available at a variety of prices.

Establishing Troubleshooting Connectivity and Communication

Most network problems occur out on the wires. The components that connect PCs and enable them to communicate are susceptible to many kinds of problems. The following sections discuss these important connectivity and communication components and some of the problems associated with them:

- ▶ Cables and connectors

- ▶ Network adapter cards

- ▶ Hubs and MSAUs

- ▶ Modems

These components were introduced in previous chapters of this book. (See Chapter 3, "Transmission Media," Chapter 6, "Connectivity Devices," and Chapter 10, "Network Adapter Cards.") This chapter concentrates on troubleshooting guidelines.

Troubleshooting Cables and Connectors

Most network problems occur at the OSI Physical layer, and cabling is one of the most common causes. A cable might have a short or a break, or it might be attached to a faulty connector. Tools such as DVMs and TDRs help search out cabling problems.

If a workstation cannot access the network, and you think the problem might be the cabling, try disconnecting the network cables and attaching them to a portable PC. If the portable reaches the network, cabling probably isn't your problem.

When troubleshooting any network, begin with the more obvious physical problems. For example, make sure that all connectors are tight and properly connected, that ground wires and terminators are used when required, and that manufacturer's specifications (such as cable grade, cable lengths, and maximum number of nodes) are met and are consistent with the specifications for the transmission medium.

Try the following checks when troubleshooting network cabling problems:

- ▶ With 10BASE-T, make sure the cable used has the correct number of twists to meet the data-grade specifications.

- ▶ Look for electrical interference, which can be caused by tying the network cable together with monitor and power cords. Outside, fluorescent lights, electric motors, and other electrical devices can cause interference.

- ▶ Make sure that connectors are pinned properly and crimped tightly.

- ▶ If excess shielding on coaxial cable is exposed, make sure it doesn't ground out the connector.

- ▶ Ensure that coaxial cables are not coiled tightly together.

- ▶ On coaxial Ethernet LANs, look for missing terminators or terminators with improper impedance ratings.

- ▶ Watch out for malfunctioning transceivers, concentrators, or T-connectors. Make sure that connectors have not been mixed up, such as ARCnet connectors used on an Ethernet network.

- ▶ Test the continuity of the cable by using the various physical testing devices discussed in the previous section, or by using a software-based cable testing utility.

▶ Make sure that all the component cables in a segment are connected. A user who moves his client and removes the T-connector incorrectly can cause a broken segment.

▶ Examine cable connectors for bent or broken pins.

▶ On Token Ring networks, inspect the attachment of patch cables and adapter cables. Remember, patch cables connect MSAUs, and adapter cables connect the network adapter to the MSAU.

> One advantage of a Token Ring network is its built-in capability to monitor itself. Token Ring networks provide electronic troubleshooting and, when possible, actually make repairs. When the Token Ring network can't make its own repairs, a process called *beaconing* narrows down the portion of the ring in which the problem is most likely to exist. (See Chapter 4, "Network Topologies and Architectures," for more information on beaconing.)

Troubleshooting Network Adapter Cards

Network problems often result from malfunctioning network adapter cards. The process of troubleshooting the network adapter works like any other kind of troubleshooting process: start with the simple. The following list details some aspects you can check if you think your network adapter card might be malfunctioning:

▶ Make sure the cable is properly connected to the card.

▶ Confirm that you have the correct network adapter card driver and that the driver is installed properly (see Chapter 10, "Network Adapter Cards"). Be sure the card is properly bound to the appropriate transport protocol (see Chapter 5, "Transport Protocols").

▶ Make sure the network adapter card and the network adapter card driver are compatible with your operating system. If you use Windows NT, consult the Windows NT hardware compatibility list. If you use Windows 95 or another operating system, rely on the adapter card vendor specifications.

▶ Test for resource conflicts. Make sure another device isn't attempting to use the same resources (see Chapter 10). If you think a resource conflict might be the problem, but you can't pinpoint the conflict using Windows NT Diagnostics, Windows 95's Device Manager, or some other diagnostic program, try removing all the cards except the network adapter and then replacing the cards one by one. Check the network with each addition to determine which device is causing the conflict.

▶ Run the network adapter card's diagnostic software.

▶ If necessary, remove the card and clean the connector fingers (don't use an eraser because it leaves grit on the card).

▶ Examine the jumper and DIP switch settings on the card. Make sure the resource settings are consistent with the settings configured through the operating system.

▶ Make sure the card fits properly in the slot.

▶ Replace the card with one that you know works. If the connection works with a different card, you know the card is the problem.

Token Ring network adapters with failure rates that exceed a preset tolerance level might actually remove themselves from the network. Try replacing the card. Some Token Ring networks also can experience problems if a 16 Mbps card is inserted into a 4 Mbps ring. (Other 16 Mbps cards can adjust to a 4 Mbps network.)

Broadcast storms (discussed later in this chapter) are often caused by faulty network adapters as well.

Troubleshooting Hubs and MSAUs

If you experience problems with a hub-based LAN, such as a 10BASE-T network, you often can isolate the problem by disconnecting the attached workstations one at a time. If removing one of the workstations eliminates the problem, the trouble may be caused by that workstation or its associated cable length. If removing each of the workstations doesn't solve the problem, the fault may lie with the hub. Check the easy components first, such as ports, switches, and connectors. Then use a different hub (if you have it) and see if the problem persists. If your hub doesn't work properly, call the manufacturer.

If you're troubleshooting a Token Ring network, make sure the cables are connected properly to the MSAUs, with ring-out ports connecting to the ring-in ports throughout the ring. If you suspect the MSAU, isolate it by changing the ring-in and ring-out cables to bypass the MSAU. If the ring is now functional again, consider replacing the MSAU. In addition, you might find that if your network has MSAUs from more than one manufacturer, they are not wholly compatible. Impedance and other electrical characteristics can show slight differences between manufacturers, causing intermittent network problems. Some MSAUs (other than the 8228) are active and require a power supply. These MSAUs fail if they have a blown fuse or a bad power source. Your problem also might result from a misconfigured MSAU port. MSAU ports might need to be reinitialized with the setup tool. Removing drop cables and reinitializing each MSAU port is a quick fix that is useful on relatively small Token Ring networks.

Isolating problems with patch cables, adapter cables, and MSAUs is easier to do if you have a current log of your network's physical design. After you narrow down the problem, you can isolate potential problem areas from the rest of the network and then use a cable tester to find the actual problem.

Troubleshooting Modems

A modem presents all the potential problems you find with any other device. You must make sure that the modem is properly installed, that the driver is properly installed, and that the resource settings are consistent and do not conflict with other devices. Modems also pose some unique problems because they must connect directly to the phone system, they operate using analog communications, and they must make a point-to-point connection with a remote machine.

The online help files for both Windows NT and Windows 95 include a topic called the Modem Troubleshooter (see fig. 13.1). The Modem Troubleshooter leads you to possible solutions for a modem problem by asking questions about the symptoms. As you answer the questions (by clicking the gray box beside your answer), the Modem Troubleshooter zeroes in on more specific questions until (ideally) it leads you to a solution. See exercise 13.1 at the end of this chapter for more on the Modem Troubleshooter.

Figure 13.1

Windows NT's Modem Troubleshooter guides the reader through a series of dialog boxes designed to identify modem problems (also available with Windows 95).

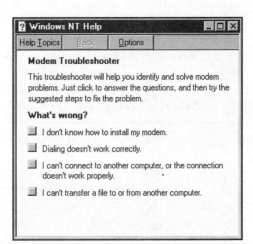

Some common modem problems (in addition to the basic device problems discussed earlier in this chapter, such as connectivity and resource settings) are as follows:

▶ **Dialing problems.** The dialing feature is improperly configured. For instance, the modem isn't dialing 9 to bypass your office switchboard, or it *is* dialing 9 when you're away from your office. The computer also could be dialing an area code or an international code when it shouldn't. Check the dialing properties for the connection.

▶ **Connection problems.** You can't connect to another modem. Your modem and the other modem might be operating at different speeds. Verify that the maximum speed setting for your modem is the highest speed that both your modem and the other modem can use. Also make sure the Data Bits, Parity, and Stop Bits settings are consistent with the remote computer.

▶ **Protocol problems.** The communicating devices are using incompatible line protocols. Verify that the devices are configured for the same or compatible protocols. If one computer initiates a connection using PPP, the other computer must be capable of using PPP.

Handling Broadcast Storms

A *broadcast storm* is a sudden flood of broadcast messages that clogs the transmission medium, approaching 100 percent of the bandwidth. Broadcast storms cause performance to decline and, in the worst case, computers cannot even access the network. The cause of a broadcast storm is often a malfunctioning network adapter, but a broadcast storm also can be caused when a device on the network attempts to contact another device that either doesn't exist or for some reason doesn't respond to the broadcast.

If the broadcast messages are viable packets (or even error-filled but partially legible packets), a network-monitoring or protocol-analysis tool often can determine the source of the storm (see Chapter 12, "Monitoring the Network"). If the broadcast storm is caused by a malfunctioning adapter throwing illegible packets onto the line, and a protocol analyzer can't find the source, try to isolate the offending PC by removing computers from the network one at a time until the line returns to normal. (For more information, see "Troubleshooting Network Adapter Cards," earlier in this chapter.)

Troubleshooting Network Performance

If your network runs slower than it used to run (or slower than it ought to run), the problem might be that the present network traffic exceeds the level at which the network can operate efficiently. Some possible causes for increased traffic are new hardware (such as a new workstation) or new software (such as a network computer game or some other network application). A generator or another mechanical device operating near the network could cause a degradation of network performance. In addition, a malfunctioning network device could act as a bottleneck. Ask yourself what has changed since the last time the network operated efficiently, and begin there with your troubleshooting efforts.

Some of the techniques described in previous chapters can help you troubleshoot network performance. A performance monitoring tool, such as Windows NT's Performance Monitor, can help you look for bottlenecks that are adversely affecting your network. See Chapter 12 for more information on Performance Monitor.

The monitoring and record-keeping procedures discussed in Chapter 12 also can help you troubleshoot network performance by providing you with baseline performance data that you can use to gauge later fluctuations.

For instance, the increased traffic could be the result of increased usage. If usage exceeds the capacity of the network, you might want to consider expanding or redesigning your network. You also might want to divide the network into smaller segments by using a router or a bridge to reduce network traffic. A protocol analyzer can help you measure and monitor the traffic at various points on your network.

Handling Other Network Problems

The following list details some other common problems that could affect your network:

- ▶ **Operating system conflicts.** Operating system upgrades sometimes can cause older programs to become incompatible with the operating system itself. This problem is compounded in network environments because, during the transition to a new network operating system, some servers will run the new version for a period of time while others are still running the previous version. Microsoft recommends that you perform a test upgrade on an isolated part of the network to ensure that all hardware and software systems function properly when the upgrade is made.

- ▶ **Server crashes.** A server disk crash can be disastrous if you aren't adequately prepared for it. You should devise a system of regular backups and, depending on the nature of your data, explore other safeguards such as a RAID fault tolerant system. (Refer to Chapter 9, "Disaster Recovery.")

- ▶ **Power fluctuations.** A small fluctuation in the power supply can make the network misbehave. If the power goes off completely—even for a moment—the whole network could shut down, causing users to lose their work in progress. A disorderly shut-down also can cause problems with file servers. The best solution is to prepare for a power outage before it happens. Connect each server to an Uninterruptible Power Supply (UPS), and encourage your users to perform occasional saves as they work.

If you implement all the measures discussed so far and you still experience problems, your next step may be to consult the experts. Or, even before you start your own troubleshooting, you may want to consult the available information to learn more about the problem. The next section discusses some online and offline sources of help.

Getting Support

You are rarely alone when you are troubleshooting network problems. An important aspect of troubleshooting is knowing where to turn for critical information on your network environment. Many online and offline sources can provide troubleshooting information. Some of these sources (in addition to the online help provided with your operating system), include the following:

▶ **Vendor documentation and help lines.** Hardware and software vendors often provide troubleshooting tips with the owner's documentation. Vendors also often provide technical assistance by phone.

▶ **Bulletin board services.** A number of electronic bulletin boards supply networking information. You can download information on Microsoft network products from the Microsoft Download Library (MSDL). (You can reach the MSDL by dialing 206-936-6735.) Other vendors also have active bulletin board systems, such as Novell's NetWire BBS. See vendor documentation for more information on how to reach a particular vendor's official BBS.

▶ **The Internet.** The major network vendors all sponsor active forums and newsgroups on the Internet, CompuServe, and other online services. See your vendor's documentation.

▶ **CD-ROMs.** Several vendors now market CD-ROMs with network and PC hardware information. Windows NT Server's Books Online (located on the Windows NT Installation CD-ROM) provides an additional layer of documentation that isn't found with online help. Microsoft's TechNet contains product information, technical information, articles, and announcements. TechNet is available on a subscription basis through Microsoft (call 800-344-2121). A Microsoft TechNet demo is included on the CD-ROM that accompanies this book. Novell's NSEPro CD-ROM is a NetWare-oriented encyclopedia of network information. The Micro House Technical Library (MHTL) is another impressive database of technical information. The MHTL addresses such items as BIOS settings for IDE drives and jumper settings for popular peripheral boards. The MHTL comes with a rich collection of informative illustrations.

Summary

Troubleshooting is an essential part of network operations. The best kind of troubleshooting is, of course, anticipating problems before they occur, but in spite of all your efforts, you'll eventually need to search down a problem that is stopping or slowing your network. This chapter looked at general troubleshooting strategies and at solutions for each of the problem areas identified by Microsoft in the Networking Essentials test objectives, as follows:

▶ Problems with communication components

▶ Connectivity problems

▶ Broadcast storms

▶ Network performance problems

This chapter also looked at online and offline sources of troubleshooting information.

Exercises

Exercise 13.1:   Modem Troubleshooter

Objective: Learn how to access Windows NT's or Windows 95's Modem Troubleshooter. This exercise addresses Microsoft's exam objective: Identify common problems associated with components required for communications.

Estimated time: 10 minutes

Modem Troubleshooter is part of Windows NT's online help system. The easiest way to access it is to start Help and search for modems in the index.

1. Click the Start button and choose Help.

2. In the Help Topics dialog box, click the Index tab. Enter **modem** in the search box at the top of the screen.

3. Look for the troubleshooting subtopic under the modems topic in the index. Double-click troubleshooting. The Modem Troubleshooter will appear (refer to fig. 13.1).

4. Browse through the Modem Troubleshooter's topics. Click the gray box to the left of each symptom for a look at possible causes or more diagnostic questions.

5. When you're finished, close the Help window.

Exercise 13.2:   Windows NT Books Online

Objective: Access Windows NT's Books Online, a CD-ROM-based source of configuration and troubleshooting information.

Estimated time: 10 minutes

1. Click the Start menu and choose Programs/Books Online.

2. Windows NT prompts you for the location of the Books Online files. The files are located on the Windows NT Installation CD-ROM in the Support directory's Books subdirectory.

continues

Exercise 13.2: Continued

3. In the Books Online main dialog box, click the Contents tab. Double-click the book icon to reveal the major subcategories for Books Online (see fig. 13.2).

Figure 13.2

Windows NT's Books Online provides configuration and troubleshooting information not found in online help.

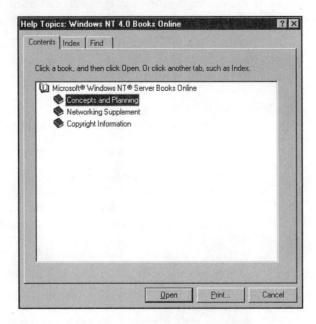

4. Browse through the topics in Books Online. Notice the extensive "Networking Supplement" section devoted to networking issues. Try to get a feeling for the kinds of questions that are best answered by Books Online.

5. When you are finished, close the Books Online dialog box.

Review Questions

The following questions test your knowledge of the information in this chapter. For additional exam help, visit Microsoft's site at www.microsoft.com/train_cert/cert/Mcpsteps.htm.

1. Which three of the following are troubleshooting steps in Microsoft's five-step troubleshooting process?

   A. Collect information to identify the symptoms.

   B. Develop a list of possible causes.

   C. Reboot the server.

   D. Set the problem's priority.

2. MSDL stands for _____.

   A. Minor Switching Delay Log

   B. Microsoft Storage Device Language

   C. Microsoft Domain License

   D. Microsoft Download Library

3. You can use a _____ to look for breaks in network cables by measuring cable voltage.

   A. protocol analyzer

   B. DVM

   C. TDR

   D. MSDL

4. Most network problems occur at the OSI _____ layer.

    A. Physical

    B. Data Link

    C. Network

    D. Session

5. A sudden, unexpected flood of broadcast messages on the network is known as a _____.

    A. net frenzy

    B. tornado

    C. broadcast storm

    D. electric shower

Pretest Answers

1. C (see the section titled "Using Troubleshooting Tools")

2. A, B, D (see the section titled "Troubleshooting Network Performance")

3. C, D (see the section titled "Troubleshooting Network Adapter Cards")

Review Answers

1. A, B, D

2. D

3. B

4. A

5. C

P a r t **5**

Appendixes

Appendix A

Overview of the
Certification Process

To become a Microsoft Certified Professional, candidates must pass rigorous certification exams that provide a valid and reliable measure of their technical proficiency and expertise. These closed-book exams have on-the-job relevance because they are developed with the input of professionals in the computer industry and reflect how Microsoft products are actually used in the workplace. The exams are conducted by an independent organization—Sylvan Prometric—at more than 700 Sylvan Authorized Testing Centers around the world.

Currently, Microsoft offers four types of certification, based on specific areas of expertise:

▶ **Microsoft Certified Product Specialist (MCPS).** Qualified to provide installation, configuration, and support for users of at least one Microsoft desktop operating system, such as Windows 95. In addition, candidates may take additional elective exams to add areas of specialization. MCPS is the first level of expertise.

▶ **Microsoft Certified Systems Engineer (MCSE).** Qualified to effectively plan, implement, maintain, and support information systems with Microsoft Windows NT and other Microsoft advanced systems and workgroup products, such as Microsoft Office and Microsoft BackOffice. The Networking Essentials exam can be used as one of the four core operating systems exams. MCSE is the second level of expertise.

▶ **Microsoft Certified Solution Developer (MCSD).** Qualified to design and develop custom business solutions using Microsoft development tools, technologies, and platforms, including Microsoft Office and Microsoft BackOffice. MCSD also is a second level of expertise, but in the area of software development.

▶ **Microsoft Certified Trainer (MCT).** Instructionally and technically qualified by Microsoft to deliver Microsoft Education Courses at Microsoft authorized sites. An MCT must be employed by a Microsoft Solution Provider Authorized Technical Education Center or a Microsoft Authorized Academic Training site.

The following sections describe the requirements for each type of certification.

For up-to-date information about each type of certification, visit the Microsoft Training and Certification World Wide Web site at http://www.microsoft.com/tran_cert. You must have an Internet account and a WWW browser to access this information. You also can call the following sources:

▶ Microsoft Certified Professional Program: 800-636-7544

▶ Sylvan Prometric Testing Centers: 800-755-EXAM

▶ Microsoft Online Institute (MOLI): 800-449-9333

How to Become a Microsoft Certified Product Specialist (MCPS)

Becoming an MCPS requires you pass one operating system exam.

The following list shows the names and exam numbers of all the operating systems from which you can choose to get your MCPS certification:

▶ Implementing and Supporting Microsoft Windows 95 #70-63

▶ Implementing and Supporting Microsoft Windows NT
Workstation 4.02 #70-73

▶ Implementing and Supporting Microsoft Windows NT
Workstation 3.51 #70-42

▶ Implementing and Supporting Microsoft Windows NT
Server 4.0 #70-67

▶ Implementing and Supporting Microsoft Windows NT
Server 3.51 #70-43

▶ Microsoft Windows for Workgroups 3.11–Desktop #70-48

▶ Microsoft Windows 3.1 #70-30

▶ Microsoft Windows Operating Systems and Services
Architecture I #70-150

▶ Microsoft Windows Operating Systems and Services
Architecture II #70-151

How to Become a Microsoft Certified Systems Engineer (MCSE)

MCSE candidates need to pass four operating system exams and
two elective exams. The MCSE certification path is divided into
two tracks: the Windows NT 3.51 track and the Windows NT 4.0
track. The "Networking Essentials" exam covered in this book can
be applied to either track of the MCSE certification path.

Table A.1 shows the core requirements (four operating system
exams) and the elective courses (two exams) for the Windows NT
3.51 track.

Table A.1

Windows NT 3.51 MCSE Track

Take These Two Required Exams (Core Requirements)	Plus, Pick One of the Following Operating System Exams (Core Requirement)	Plus, Pick One of the Following Networking Exams (Core Requirement)	Plus, Pick Two of the Following Elective Exams (Elective Requirements)
Implementing and Supporting Microsoft Windows NT Server 3.51 #70-43	Implementing and Supporting Microsoft Windows 95 #70-63	Networking Microsoft Windows for Workgroups 3.11 #70-46	Microsoft SNA Server #70-12
AND Implementing and Supporting Microsoft Windows NT Workstation 3.51 #70-42	*OR* Microsoft Windows for Workgroups 3.11–Desktop #70-48	*OR* Networking with Microsoft Windows 3.1 #70-47	*OR* Implementing and Supporting Microsoft Systems Management Server 1.0 #70-14
	OR Microsoft Windows 3.1 #70-30	*OR* Networking Essentials #70-58	*OR* Microsoft SQL Server 4.2 Database Implementation #70-21
			OR Microsoft SQL Server 4.2 Database Administration for Microsoft Windows NT #70-22
			OR System Administration for Microsoft SQL Server 6 #70-26
			OR Implementing a Database Design on Microsoft SQL Server 6 #70-27

Take These Two Required Exams (Core Requirements)	Plus, Pick One of the Following Operating System Exams (Core Requirement)	Plus, Pick One of the Following Networking Exams (Core Requirement)	Plus, Pick Two of the Following Elective Exams (Elective Requirements)
			OR Microsoft Mail for PC Networks 3.2-Enterprise #70-37
			OR Internetworking Microsoft TCP/IP on Microsoft Windows NT (3.5–3.51) #70-53
			OR Internetworking Microsoft TCP/IP on Microsoft Windows NT 4.0 #70-59
			OR Implementing and Supporting Microsoft Exchange Server 4.0 #70-75
			OR Implementing and Supporting Microsoft Internet Information Server #70-77
			OR Implementing and Supporting Microsoft Proxy Server 1.0 #70-78

Table A.2 shows the core requirements (four operating system exams) and elective courses (two exams) for the Windows NT 4.0 track. Tables A.1 and A.2 have many of the same exams listed, but there are distinct differences between the two. Make sure you read each track's requirements carefully.

Table A.2

Windows NT 4.0 MCSE Track

Take These Two Required Exams (Core Requirements)	Plus, Pick One of the Following Operating System Exams (Core Requirement)	Plus, Pick One of the Following Networking Exams (Core Requirement)	Plus, Pick Two of the Following Elective Exams (Elective Requirements)
Implementing and Supporting Microsoft Windows NT Server 4.0 #70-67	Implementing and Supporting Microsoft Windows 95 #70-63	Networking Microsoft Windows for Workgroups 3.11 #70-46	Microsoft SNA Server #70-12
AND Implementing and Supporting Microsoft Windows NT Server in the Enterprise #70-68	OR Microsoft Windows for Workgroups 3.11-Desktop	OR Networking with Microsoft Windows 3.1 #70-47	OR Implementing and Supporting Microsoft Systems Management Server 1.0 #70-14
	OR Microsoft Windows 3.1 #70-30	OR Networking Essentials #70-58	OR Microsoft SQL Server 4.2 Database Implementation #70-21
	OR Implementing and Supporting Microsoft Windows NT Workstation 4.02 #70-73		OR Microsoft SQL Server 4.2 Database Administration Microsoft Windows NT #70-22
			OR System Administration for Microsoft SQL Server 6 #70-26

Take These Two Required Exams (Core Requirements)	Plus, Pick One of the Following Operating System Exams (Core Requirement)	Plus, Pick One of the Following Networking Exams (Core Requirement)	Plus, Pick Two of the Following Elective Exams (Elective Requirements)
			OR Implementing a Database Design on Microsoft SQL Server 6 #70-27
			OR Microsoft Mail for PC Networks 3.2–Enterprise #70-37
			OR Internetworking Microsoft TCP/IP on Microsoft Windows NT (3.5–3.51) #70-53
			OR Internetworking Microsoft TCP/IP on Microsoft Windows NT 4.0 #70-59
			OR Implementing and Supporting Microsoft Exchange Server 4.0 #70-75
			OR Implementing and Supporting Microsoft Internet Information Server #70-77
			OR Implementing and Supporting Microsoft Proxy Server 1.0 #70-78

How to Become a Microsoft Certified Solution Developer (MCSD)

MCSD candidates need to pass two core technology exams and two elective exams. Unfortunately, the "Networking Essentials" (#70-58) exam does NOT apply toward any of these requirements. Table A.3 shows the required technology exams, plus the elective exams that apply toward obtaining the MCSD.

The "Networking Essentials" (#70-58) exam does NOT apply toward any of the MCSD requirements.

Table A.3

MCSD Exams and Requirements

Take These Two Core Technology Exams	Plus, Choose from Two of the Following Elective Exams
Microsoft Windows Operating Systems and Services Architecture I #70-150	Microsoft SQL Server 4.2 Database Implementation #70-21
AND Microsoft Windows Operating Systems and Services Architecture II #70-151	*OR* Developing Applications with C++ Using the Microsoft Foundation Class Library #70-24
	OR Implementing a Database Design on Microsoft SQL Server 6 #70-27
	OR Microsoft Visual Basic 3.0 for Windows–Application Development #70-50
	OR Microsoft Access 2.0 for Windows–Application Development #70-51
	OR Developing Applications with Microsoft Excel 5.0 Using Visual Basic for Applications #70-52
	OR Programming in Microsoft Visual FoxPro 3.0 for Windows #70-54

Take These Two Core Technology Exams	Plus, Choose from Two of the Following Elective Exams
	OR Programming with Microsoft Visual Basic 4.0 #70-65
	OR Microsoft Access for Windows 95 and the Microsoft Access Development Toolkit #70-69
	OR Implementing OLE in Microsoft Foundation Class Applications #70-25

Becoming a Microsoft Certified Trainer (MCT)

To understand the requirements and process for becoming a Microsoft Certified Trainer (MCT), you need to obtain the Microsoft Certified Trainer Guide document (MCTGUIDE.DOC) from the following WWW site:

http://www.microsoft.com/train_cert/download.htm

On this page, click on the hyperlink MCT GUIDE (mctguide.doc) (117 KB). If your WWW browser can display DOC files (Word for Windows native file format), the MCT Guide displays in the browser window. Otherwise, you need to download it and open it in Word for Windows or Windows 95 WordPad. The MCT Guide explains the four-step process to becoming an MCT. The general steps for the MCT certification are as follows:

1. Complete and mail a Microsoft Certified Trainer application to Microsoft. You must include proof of your skills for presenting instructional material. The options for doing so are described in the MCT Guide.

2. Obtain and study the Microsoft Trainer Kit for the Microsoft Official Curricula (MOC) course(s) for which you want to be certified. You can order Microsoft Trainer Kits by calling

800-688-0496 in North America. Other regions should review the MCT Guide for information on how to order a Microsoft Trainer Kit.

3. Pass the Microsoft certification exam for the product for which you want to be certified to teach.

4. Attend the MOC course for which you want to be certified. This is done so you can understand how the course is structured, how labs are completed, and how the course flows.

You should use the preceding steps as a general overview of the MCT certification process. The actual steps you need to take are described in detail in the MCTGUIDE.DOC file on the WWW site mentioned earlier. Do not misconstrue the preceding steps as the actual process you need to take.

If you are interested in becoming an MCT, you can receive more information by visiting the Microsoft Certified Training (MCT) WWW site at http://www.microsoft.com/train_cert/mctint.htm; or by calling 800-688-0496.

Appendix

Study Tips

B

Self-study involves any method that you employ to learn a given topic, with the most popular being third-party books, such as the one you hold in your hand. Before you begin to study a certification book, you should know exactly what Microsoft expects you to learn.

Pay close attention to the objectives posted for the exam. The most current objectives can always be found on the WWW site http://www.microsoft.com/train_cert. This book was written to the most current objectives, and the beginning of each chapter lists the relevant objectives for that chapter. As well, you should notice a handy tear-out card with an objective matrix that lists all objectives and the page you can turn to for information on that objective.

If you have taken any college courses in the past, you have probably learned which study habits work best for you. Nevertheless, consider the following:

- ▶ Study in bright light to reduce fatigue and depression.

- ▶ Establish a regular study schedule and stick as close to it as possible.

- ▶ Turn off all forms of distraction, including radios and televisions; or try studying in a quiet room.

> ▶ Study in the same place each time you study so your materials are always readily at hand.

> ▶ Take short breaks (approximately 15 minutes) every two to three hours or so. Studies have proven that your brain assimilates information better when this is allowed.

Another thing to think about is this: humans learn information in three ways: visually, audially, and through tactile confirmation. That's why, in a college class, the students who took notes on the lectures had better recall on exam day; they took in information both audially and through tactile confirmation—writing it down.

Hence, use study techniques that reinforce information in all three ways. For example, by reading the book, you are visually taking in information. By writing down the information when you test yourself, you are giving your brain tactile confirmation. And lastly, have someone test you out loud, so you can hear yourself giving the correct answer. Having someone test you should always be the last step in studying.

Pretesting Yourself

Before taking the actual exam, verify that you are ready to do so by testing yourself over and over again in a variety of ways. Within this book, there are questions at the beginning and end of each chapter. On the accompanying CD-ROM, there is an electronic test engine that emulate the actual Microsoft test and enable you to test your knowledge of the subject areas. Use these over and over and over again, until you are consistently scoring in the 90 percent range (or better).

This means, of course, that you can't start studying five days before the exam begins. You will need to give yourself plenty of time to read, practice, and then test yourself several times.

New Riders's TestPrep electronic testing engine, we believe, is the best one on the market. Although it is described in Appendix D, "All About TestPrep," here it's important for you to know that TestPrep will prepare you for the exam in a way unparalleled by most other engines.

Hints and Tips for Doing Your Best on the Tests

In a confusing twist of terminology, when you take one of the Microsoft exams, you are said to be "writing" the exam. When you go to take the actual exam, be prepared. Arrive early, and be ready to show two forms of identification and to sit before the monitor. Expect wordy questions. Although you have approximately 90 minutes to take the exam, there are 58 questions you must answer. This gives you just over one minute to answer each question. That might sound like ample time for each question, but remember that most of the questions are lengthy word problems, which tend to ramble on for paragraphs. Your 90 minutes of exam time can be consumed very quickly.

It has been estimated that approximately 85 percent of the candidates taking their first Microsoft exam fail. It is not so much that they are unprepared and unknowledgeable. It is more the case that they don't know what to expect and are immediately intimidated by the wordiness of the questions and the ambiguity implied in the answers.

For every exam Microsoft offers, there is a different required passing score. The "Networking Essentials" required score is 793, or 79.3 percent. Because there are 58 questions on the exam (randomly taken from a pool of about 150), you must correctly answer 45 or more to pass.

Things to Watch For

When you take the exam, look closely at the number of correct choices you need to make. Some questions require that you select one correct answer; other questions have more than one correct answer. When you see radial buttons next to the answer choices, remember that the answers are mutually exclusive; there is only one right answer. On the other hand, check boxes indicate that the answers are not mutually exclusive and there are multiple right answers. On the "Networking Essentials" exam, as opposed to several others, the number of correct choices is always stated on-screen. Be sure to read the questions closely to see how many correct answers you need to choose.

Also, read the questions fully. With lengthy questions, the last sentence often dramatically changes the scenario. When taking the exam, you are given pencils and two sheets of paper. If you are uncertain of the meaning of the question, map out the scenario on paper until you have it clear in your mind. You're required to turn in the scrap paper at the end of the exam.

Marking Answers for Return

You can mark questions on the actual exam and refer back to them later. If you get a wordy question that will take a long time to read and decipher, mark it and return to it when you have completed the rest of the exam. This will save you from wasting time and from running out of time on the exam. Remember, only 90 minutes are allotted for the exam, and it ends when those 90 minutes expire—whether or not you are finished with the exam.

Attaching Notes to Test Questions

At the conclusion of the exam, before the grading takes place, you are given the opportunity to attach a message to any question. If you feel that a question was too ambiguous, or tested on knowledge you did not need to know to work with the product, take this opportunity to state your case. Microsoft has never changed a test score as a result of an attached message; however, it never hurts to try—and it helps to vent your frustration before blowing the proverbial 50-amp fuse.

Good luck.

What's on the CD-ROM

This appendix is a brief rundown of what you'll find on the CD-ROM that comes with this book. For a more detailed description of the TestPrep test engine, exclusive to New Riders, please see Appendix D, "All About TestPrep."

New Riders's Exclusive TestPrep

A new test engine was developed exclusively for New Riders. It is, we believe, the best test engine available because it closely emulates the actual Microsoft exam, and it enables you to check your score by category, which helps you determine what you need to study further. For a complete description of the benefits of TestPrep, please see Appendix D.

New Riders's Exclusive FLASH! Electronic Flash Card Program

You can use the FLASH! Electronic Flash Card program to convert some of the questions in the test engine database to a fill-in-the-blank format. Run the FLASH! Program and select the categories on which you want to be tested. The engine then goes through the database in sequential order and tests your knowledge without multiple choice possibilities.

Exclusive Electronic Version of Text

Use the electronic version of this book to help you search for terms or areas that you need to study. It comes complete with all figures as they appear in the book.

Copyright Information

New Riders TestPrep test engine: Copyright 1997 New Riders Publishing. All rights reserved. Made in the U.S.A.

FLASH! Electronic Flash Cards: Copyright 1997 New Riders Publishing. All rights reserved. Made in the U.S.A.

Appendix

D

All About TestPrep

The electronic TestPrep utility included on the CD-ROM accompanying this book enables you to test your Networking Essentials knowledge in a manner similar to that employed by the actual Microsoft exam. When you first start the TestPrep exam, select the number of questions you want to be asked and the objective categories in which you want to be tested. You can choose anywhere from one to 58 questions and from one to 4 categories, of which the real exam consists.

Although it is possible to maximize the TestPrep application, the default is for it to run in smaller mode so you can refer to your Windows 95 Desktop while answering questions. TestPrep uses a unique randomization sequence to ensure that each time you run the program you are presented with a different sequence of questions—this enhances your learning and prevents you from merely learning the expected answers over time without reading the question each and every time.

Question Presentation

TestPrep emulates the actual Microsoft "Networking Essentials" exam (#70-58), in that radial (circle) buttons are used to signify only one correct choice, while check boxes (squares) are used to signify multiple correct answers. Whenever more than one answer is correct, the number you should select is given in the wording of the question.

You can exit the program at any time by choosing the Exit key, or you can continue to the next question by choosing the Next key.

Scoring

The TestPrep Score Report uses actual numbers from the "Networking Essentials" exam. For Networking Essentials, a score of 793 or higher is considered passing; the same parameters apply to TestPrep. Each objective category is broken into categories with a percentage correct given for each of the four categories.

Choose Show Me What I Missed to go back through the questions you answered incorrectly and see what the correct answers are. Choose Exit to return to the beginning of the testing routine and start over.

Non-Random Mode

You can run TestPrep in Non-Random mode, which enables you to see the same set of questions each time, or on each machine. To run TestPrep in this manner, you need to create a shortcut to the executable file, and place the CLASS parameter on the command line calling the application, after the application's name. For example:

```
C:\TESTENG\70_58.EXE CLASS
```

Now, when you run TestPrep, the same sequence of questions will appear each and every time. To change the sequence but stay in Non-Random mode (for example, if you're in a classroom setting, where it is important that everyone see the same questions), choose Help, Class Mode on the main screen. This lets you enter a number from 1 to 8 to select a predefined sequence of questions.

Instructor Mode

To run TestPrep in Instructor mode (seeing the same set of questions each time, or on each machine), create a shortcut to the executable file, and place the INSTR parameter following CLASS on the command line calling the application, after the application's name. For example:

```
C:\TESTENG\70_58.EXE CLASS INSTR
```

Now, when you run TestPrep, the same sequence of questions will appear each and every time. Additionally, the correct answer will be marked already, and the objective category from which the question is coming will be given in the question. To change the sequence of questions that appear, choose Help, Class Mode on the main screen. This prompts you to enter a number from 1 to 8 to select a predefined sequence of questions; increment that by 100 and the sequence will be presented in Instructor mode.

Flash Cards

As a further learning aid, you can use the FLASH! Electronic Flash Cards program to convert some of the questions in the database into a fill-in-the-blank format. Run the FLASH! program and select the categories on which you want to be tested. The engine then goes through the database in sequential order and tests your knowledge without multiple choice possibilities.

I n d e x

G

R

X-Z

REGISTRATION CARD

MCSE Training Guide: Networking Essentials

Name _____ Title _____

Company _____ Type of business _____

Address _____

City/State/ZIP _____

Have you used these types of books before? ☐ yes ☐ no

If yes, which ones? _____

_____

How many computer books do you purchase each year? ☐ 1–5 ☐ 6 or more

How did you learn about this book? _____

Where did you purchase this book? _____

Which applications do you currently use? _____

_____

Which computer magazines do you subscribe to? _____

_____

What trade shows do you attend? _____

_____

Comments: _____

_____

_____

Would you like to be placed on our preferred mailing list? ☐ yes ☐ no

☐ **I would like to see my name in print!** You may use my name and quote me in future New Riders products and promotions. My daytime phone number is: _____

New Riders Publishing 201 West 103rd Street ◆ Indianapolis, Indiana 46290 USA

Fax to **317-817-7448**

Fold Here

BUSINESS REPLY MAIL
FIRST-CLASS MAIL PERMIT NO. 9918 INDIANAPOLIS IN

POSTAGE WILL BE PAID BY THE ADDRESSEE

NEW RIDERS PUBLISHING
201 W 103RD ST
INDIANAPOLIS IN 46290-9058

Getting Started with the CD-ROM

This page provides instructions for getting started with the CD-ROM.

Windows 95/NT Installation

Insert the disc into your CD-ROM drive. If autoplay is enabled on your machine, the CD-ROM setup program starts automatically the first time you insert the disc.

If setup does not run automatically, perform these steps:

1. From the Start menu, choose Programs, Windows Explorer.

2. Select your CD-ROM drive under My Computer.

3. Double-click SETUP.EXE in the Contents list.

4. Follow the on-screen instructions that appear.

5. Setup adds an icon named CD-ROM Contents to a program group for this book. To explore the CD-ROM, double-click on the CD-ROM Contents icon.

How to Contact New Riders Publishing

If you have a question or comment about this product, there are several ways to contact New Riders Publishing. For the quickest response, please send e-mail to support@mcp.com.

If you prefer, you can fax New Riders at 1-317-817-7448.

New Riders's mailing address is as follows:

New Riders Publishing
Attn: Publishing Manager
201 W. 103rd Street
Indianapolis, IN 46290

You can also contact us through the Macmillan Computer Publishing CompuServe forum at GO NEWRIDERS. Our World Wide Web address is http://www.mcp.com/newriders.

MACMILLAN COMPUTER PUBLISHING USA

A VIACOM COMPANY

Technical ·····┐
               └···· **Support:**

If you cannot get the CD/Disk to install properly, or you need
assistance with a particular situation in the book, please feel
free to check out the Knowledge Base on our Web site at
http://www.superlibrary.com/general/support. We have
answers to our most Frequently Asked Questions listed there.
If you do not find your specific question answered, please
contact Macmillan Technical Support at **(317) 581-3833**.
We can also be reached by e-mail at **support@mcp.com**.